The Newly Qualified Teacher's Handbook

Second edition

Elizabeth Holmes

 Routledge
Taylor & Francis Group

LONDON AND NEW YORK

Publisher's note

This book contains information and guidance on a variety of legal and healthcare issues. Every effort has been made to ensure that this information is correct at the time of going to press and sources of additional information have been given where possible. However, this book does not replace the advice of qualified practitioners, and neither the author nor the publisher can be held responsible for any consequence incurred by those following the guidance herein.

First published 2003 by Kogan Page Ltd

Reprinted 2004, 2005 by RoutledgeFalmer

This edition published 2009
by Routledge
2 Park Square, Milton Park, Abingdon, Oxon OX14 4RN

Simultaneously published in the USA and Canada
by Routledge
270 Madison Avenue, New York, NY 10016

*Routledge is an imprint of the Taylor & Francis Group,
an informa business*

© 2009 Elizabeth Holmes

Typeset in Garamond by
RefineCatch Limited, Bungay, Suffolk
Printed and bound in Great Britain by
TJ International Ltd, Padstow, Cornwall

British Library Cataloguing in Publication Data
A catalogue record for this book is available from the British Library

Library of Congress Cataloging in Publication Data
A catalog record for this book has been requested

ISBN10: 0–415–44595–7 (hbk)
ISBN10: 0–415–44596–5 (pbk)

ISBN13: 978–0–415–44595–5 (hbk)
ISBN13: 978–0–415–44596–2 (pbk)

For my parents, Dorothy and Tony

Contents

Acknowledgements

This book could not have been written without the input of the many people who freely offered time, ideas, support and encouragement. In particular, I would like to thank:

- Charlotte Howard of Fox and Howard Literary Agency;
- all members of the publishing teams that have worked on *The Newly Qualified Teacher's Handbook* over the years, in particular, Philip Mudd;
- Emma Martin, whose input in the very first edition of this book was invaluable;
- all those at the Training and Development Agency for Schools, the General Teaching Council for England and the Department for Children, Schools and Families, past and present, who responded to my many enquiries;
- the ever-growing group of NQTs, teachers and induction tutors who contribute ideas and respond to my questions;
- the teaching unions and professional associations, all of which contributed information;
- the many local authority staff who offered insights into local practice;
- my family and friends.

Preface

Over the years since *The Newly Qualified Teacher's Handbook* was first published, there have been many changes to the way in which teachers operate in the classroom. New initiatives have been developed to help bring about improvements in teaching and learning and those working in schools have had to grapple with a wide range of new requirements. National agendas such as *Every Child Matters* also permeate all aspects of school life now and those working with children must incorporate this into their daily routines. These are all major considerations for those who are newly qualified and yet many core values that have always been linked to the job still remain.

This new edition of *The Newly Qualified Teacher's Handbook* is utterly realistic in what it expects new teachers to embrace, while ensuring that all the essentials are covered and a wide range of additional and helpful material is offered as a resource to dip into whenever appropriate.

Keeping completely up to date at all times is rarely possible, especially for those who are getting into their new careers and coping with the nitty gritty of induction. For this reason, throughout this book, I offer all the main sources of up to the minute information about all aspects of your work. These signposts direct you to precisely where you need to go for the latest updates, meaning that, whenever you pick up this book, you can be assured that you have access to all that you need.

I am often asked for my top tips for newly qualified teachers as they set out on their careers in the profession. This is an impossible question to answer; just as we are working hard at personalising our teaching for the needs of the pupils in our care, so too is it desirable to personalise top tips for new teachers. But if there is one thing you do before setting foot in the classroom, make sure it is this: read and fully absorb the professional standards for teachers (you can find these in an appendix at the back of this book). In particular, you will need to be completely familiar with the Standards for Qualified Teacher Status and the Core Standards. Knowing these, how they relate to your work and how you can use them to help build possible directions for professional development will greatly add to the firm foundations you already have from your initial teacher training – use them and this book well, and thoroughly enjoy your new career!

Elizabeth Holmes, 2008

Introduction

Rewarding and stimulating as it can be, teaching is an extremely complex career requiring high-level expertise in many skills areas. It is also a profession in which the nation is permanently interested, and of which seemingly increasing levels of accountability are demanded. You only have to glance at a newspaper or listen to the news to see how frequently education issues are, sometimes inaccurately, discussed. Add to this the pace of change in education, and you could easily find yourself confused, however satisfying your job is.

The purpose of *The Newly Qualified Teacher's Handbook* is to provide newly qualified teachers (NQTs) in primary and secondary schools, as well as those considering a return to teaching and supply teachers, with a valuable resource for their first few years in the profession. It includes ideas on easing your way into your new career and draws from the Standards for the Award of Qualified Teacher Status and the Core Standards, as well as dealing with the other needs of new teachers, such as finding a job, how to deal with work-related stress and union membership, to name a few.

Keeping up with the latest developments in a profession such as teaching can be a challenge. Working as a teacher requires that you be familiar with a wide variety of laws, circulars and guidance, strategies and initiatives, not to mention the latest curriculum and requirements of Qualified Teacher Status (QTS). All of these aspects of teaching in England necessarily develop as time passes and, for this reason, *The Newly Qualified Teacher's Handbook* has been thoroughly updated.

Some teachers experience teaching as a relatively lonely career, with many NQTs feeling that they must cope with the job alone. This book is designed to help you to accept that you don't have to muddle through – that there are lines of support that you can follow and lean on. Your first few years of teaching should not be about 'getting through' induction and surviving the profession; surviving is only a marginal improvement on barely existing, and no one can teach effectively under those circumstances. Your induction year is about building on your sense of security in your job, as well as developing and encouraging enjoyment of it.

The Newly Qualified Teacher's Handbook is not an academic textbook, relying heavily on teaching and learning theory. It doesn't attempt to tell you how to teach – a skill that you will continue to perfect throughout your career – and neither is it a digest of academic papers and texts. It does, however, seek to draw together good practice and a heavy dose of common sense in an easily accessed way. It is a practical, functional guide for everyday use – for you to reach for and dip into whenever you need an idea, support or inspiration. It seeks to enable rather than preach, to help you guard against misinformation and dogma and to encourage you to develop your own ideas about the best way of managing your job with integrity.

The following features have been used in the book:

- *Checklists.* For ease of information retrieval, many hints have been organized into lists. It is not intended that you should follow each list slavishly; rather use them as a springboard for your own ideas. They are designed to be a time-saving device for you. Simply dip in, select the information you need, and go.
- *'Action' features.* These have not been written around hypothetical issues, requiring you to spend time on hypothetical answers. Rather, they are intended to draw from your own wealth of resources for problem solving. Again, there is no need to work through them systematically.
- *'Example' features.* All of the examples have been drawn from the real experiences of teachers, although some of the names have been changed. They have been included to illustrate points in the text, and some deal with relatively unusual situations.
- *'About' boxes.* These boxes contain succinct information covering the many issues and situations that face new teachers.
- *Find out more features.* At the end of every chapter there is a suggestion for where you might start a search for further information. This is because there is an ever-developing body of support out there too great to be itemised in this book, but worth exploring from these starting points.

No book is perfect, and there are bound to be comments and ideas that you, as an NQT, would wish to make about the material presented here. If you would like to make your thoughts known, then you can e-mail me at: *eh@elizabeth-holmes.info*. Feedback from trainees, trainers, induction tutors, headteachers and NQTs themselves inspired many of the improvements that have been made in all of the editions of *The Newly Qualified Teacher's Handbook* and there is no doubt that this has contributed to the evolutionary nature of this book.

Finally, I offer my good wishes to all of you working through your induction and your first few years of teaching, and sincerely hope that *The Newly Qualified Teacher's Handbook* will be an important companion, helping you to find your job valuable, rewarding, exciting and, at times, exhilarating.

Chapter 1

Applying for jobs

Nothing is really work unless you would rather be doing something else.
(James M Barrie)

The very first stage of progressing your teaching career beyond training is to apply for a job. While this may seem straightforward, there are several key points to keep in mind when going through this all-important process. To reflect that, this chapter explores:

- Choosing a location
- The maintained sector
- The independent sector
- Contract types
- Part-time teaching
- Job sharing
- Careers related to teaching
- Making your application.

Location, location, location: where do you want to teach?

Completing your initial teacher-training (ITT) course leaves you with many decisions to make. You have to decide not only whether you would like to continue your teaching career in education but, also, in which type of school you would like to work – independent or state, community or voluntary-aided, mixed or single-sex, inner-city or rural. You may even decide that you would prefer to work in a profession related to teaching.

Rather than falling into the first vacancy that comes your way, it is worth considering all the options available to you. What kinds of experience do you want to gain? Do you want to consolidate your training in a school similar to, or the same as, your teaching practice school? Are you eager for a complete change? Just be aware of the extent to which your first job can help to shape your career. It's well worth avoiding false starts if you can!

Joining the mainstream

By far the largest percentage of all schools falls into the category of mainstream education, including state maintained and independent schools, voluntary-aided schools, voluntary-controlled schools, academies, city technology colleges and colleges of further education.

Maintained schools

Maintained schools are those that receive funding, or rather, are maintained by the state (as opposed to charging fees to cover running costs). As an NQT, you need to be aware of which institutions can provide an induction period. It is also important to be aware of whether your employer would be the local authority or the governing body of the school. If you are not certain about any of these answers, make sure you find out (by ringing the school in question) before attending an interview.

In England in particular, there is a range of school types in the mainstream maintained sector. It may not matter to you where you end up teaching, but it is worth finding out about the category of any school that you are thinking of applying to so that you know exactly what the context is in which the school operates. A school is not simply a school!

ABOUT SCHOOL CATEGORIES

In England, there are three main categories of school: community schools (the local authority is the employer of staff and it owns the school buildings and land), foundation schools (the governing body is the employer, and can also own the school building and land), and voluntary schools (the governing body is the employer for voluntary aided schools and the local authority is the employer for voluntary controlled schools).

There are also specialist schools (any maintained school in England can apply for specialist designation), City Technology Colleges, Academies, Pupil Referral Units, Secure Training Units, Local Authority Secure Units and Grammar Schools among others.

When thinking about where to work, these are the key considerations:

Faith schools – While all schools have to have an element of spiritual teaching, joining a faith school carries specific obligations on the part of the teacher. You will usually be expected to at least respect, if not live according to, the doctrines and tenets that the school represents. There are currently faith schools in England of (at least) the following denominations (with a number of different faiths represented by the 'other' category):

- Church of England
- Roman Catholic
- Jewish
- Muslim
- Sikh.

Post-16 – these are very tempting for those with a real love of their subject. However, do think about how committed you are to this age range, because it could be difficult to adjust to secondary level once you have worked with the 16–19s, should you subsequently decide to work in a school. Another consideration is that post-16 colleges are totally independent of the local authority and the salary you can expect *may* be slightly lower than that of an NQT teaching in a school. There are also implications regarding the developments in the 14–19 curriculum to consider (check out www.dcsf.gov.uk/14–19/ for the latest information on this).

Single-sex schools – opinion about single-sex education seems to change with great frequency, as do ideas on the merits of working in such a school. Girls' schools are very different places from boys' schools and it would be worth spending a few days observing in each to assess whether single-sex teaching is for you. You may also like to consider the fact that you may be in the minority if you teach in a single-sex school of the opposite sex to your own.

Special schools – It is possible to gain employment in a special school for your first post, and if you are sure that this type of teaching is for you then all is well. However, it is often a good idea to consolidate your experience in mainstream-ability ranges first, before specializing. You can use this time to become involved with special education needs (SEN) at your school and gather skills and experience.

ABOUT INVESTORS IN PEOPLE

Some schools are Investors in People (IiP) schools, meaning that they use the IiP framework to meet national standards. This framework helps schools to manage all they must do and achieve as well as any additional activities they choose to do. The core purpose of the IiP Standard is to support the development of staff so that the performance of the school improves.

The IiP Standard has three main principles:

- developing strategies to improve the performance of the organisation;
- taking action to improve the performance of the organisation;
- evaluating the impact on the performance of the organisation.

These principles are supported by indicators and evidence requirements that would show that they are being met. You can find out more about IiP at www.investorsinpeople.co.uk

The independents

Independent schools vary in size and ethos just as much as maintained schools do. There are currently approximately 2,500 non-maintained mainstream schools (the broad term the Department for Schools, Children and Families (DSCF) gives to independent schools) in the UK, with over 650,000 pupils between them (roughly 7 per cent of the school-age population). They invariably involve the payment of fees, although the parental burden can vary tremendously as some children will be eligible for bursaries, scholarships and sponsorships (at the time of writing, bursaries and scholarships currently cost independent schools approximately £300 million per year). Independent schools do not come under the guidance of a local authority and are free to develop the curriculum and teaching styles as they see fit. That said, many do use the National Curriculum as a framework and offer the opportunity for pupils to prepare for and take national qualifications. In direct contrast to the state system, the headteacher of an independent school usually has the final say over the way in which the school is run, with a board of governors adopting an advisory and ratifying role.

ABOUT THE INDEPENDENT SCHOOLS COUNCIL

The Independent Schools Council (ISC) brings together the seven independent schools' associations in a single unified organization. It serves to promote independent schools' common interests. ISC schools undergo inspection by the Independent Schools Inspectorate (ISI) every six years following a framework agreed with the Department for Schools, Children, and Families (DCSF). You can find out more about the ISC here: www.isc.co.uk; and the ISI here: www.isi.net

For the teacher, working in an independent school is a different experience from working in a maintained school. Although, in both kinds of establishment, an educational package is being offered to parents and pupils, in the independent sector market forces do seem to play a more central role. Naturally, when parents are choosing which product to buy, they are going to be conscious of the quality of education on offer. This can create a culture of exceptionally high expectations being placed on teachers by:

- the school management (wanting to keep the standards high enough to attract more clients);
- the parents (who are aware of value for their money);
- the pupils (who often understand their relatively powerful position at the centre of these dynamics).

Interestingly, the ISC reports that more than half of children now entering independent schools have parents who were educated in maintained schools. The ISC also reports that mobility between independent and maintained schools is very common among teachers.

If you do decide to apply for a job in the independent sector, be aware that pay and conditions of service vary throughout the sector. You may be eligible for additional pay as a member of house or pastoral staff in a boarding school, for example.

Get answers to these questions before accepting an offer of a teaching post at an independent school:

- Will you be able to do your induction at this school?
- Does the school adopt the same pay spine as the maintained sector?
- Is your contract comparable to one you would receive in the maintained sector?
- Under what circumstances could your contract be terminated?
- What are the arrangements for your pension?
- What expectations will be made of you in terms of extra-curricular activities?

Teaching in independent schools

Pros are:

- Misbehaviour is generally thought to be less common.
- Class sizes can be considerably smaller than in most maintained schools.
- Parental support for the school can be greater.
- Independent schools can sometimes offer a wider variety of subjects, which may suit your interests.
- An anti-staff subculture is relatively uncommon.
- Holidays are longer in an independent school.

Cons are:

- You may not be able to serve an induction period.
- Teachers can be expected to perform duties outside the teaching day, e.g. sports training, clubs etc.
- Independent schools are exclusive on the grounds of the fees payable (although many offer bursaries and scholarships).
- You may not be paid on the same scale as NQTs in the maintained sector.
- The pension arrangements may be down to you.
- It can prove difficult to move from the independent sector into the state sector.

ABOUT WHERE YOU CAN DO YOUR INDUCTION

According to the Statutory Guidance on Induction for Newly Qualified Teachers in England (DCSF reference: 00364–2008), the induction period can be undertaken in the following institutions (under specific conditions – be sure to check with the Guidance mentioned above for exact details): maintained schools; non-maintained special schools; maintained nursery schools; nurseries that form a part of a maintained school; local authority maintained children's centres; independent schools (including academies and city technology colleges); FE colleges; sixth form colleges; and schools and colleges in Wales in which induction may be served under Welsh regulations. You may *not* serve complete induction in the following (again, conditions apply so read the Guidance for clarity): pupil referral units; secure training centres; schools requiring special measures (this is *sometimes* acceptable); FE institutions which are deemed unsuitable by Ofsted; independent schools which don't meet the conditions; private nurseries and other early years settings that don't meet the conditions; and schools abroad including British schools.

Remember, you are only legally able to start your induction once you have been awarded Qualified Teacher Status by the General Teaching Council for England *wherever* you undertake it.

Vacancies for jobs in independent schools are advertised in the educational press and on Internet recruitment sites.

A word about contracts

The type of contract that you might be offered may not seem important when you have just secured your first teaching job, but always make sure you are fully aware of its implications.

You may be offered a temporary contract or a permanent contract. Temporary contracts can be for a fixed term or until the post-holding teacher returns to work (for example, following maternity leave). Don't automatically avoid temporary contracts as they can be appropriate in certain circumstances. You may want to gain experience in a variety of settings before committing to one particular type of school, or you may need to move your home mid-year, making a permanent contract less important.

The references you can pick up from your employment on a temporary contract are far more detailed regarding your skills once in post than anything your tutors are in a position to write. In that respect, they add greatly to the value of your CV. Don't forget, there really is no such thing as a job for life!

If you do accept a temporary contract, keep these points in mind:

- Regardless of the type of contract you accept, as an NQT you are entitled to an induction programme and should be offered the same opportunities as NQTs on permanent contracts. Don't miss out. You need to find out from the school how much of your induction you can do and when you will be deemed to have completed your induction period if you take a temporary contract.
- Taking over from another teacher mid-year can be difficult, especially if the pupils know that you are not a permanent member of staff. Support from your school at this stage is crucial. Make your mark on each class you teach; you are not simply a babysitter, and can do things 'your way'.
- Make sure you know the termination date of your contact, its type and the reason why it is temporary. Seek advice from your union if you feel you have been treated unfairly.
- Make sure that you will be receiving the correct remuneration. Again, you union will be able to help you with this.

Part-time teaching

Current legislation means that there are few, if any, differences between full- and part-time employees apart from hours worked. All employees are equal. This means that part-timers have the same holiday and sick pay entitlements (pro rata) as full-time employees. For this reason, part-time teaching can be attractive to some teachers, providing you can afford to accept the necessary reduction in salary! It also offers these benefits:

- It gives you the chance to pursue other career options.
- It can allow you to continue your career at a time when you have domestic pressures such as child rearing or caring for a relative.
- It frees time to concentrate on further professional development such as obtaining additional qualifications.
- There is usually flexibility to increase your working hours, often through covering for absent staff.

ABOUT TAKING CARE OVER CONTRACTS

It can feel as though you are being unnecessarily meticulous if you question the finer details of your contract, but it is important to protect yourself against possible future disputes, which can drain your energy and place a negative focus on your career. There is no reason why a contract that is fair to both you and the school cannot be negotiated. Your union and local authority human resources office are able to offer contract advice and some lawyers will also do this free of charge. Make sure you clearly understand your contractual

obligations, so that you are free to commence your career from a position of knowledge and security. Above all, do not sign or agree to anything unless you are happy with the implications – if not, your first job could be your worst job!

However, even if it has been possible to negotiate part-time hours at your school, there are always disadvantages that should be considered:

- It can feel as though you are not fully involved in the life of the school when you only attend at certain times.
- Liaising with colleagues can become difficult because of your work patterns.
- Part-time teachers invariably spend more time than their pay suggests in preparing for lessons and marking/assessing.
- Career progression can become difficult (and in some schools impossible).
- Depending on how efficient your school is at disseminating information, it can be very difficult to stay fully informed of the latest changes.
- You will probably spend a disproportionate amount of time travelling to and from school if you do not work full days.

Job sharing

As the work profile of the nation changes and increasing numbers of people are looking for more flexibility in their work, job sharing seems to have become an interesting option. Many schools have job-sharing schemes in place, which can offer all the advantages (and disadvantages) of part-time teaching, as well as the added bonus of having ready-made cover should you need time off for any reason. You should, however, be aware of these factors:

- Job sharing can be an extremely good deal for the school – the sum of two half-teachers is often greater than one!
- Time must be spent liaising with your colleague for the purposes of planning, marking and assessment.

- Difficulties can arise if one side of the partnership leaves and good working dynamics have to be established quickly with a newcomer.
- As with any job, full-time, part-time or shared, always check the finer details of your contract, and consider the implications for your pension.

Careers related to teaching

Receiving QTS does not mean that you are obliged or committed to take a job as a teacher, or to teaching in this country. There are many opportunities for qualified teachers – in fact, people with teaching qualifications are often sought by industry because of the transferable skills they possess. These include skills such as the ability to multi-task, to work to extremely tight deadlines, to relate to a variety of different people within each working day and to adjust the time spent working each day as appropriate.

Here are just some ideas you may like to consider.

Choices within teaching

You may not want to take a permanent job in a British school, but there are many other ways of earning money from teaching.

Teaching English as a foreign language

Teaching English as a foreign language (TEFL) can offer excellent opportunities to work with students of all ages and even travel around the world. Some language schools insist on specific TEFL qualifications, which can be gained by attending various courses, either full- or part-time. Training is advisable, as it will enhance employment opportunities, particularly if you go through the British Council (see www.britishcouncil.org for further information). There will always be a world market of people keen to learn English, as either a second or a third language, or for specific purposes such as business.

ABOUT SEEKING CAREERS ADVICE

Most institutes of higher education offer students and ex-students careers advice free of charge, specifically for people with higher-education qualifications. This is probably the best place to start. You may be able to get careers advice from the university/college in your home area as well as the university/college you attended, but this will probably mean waiting for an appointment, as university careers services will put their own students first.

You can also get advice from independent careers offices, but it is a good idea to use a local authority service that employs trained careers advisers. There is usually a charge for the advice they give, but the time, resources and follow-up care that you are given can be worth the investment.

It is also worth taking a look at the Training and Development Agency for Schools website (www.tda.gov.uk).

Teaching in developing countries

Voluntary Service Overseas (VSO) can offer opportunities for graduate teachers to teach overseas, normally for at least two years. Payment is at local rates. Some aid agencies and religious organizations also employ teachers to work abroad. Embassies and the educational press often have details of overseas teaching opportunities.

Other work abroad

Opportunities in the USA, Canada, Australia, New Zealand and non-European Union countries appear to be relatively limited, but European Union (EU) countries offer some possibilities. Again, the relevant embassies or high commissions will be able to advise as to how to obtain employment. Also, the careers section of your local library will have information on job opportunities in EU countries.

ABOUT RETURNING AFTER WORKING ABROAD

If you spend time in your career teaching abroad, there will inevitably be some employers who do not value the extra experience you will have gained. In order to capitalize on your breadth of experience, carefully select elements of your work abroad that have specific application to teaching in this country. Find ways of working this information into any interviews that you have on your return. Unfortunately, some schools may not recognize work abroad as a justification for an additional point on the salary scale.

It is worth noting that you will have to complete an induction period if you have not already done so in order to be eligible to teach in a maintained school or a non-maintained special school.

For information on taking a gap year, take a look at www.yearoutgroup.org and www.gapyear.co.uk

Private tutoring

There are often advertisements for teachers to work as private tutors in families, both in this country and abroad, in the educational press. Some teaching agencies maintain registers of private tutors, although obtaining work through such agencies can result in having to pay a fee for the introduction, or a percentage of any earnings that you receive from work through the agency.

For this reason, it can be more lucrative to advertise your teaching services in your local press. Such advertisements usually cost around £25. If timed well, for example around Easter time to catch the exam crammers and the beginning of September for those students whose parents want them to improve on their performance in the previous year, you can quickly recoup your expenses. Do remember that any earnings from private tutoring form part of your taxable income.

Many teachers find private tutoring extremely rewarding, as it allows an opportunity to focus on teaching and interacting without the need to consider the dynamics of a large group. Your union will be able to advise on what is the current rate for private tutoring.

Supply teaching

Supply teaching is quite a tough route to take as a newly qualified teacher. As you move from school to school covering for absent staff, your abilities to adapt to different institutions, subjects and age groups will need to be well honed. However, there seem to be increasing opportunities whereby supply teaching leads to a temporary contract, which could in turn become a permanent one.

Day-to-day supply teaching makes it virtually impossible to gain a valuable induction into the teaching profession if you are not based in one school for a term or more, and this has grave implications for your chances of satisfying the requirements of what should be your first year of teaching. Professional support is likely to be patchy too, at a time when behaviour management will be most challenging. For this reason, you might want to avoid supply teaching unless you are unable to secure a permanent position.

The best way into supply teaching is through your own contacts. If you have connections with a particular school, ask the headteacher for an informal interview with a view to being added to the school's list of supply teachers. Alternatively, if there is a school you would like to work in, doing some voluntary work as a precursor to paid employment is a great way of convincing the powers that be of your skills and abilities.

Local authorities maintain a list of teachers available for supply work that is distributed to schools within its remit. Contact the appropriate authority's education human resources office for details.

It is possible to complete your induction through supply teaching contracts of a term or more in duration. The overall length of your induction would be calculated pro rata if you were teaching part-time. You can find out more about the restrictions which apply to supply teaching and induction from the Statutory Guidance on Induction for Newly Qualified Teachers in England (DCSF reference: 00364–2008). Make sure you know what is and is not acceptable.

Choices outside teaching

You're not selling your soul if you decide to go for work outside teaching. There is tremendous scope for using your qualifications, and the profession will invariably welcome any experience you gain should you decide to return to teaching at a later date.

Project work

Look in the education press for advertisements for trained teachers to take part in projects. These are usually research-based, fixed-term contracts, which offer the chance to become involved in a specialist area of education.

Resource development

Most teachers write their own materials on occasion (if not all the time) and there are opportunities within publishing to become involved in book and resource package projects. Either approach suitable publishers directly with a brief synopsis of your idea (the *Writers' and Artists' Yearbook*, published by A & C Black, is invaluable for information on publishing companies) or look out for 'creative' and 'media' advertisements in the quality press.

Multi-media educational-resource development is another growth area and one in which it could be wise for teachers to become involved.

Education administration

There are opportunities at many levels in local authority administration from planning and budgeting to policy implementation and problem solving. Vacancies will usually be advertised in the local press, but it is also worth arranging some work experience or talking to key personnel in your local authority. Many such jobs still allow for close contact with schools.

Education officer posts

Most museums, heritage and conservation sites, large companies and major charities have education officers whose job it is to liaise with visitors and generally inform the public of the work of the organization. This may be through writing worksheets and newsletters or organizing exhibitions and fund-raising.

Often, such jobs are advertised in the education press but, again, if there is a particular organization you would like to work for, make your own introductions through speculative applications, work experience and voluntary work.

Training in industry and commerce

The training department of any company performs a vital role, especially now that the pace of change within the workplace is so rapid. The skills you need for a job in training are very similar to those needed in the teaching profession, i.e. good communication, motivation, organization, analysis and problem solving.

As training departments in companies are often part of the human resources services, you may need to do some further study to acquire the relevant professional qualifications.

Caring work

This general term covers all jobs involving caring for others, such as social work, youth and community work, educational welfare and residential care. Caring work often allows you to develop solid relationships with those you are working with over a long period of time and will demand many skills.

Jobs in other areas

These job areas are also worth considering:

- retail management;
- public relations;
- marketing;
- librarianship;
- broadcasting;
- research;
- leisure;
- careers advising;
- counselling;
- writing;
- journalism.

Making your application

Unless you fall into the relatively small category of trainee teachers who are offered a job in their teaching practice school and want to accept that job, you will have to apply to an unfamiliar school for a teaching post at some stage. This may seem daunting, but if you view the challenge as a project that can easily be broken down into stages you could not only be successful in receiving a job offer but also in ensuring that it is suitable.

Finding vacancies to apply for

Somewhere, your ideal job will be advertised and, if you are not looking in the right places, it will be offered to someone else. The best way to start the great hunt is to decide on the geographical area in which you are prepared to work. Obviously, the smaller your chosen area the more limited your search, but that is no reason to force yourself into applying for jobs in areas about which you have doubts. Once you have a list of places in which you would be happy to work, pursue every lead in the hunt for the ideal vacancy.

Covering every option

Resignations of teaching posts are typically made to three deadlines throughout the year – 31 October, 28 February and 31 May – although these deadlines may be waived if both parties agree. Naturally, the few weeks following these deadlines are particularly good times to search for job advertisements.

The national press

Most vacancies in the teaching profession are advertised in the *Times Educational Supplement* so make sure that you look at it each week (take a look at its website too: www.tes.co.uk). Although online advertising is increasingly popular with schools, it is also worth looking at the *Guardian* and the *Daily Telegraph*.

If you are looking for a post in a faith school, it's also worth looking in the relevant specialist press such as the *Church Times* for Church of England schools.

The local press

As only vacancies for heads and deputies have to be advertised nationally, it is well worth scrutinizing the local press. If you are not living where you would eventually like to be working, contact the appropriate local paper and they will arrange to send you the copies you require if their job ads are not placed online.

Local Authority bulletins

These are invaluable to the job-searching NQT, as vacancies will often be advertised here before they go into the national press. Arrange with relevant authorities to have newsletters posted to you. Contacting the appropriate education human resources department is usually enough to get this set up if such jobs aren't posted online on their website.

The Internet

Many local authorities (or equivalent) have channelled resources into creating sophisticated websites where current vacancies, amongst other things, may be posted. These are worth browsing regularly to see what you can find.

Another 'must see' website for jobs is www.tes.co.uk, and www.eteach.com also carries job ads for NQTs. A search online will also come up with several other websites that you can browse for jobs in your area.

ABOUT WHAT TO LOOK FOR IN A VACANCY

Although it is important to be enthusiastic and have high aspirations, you should never accept extra responsibility points in your first year of teaching. Leave the promotions until you have completed your induction period.

Go for vacancies that either specifically refer to NQTs or are advertised as being on the main scale. A school that is prepared to offer an NQT extra responsibilities is probably thinking more of the budget than of your abilities to cope, and the additional support you will need is unlikely to be forthcoming.

If you are returning to the profession, your new post should be a supportive one that will enable you to settle into teaching at a reasonable pace. If this means taking a 'backward step', do it; this approach will almost certainly gain you time in the long run. If you need advice on what salary to expect, get in touch with your union, which should be able to give you a salary assessment.

Contacts made during teaching practice

Don't underestimate how valuable networking can be when you have the opportunity during training to visit a variety of schools. Utilize any contacts you have made and you may be privy to information about a vacancy before it is advertised to the general public. Such contacts could be mentors, heads and deputies, course tutors (who invariably retain close links with local schools) and any inspectors and advisers you may have come across in the course of your studies. A phone call, letter or e-mail could provide you with a specific piece of information that puts you at an advantage.

Deciding to apply

Actually deciding to apply for a teaching vacancy is a commitment to a fair amount of work and, therefore, not to be undertaken lightly. Minimize the possibility of pulling out at any stage by finding out as much as you can about the school.

The job advertisement will give limited information and, if this sounds tempting, request an application form and job description. You can do this by telephone, e-mail or post, although some schools may request that you send in a stamped, addressed envelope. It is essential not to apply for a job unless you have been sent the application form and job description.

The job description should contain at the very least the following information:

- the title of the post (e.g. class teacher, history teacher etc.);
- the salary;
- details of the person to whom the post is responsible (e.g. head of department);
- what the responsibilities are;
- any extra duties;
- an indication of the timetable;
- an applicant profile.

Vacancies can be advertised on the basis of a verbal resignation. Whilst retraction of the resignation is extremely unlikely, do bear in mind that this could, in theory, happen. Before sitting down to complete the necessary forms, do some mental questioning to establish whether, based on the information available to you at this stage, you would accept the job if offered. It will be helpful to consider these questions:

- Is it suitable for an NQT?
- Would you be able to complete your induction there?
- Would the job allow you to live in an area in which you want to live?
- Is it in the type of school of which you would like to be a part?
- Would you be teaching subjects you have specialized in?
- Would you be teaching an age group you have specialized in?

Completing the necessary forms

The method of application varies among schools and local authorities, so it is essential to follow any guidance given carefully, especially if you are making applications in different authorities. The minimum that you will have to do is fill in an application form, including a supporting statement in which you have the opportunity honestly to sell your skills. Most schools require a medical form as well.

It is a good idea to have a current CV printed and ready to send at short notice. Your training institution will be able to offer advice on how it should be set out. However, even if you are employed on the basis of your CV, most human resources departments still require a completed application form for their records. Before you start to complete the form, take a photocopy so that you can have a dry run. There may also be the option of downloading an application form or applying online so do check on the relevant local authority website.

ABOUT SPECULATIVE APPLICATIONS

If you have set your heart on a particular school but have not seen an advertisement for a vacancy, send in a speculative application.

Points to remember:

- Plan your letter carefully, being sure to include any achievements and outstanding skills. Keep it punchy and use bullet points as appropriate. One side of A4 paper should be ample, as you will be sending a current CV with the letter. Remember, don't plead; the idea is for the school to feel that they can't function without you!
- Write or type on good-quality paper.
- First state what kind of vacancy you are interested in.
- Match your skills and experience to what you know of the school.
- State some attributes that you can bring to the school.
- Ask for an interview – offer broad suggestions for possible dates.
- End with the expectation of a reply, e.g. 'I look forward to hearing from you', and include an SAE.
- If you don't hear within a week, make a follow-up call – ask to speak to the person to whom you wrote.

Selling your skills

The application form is designed to elicit basic information about you, your education and employment history. This alone will not make you stand out from the crowd, but your real opportunity to shine is in the supporting statement.

Your main goals when writing your supporting statement must be to match your skills to the job description and to include your unique selling points. Don't simply write about the experiences you have had. There are many experienced teachers, but are they necessarily skilled? Inform your future employers of your achievements. Your leading sentence must engage the reader immediately, giving a sense of your personality. Always optimize your positive aspects and end with something memorable.

Although the supporting statement is by far the most trying part of the application process, don't be tempted to reproduce it for all your applications, without relating it directly to respective job descriptions.

ACTION

What are your unique selling points? This can be hard to think about without some feedback from other people. Talk to at least two trusted friends (preferably with whom you have worked). Ask them what your outstanding skills are and you should end up with a list that will get you started.

Checklist for writing a supporting statement

- Before starting, write a list of key points from the job description (e.g. year 3 class teacher, class contains pupils with special needs, strong singing tradition in the school etc.).
- Write a list of your unique selling points, ensuring that they relate directly to your first list (see above).
- Begin with impact and end unforgettably!
- Convey a sense of your personality.
- Fill the main body of the statement with your skills and achievements, always optimizing the positive. Include an explanation of your motivation to teach.
- Use impeccable grammar throughout, avoiding lengthy sentences and aimless paragraphs. Brevity is the key. Use so-called 'action' words to avoid overuse of 'I did'. The following may be helpful:

accomplished	compiled
achieved	composed
acquired	conceived
addressed	concluded
advised	conducted
analysed	consolidated
arranged	counselled
assessed	created
assimilated	cultivated
averted	defined
collaborated	delivered

demonstrated
designed
developed
devised
diversified
documented
effected
eliminated
enacted
engaged
established
evaluated
expanded
formulated
generated
implemented
improved
improvised
incorporated
initiated
inspired
instigated
instructed
integrated
intervened
introduced
invented
launched
led
maintained
managed
modernized
monitored
observed
organized
originated

performed
pioneered
predicted
prevented
produced
promoted
proposed
provided
recommended
redesigned
reduced
regulated
renegotiated
reorganized
resolved
reviewed
revised
revitalized
shaped
simplified
specified
standardized
streamlined
strengthened
structured
supported
tightened
uncovered
unified
unraveled
utilized
visualized
vitalized
vivified
volunteered

- Express what your teaching practice has taught you, and convey an idea of your philosophy of teaching.
- Include information on any travel, hobbies and voluntary work that you have done, and how this equips you for the job.
- If possible, or unless requested otherwise, type your statement.

ABOUT REFEREES

Think carefully about whom you ask to be your referees. Employers will look closely at their status and how recent your contact was, so your favourite primary teacher or best mate from the pub are probably bad choices! Choose referees who will be in a position to match your qualities and capabilities to the job's requirements and be as supportive as possible. Perhaps a past employer and your tutor from your ITT institution would be good choices. Make sure you have their permission before listing them as referees.

ABOUT APPLYING TO A POOL

Some local authorities operate a pool system whereby applicants apply to work in a school in that authority rather than in a specific school. Successful applicants are then matched as closely as possible with suitable schools. The application form for a pool job will be very similar to the forms used by individual schools, and the supporting statement will still be an important section. Interviews for pool jobs are usually conducted in a central location in the local authority and you should expect to be interviewed by a panel consisting of representatives from the authority and local teachers and headteachers. Questions won't be specific to a school or post, but will be based in generic aspects of teaching such as behaviour management learning styles, underachievement, national strategies, personalization and so on. Interviews for pools are usually around 20 minutes long.

By applying to a pool you are declaring your desire to work in a particular authority, so it is a good idea to express clearly why you want to work there. Be sure to get your application in on time, as it will almost certainly not be looked at if it arrives during the short-listing stage.

Sending in your application

Always use an A4 (preferably cardboard-backed) envelope for your application so that it does not have to be folded. Write down a checklist of items that need to be included, for example the application form, CV and medical form, and tick them off as you put them in the envelope. Send in the originals, but keep a photocopy of everything so that you can refer to them before an interview. If you are applying online or via email do check to see if you need to send anything that you also need to send in by post. Make sure you print off a copy of what you submit too.

If at all possible, deliver your application to the school. If you do have to post it, include a stamped, self-addressed postcard that can be sent to you as acknowledgement of receipt. Schools rarely do this unless you provide the stamp. Now, all you have to do is sit back and wait for an invitation to an interview!

ABOUT NOT BEING INVITED FOR AN INTERVIEW

If you are not asked to attend for an interview, try not to think about it as a disaster. It is certainly frustrating that your hard work has not apparently paid off, but there are always positive aspects in any situation. Cultivate the attitude that perhaps the job was not as suited to you as you first thought and that the experience has been a valuable one. Think how much easier future applications will be now that you have gone this far. Do, however, take the opportunity to reassess your application to see if there are any obvious weaknesses that can be tightened up in future. Some schools may offer feedback if asked so it can be worth trying this if you want to find out exactly why you weren't shortlisted. However don't be disappointed if your request is refused. Some vacancies attract piles of applications making feedback difficult. Always worth a try though! If you suspect ageism may be the problem, contact your union.

Find out more . . .

It's amazing how many applications from perfectly competent teachers don't make it through the selection process due to shoddy presentation and carelessness. Don't let this be you! Keep a close eye on the education press and websites such as www.teachingexpertise.com for advice on getting a job at key times of the academic year.

Make sure that you are really familiar with the Statutory Guidance on Induction for Newly Qualified Teachers in England (DCSF reference: 00364–2008). You can download this from Teachernet: www.teachernet.gov.uk. It's worth printing off and keeping somewhere accessible!

Chapter 2

Succeeding in interviews

> You have to learn the rules of the game. And then you have to play better than anyone else.
>
> (Albert Einstein)

It doesn't matter how superb your lessons are, how dynamic and developmental you are as a teacher or how scintillating your coursework assignments have been for your initial teacher training, if you can't perform at interviews the chances are you won't get the chance to show off your skills as a teacher. Knowing how to give yourself the best chance during an interview is essential if you are to make progress in the way you deserve to in this profession. This chapter looks at:

- Preparing for interviews
- Tackling interview questions
- Selling yourself
- Moving to a new area.

Attending for an interview

The interview is an opportunity for both sides to gather the additional information needed before a commitment to employment can be made. At this stage, a positive attitude is at least as important as any other factor in securing a job offer.

Preparing for the day

While it is important to be prepared for an interview in terms of physical appearance, knowledge of the job and of the school etc., there is something to be said for maintaining a balance. Over-rigorous preparation can lead to excessive anxiety that will inevitably limit your chances of success.

As soon as possible after receiving your invitation to an interview, send a reply confirming the arrangements. At this stage, you can ask if the school will be paying your interview expenses and, if so, at what rate. Only in extreme circumstances would you be justified in attempting to change the arrangements suggested by the school.

You should have been sent a map and advice on accommodation if you will be travelling a long distance, together with additional information about the school, such as a description of the surrounding area, site and buildings, an outline of the staffing structure and details of the governing body, along with the interview format. Much of this information is likely to be on the school's website too.

What are the interviewers looking for?

Interviewers are looking for:

- the person who matches the job criteria most closely;
- the person who will fit in with the existing staff;
- the person who will be able to make a valuable contribution to the work of the school;
- your attitudes to management and governance;
- your personal philosophy of teaching;
- your motivations, satisfactions and any dissatisfactions;
- your attitude to change and development;
- your ability to assert yourself.

That said, the success of the interview in terms of extracting this information depends on the skills of those asking the questions.

Dressing to win

> I have yet to meet a man as fond of high moral conduct as he is of outward appearances.
>
> (Confucius)

It sounds totally irrational, but instant judgements will be made of you based on your appearance. For this reason, there are some basic ground rules to follow when deciding what to wear on the big day.

Schools vary tremendously in their dress codes. From jeans and T-shirts to suits and ties, there is a school at every point on the spectrum. As far as is possible, try to find out what the dress code is for your school. If it is local, catching a glimpse of staff is useful, or arranging an informal visit will allow you to check out these kinds of details. Otherwise, ring the headteacher and ask if there is a dress code. This enables you to establish whether you need to wear a suit, or toning separates. Feeling inappropriately dressed, whether too formal or too casual, will not boost your confidence on the day.

Use these guidelines:

- Darker, coordinated colours are most appropriate.
- Avoid extremes in style, e.g. nothing too short, baggy, striped or patterned.
- Go for comfort. Your clothes should be an extension of your body, i.e. you shouldn't have to think about them. Constant tweaking will only annoy!
- If you will be wearing tights or stockings, take a spare pair with you.
- Get your hair trimmed and wear it in a style that won't need constant adjustment.
- Be moderate in your use of jewellery, make-up and perfume or aftershave.

ABOUT PORTFOLIOS

There is an unwritten expectation now that NQTs will take a portfolio of examples of their work and training to interviews. You will probably have received guidance from your training institution on how best to build a port-folio but if not, the ideas below will help:

- An A3 folder is the ideal size. Portfolio folders are readily available in good-quality stationery shops. Avoid the folders with plastic inner pockets so that you can easily retrieve contents.
- Include items that show the breadth of experience you have. For example:
  - samples of planning (if possible, short-term and long-term planning, although you may not have had the opportunity to do long-term planning on teaching practice);
  - photographs of displays or special events that you have been involved in;
  - examples of your assessment of pupils' work;
  - samples of work that, if possible, show an idea of your teaching philosophy or, at least, your understanding of current priorities in education.
- Don't shy away from including examples of work that did not go down well. This will give you the opportunity to demonstrate the fact that you are a reflective practitioner and to explain how you dealt with the situation.
- Before each interview, select for your portfolio only those items that will enable you to link specifically to the job in question.
- Organize the contents of your portfolio so that you can retrieve items in the order in which you will discuss them. This will avoid having to fumble around pulling out samples of work at random!

By offering your interviewers a portfolio of your best work to peruse, you are handing them a positive focus for questioning. That has to be a good thing and invariably interviewers will love looking it.

Before the big day

It is so easy to get anxious about events like job interviews, especially if your heart is set on a positive outcome. Yet this anxiety can rapidly backfire and severely affect performance on the day if you don't actively strive for balance. For this reason, physical and mental preparation needs to begin a few days in advance.

Here are some ideas on maximizing your chances:

- Do eat sensibly. A diet high in fresh fruits and vegetables will provide you with the extra energy you need to sail through the interview.
- Do focus on your breathing. Slow, deep breaths are instantly calming in stressful situations.
- Do plan your route to the interview and aim to arrive about 30 minutes early. This will give you not only extra time in case you are delayed but also the chance to freshen up when you arrive, familiarize yourself with your surroundings and practise some deep breathing if you are nervous.
- Do read the education press or visit education-based web sites to ensure that you are familiar with current developments and popular jargon.
- Don't let negative thinking spoil your day. Say to yourself that the interview will be a success and the outcome will be the best possible one for you.

ABOUT OPTIMISM

The optimist sees the doughnut; the pessimist sees the hole.

(Anonymous)

According to *The New Oxford Dictionary of English*, the noun 'optimism' means: 'hopefulness and confidence about the future or the successful outcome of something'. The extent to which we are in control of our levels of optimism has been fiercely debated and, no doubt, will continue to be, but the fact that we can have at least some influence over the way we think about a future event is certain.

Nurturing optimism can be the difference between success and failure; winning and losing. Most sportsmen and women, and death-defying adventurers such as those who conquer Everest, cultivate utterly positive outlooks; after all, climbing through the 'death zone' while muttering under your oxygen-starved breath that you will probably not make it safely down to base camp could well become a self-fulfilling prophecy! Likewise, attending an interview with a pessimistic attitude is sure to produce the very outcome you are drawing towards you.

There are many books on optimism, and the Internet is a fine source of information on this topic. If low self-esteem is preventing you from making the conscious decision to be optimistic, there are many good exercises in Dr David Burns's book, *Ten Days to Great Self-Esteem*, published by Vermilion. A good search on Amazon will throw up other ideas that are suitable for you too.

- Don't smoke anywhere near your interview clothes.
- Don't drink alcohol for 24 hours before the interview. It affects physical appearance, not to mention wits!
- Don't worry about potential problem areas in your application such as gaps in employment or a long period of illness. Work out ways of expressing this in positive terms, e.g. what adversity taught you.

ACTION

If anxiety can be a problem, you need to be able to control it with your breathing. This can be done surreptitiously. Relax your jaw by unclenching your teeth, placing your lips lightly together and teeth slightly apart. It is virtually impossible to retain tension in your face in this position. Then start 4–2–4–2 breathing, i.e. breathe in to a count of four; hold for two, breathe out to a count of four, pause for two. Keep going until you feel noticeably better.

Interview scenarios

Interviews for teaching jobs generally involve a tour of the school, possibly some food or a drink and questioning by a panel, usually comprising the headteacher, a deputy, head of department or year and at least one governor. Each member of the panel should be introduced to you and his or her position in the school made clear. If not, you are justified in tactfully asking. Although the governors of a school hold a good deal of power, they may draw heavily on the expertise of the senior leadership team. There are distinct advantages in panel interviews, as personal biases are less likely to be strong deciding factors.

The practice of asking interviewees to perform a task or teach a sample lesson has become the norm in most schools. This can be of limited value in terms of determining which candidate will be most suitable in the long run unless your interviewers are highly skilled in their interpretation of the results.

If you are asked to perform in your interview, you should have been given plenty of advance warning. Anything sprung on you unexpectedly, besides the usual panel questioning, is not acceptable practice and you may even consider the implications for your possible employment at the school. Do you want to work for this type of leadership team?

Assuming you have been given prior warning of anything you might have to do, you owe it to yourself to prepare thoroughly, asking advice from tutors and mentors and gathering resources where appropriate. View it as an exciting challenge.

Remember, if you feel that to continue with the interview would weaken your confidence, thus jeopardizing future interviews, or you simply don't want to work at the school, you may politely withdraw from the proceedings at any stage.

EXAMPLE

Some NQTs have had bizarre interview experiences. From being asked to write an unseen lesson plan in 30 minutes, to being asked to teach a group of pupils a lesson that the same group had been taught by three other candidates that day, there are clearly some strange views prevailing on how best to judge interviewees! One NQT was even asked to give a presentation on the role of middle management; even though this is of dubious relevance to a first position.

Another complaint that has been raised by NQTs is the rather unsubtle way in which some schools distinguish between those candidates whom they are genuinely interested in and those who are simply making up the numbers. It has even been reported by some that they were not interviewed by the full interview panel whereas other interviewees were. If anything like this happens to you, there are two ways of looking at it. You could feel satisfied that you have had a close escape. This is an underhand way of approaching interviewing and there are grave implications for the way the school is run and the general treatment of staff. Or, you could raise the issue with your union, which may want to investigate what is going on at the school and perhaps lodge a complaint. Whatever you decide to do, remember that not all schools are the same and the chances are that your next interview will be a much more positive experience.

Seating arrangements

Be prepared for a wide variety of creative seating plans. Ideas on the optimum arrangement are changing all the time and you could find yourself:

- facing the panel across a desk;
- sitting around a table with the panel;
- in comfortable chairs around a coffee table;
- in comfortable chairs with no table;
- most oddly, sitting in front of a panel, the members of which are seated in a row with no desk – formal informality!

EXAMPLE

Armena was surprised to get all the way through her interview to the stage of being offered the job without being introduced to her future head of department. Be extremely suspicious if you are not given the opportunity to meet the key personnel with whom you would be working. Ask yourself (and your interviewers) why you have not been introduced and draw your own conclusions.

ABOUT BODY LANGUAGE

> Mortals can keep no secret. If their lips are silent, they gossip with their fingertips; betrayal forces its way through every pore.
>
> (Sigmund Freud)

Body language can shout louder than any other form of communication, so utilize it and make it work for you. Without being aware of it, we are all experts at reading body language, but often allow it to give away our innermost thoughts. When greeting your interviewers, use a firm grip for handshakes, and smile. This indicates cooperation and friendliness. Be aware of your posture when walking and, when invited to sit, keep your back straight. Avoid crossing your legs.

Eye contact is essential. Maintain it without letting it deteriorate into a staring contest! A calm, steady gaze that follows the speaker's hands when a point is being made will be read as confident. If you need glasses or contact lenses, wear them.

Other positive signals are to lean forward slightly and smile or nod in agreement. Aim to keep your hands lower than your elbows and limit your movements. This will give you at least the appearance of calm serenity.

Negative signals to be avoided are folding your arms or holding something in front of your body, clasping your hands behind your head, putting your hands in your pockets, fidgeting with fingers or things (holding your fingers in a 'steeple' can control active digits), adjusting hair or clothing and slouching.

Questions to answer and questions to ask

Every interview offers the opportunity to show your appropriateness for the job through the answers you give and the questions you ask. However, there are two golden rules that should always be remembered:

1   listen carefully to every question and answer so that you don't misinterpret what is being said;
2   never begin your answer until you know how you intend to end.

If you do find you have not understood a question or have allowed your mind temporarily to wander, there is no harm in asking for it to be repeated. Likewise, if you begin an answer and lose your thread, own up as soon as possible to avoid an embarrassing ramble.

When putting your answers together, try not to use vague, tentative, colloquial language like 'sort of' or 'You know what I mean, right?' At the same time, avoid appearing to be dogmatically fixed in your beliefs to the point of becoming argumentative with questioners. If you're flappable with adults, what is going to happen in the classroom? A balance must be struck through the use of appropriate language delivered at a steady pace and moderate pitch and volume.

Be yourself and be honest. Don't say anything that can be challenged or contradicted (worst of all by you!) at a later date. Cut the blather – if you get the job, you're going to have to live with your words!

You will be asked two different kinds of questions. The key is to know the difference.

Types of questions

Open questions

Example: 'You had the opportunity to teach A level during your initial teacher training. Was that something you enjoyed?' These require more than short, factual answers.

Advantages of open questions are that they give the opportunity to add depth to your answers and to expand on ideas; and they offer the chance to reveal aspects of your character.

Disadvantages are that they can trip you up if you have misunderstood the question and lead you to 'waffle'; and they could show that you can be side-tracked off the key issues and that you haven't thought your answer through.

Closed questions

Example: 'How long have you lived in Sussex?' These require short, factual answers. They are not trick questions!

Advantages of closed questions are that they don't demand creativity or the ability to 'think on your feet'; and they allow the interview to move on at a pace.

Disadvantages are that they don't allow you to expand and justify answers you give; and if they are over-used they can make you feel as though you are on a programme like *University Challenge*!

Although you will be expected to do most of the talking in an interview, apparently the more your questioners talk, the more likely it is that they are impressed with you. So if you can't get a word in, you're doing well!

The following lists of general questions and questions for recent graduates contain some of those that are being asked in teaching interviews today. A list of tricky questions has also been included, with some suggestions on how to tackle them.

Expect to be asked a variety of questions. You will also be asked specifically about your age group or subject specialisms so be up to date with recent developments. Tutors and mentors will be invaluable here.

ABOUT REVEALING PERSONAL AND PROFESSIONAL SKILLS

There are key skills that employers want to see in applicants and these fall into two broad categories: personal and professional. Under the heading 'personal skills', expect to find drive, motivation, communication abilities, energy, determination and confidence. Under 'professional skills' fall reliability, honesty and integrity, loyalty, pride and skills of analysis and listening. Formulate your answers to reveal these characteristics.

General questions that you may be asked

- 'Give examples of methods of teaching you have used.'
- 'How would you deal with potential problems, like difficult parents or troublesome pupils?'
- 'What are your major accomplishments?'
- 'What are your career aspirations?'
- 'Describe your worst experience on teaching practice.'

- 'What interests you most about this job?'
- 'How do you relate the Every Child Matters agenda to your work in the classroom?'
- 'How do you handle stress?'
- 'What do you feel about taking work home?'
- 'How do you plan for personalized learning?'
- 'Are you a team player?'
- 'What is your greatest strength?'
- 'What can you offer outside your subject/age specialism?'
- 'What are your views on school uniform?'
- 'What do you know about assessment for learning?'

And even:

- 'What was the last book you read?'
- 'What film did you last see?'

Questions for recent graduates

- 'Why do you want to be a teacher?'
- 'So many teachers leave the profession; what makes you think you'll stay?'
- 'Tell me about your dissertation work.'
- 'What issues in education interest you?'
- 'What are you looking for in your career?'
- 'What direction do you think your career will take?'
- 'What have you done that shows initiative?'
- 'What motivates you?'

Tough questions that you may be asked

- 'Tell me about yourself.' This is a tricky question. 'How long have you got?' might be on the tip of your tongue. Rather than begin a monologue on your best characteristics, it might be better to ask, 'Is there a particular aspect that interests you?'
- 'What did you dislike about the last school you taught in?' This is the one situation when honesty may not be the best policy. 'I hated the head – he was amoral' is probably not going to win you favours! Even if your experience of the school showed it to be run by mavericks and attended by thugs, say something tactful about what you learnt there and express your desire to expand your horizons.
- 'Why did you take a job strawberry picking?' Every job, no matter how apparently menial, has given you experience and taught you some skills. Formulate an answer that reflects this and shows that you can extract

positive benefits from every situation. If you can possibly relate it to teaching, then do so.

- 'Why did you choose to train at . . . institution?' Avoid answers like 'Because my Dad went there', 'Because it was the only one that would have me' or 'It meant that I didn't have to leave home.' You have spent at least a year there so speak about its strong points and how much you enjoyed being a part of the institution.

- 'Why do you think you would like this post?' Regardless of the truth, you must relate your answer to the job specification. Tell the panel what they want to hear. When you have done that, there is no harm in injecting a little humour into the proceedings and admitting, for example, that it would allow you to live on the doorstep of your favourite football team. At this stage, they will have made a decision and you can afford to reveal more aspects of your character.

- 'What do you know about this school?' Be honest about what you know. Do not be tempted to bluff. If you have to think on your feet, mention aspects you have learnt since being at the school for the interview. Outsiders' perceptions are always very helpful for a school to understand how it is viewed by the world. The key points here are honesty, tact and diplomacy. There is also a great amount you can find out from a school's web site. (Even if they don't have one, that tells you something!) Also look up their OFSTED report on the Internet, available through the OFSTED site (www.ofsted.gov.uk).

- 'What aspects of the job are most crucial?' Do not focus on the parts that you would most like to do. They are looking for tendencies towards task avoidance and your abilities to prioritize. Teaching and learning, raising achievement and national agendas such as *Every Child Matters* are key things to mention here.

- 'What are your energy levels like?' Everyone goes through periods when their energy levels are low; it is in our nature to experience these fluctuations. However, prospective employers, some of whom think that because you are (probably) young you will be able to keep a consistent pace indefinitely, do not always understand this. Rather than speak about how you have a tendency to get tired if you work too hard, focus on what you do to maintain good health, such as eating sensibly, taking regular exercise, going to a relaxation class, etc.

- 'How long do you think you would stay in the job if we offered it to you today?' This is a really difficult one! How could you possibly know or answer with any accuracy? You could say something like 'I intend to commit to this job and work conscientiously. I would be delighted if it was offered to me and do not envisage any need to move jobs in the foreseeable future.'

ABOUT UNFAIR DISCRIMINATION

Interviewers have a moral and legal duty to avoid unfair discrimination on the grounds of disability, race, ethnic background, religion (with the exception of church-aided schools), marital status, political preferences (including trade union membership), sexual orientation, age and gender. While it is not illegal for you to be questioned on any of these areas, it is generally considered to be bad practice, and any questions asked of you must also be asked of all the other candidates if unfair discrimination is to be avoided. However, many candidates are asked such questions and are happy to answer.

The best policy if you are asked such a question is to take one of two options. Either answer it, taking care to remember the context in which the question was asked for future reference, or politely explain that you would rather not answer that question. Only if your interviewers persist should you offer further explanation of your decision.

Interview questions should be based on the person specification for the job, rather than the private life of the individual. If a school goes beyond this boundary, ask yourself, why do they want this information, and what are they going to do with it?

Questions that you may like to ask

At some stage in the interview, you should be offered the opportunity to ask some questions. It is wise to have some ready to show how well you have prepared and your interest in the school and the job. Alternatively, if absolutely everything has been discussed and you can think of no further comments to make, say that you are happy that all of your questions have been covered. This implies that you had thought of some in advance!

The following should give you some ideas:

- Has the school had an OFSTED inspection recently? What was the outcome?
- Who would be your employers, the governing body or the local authority?
- Will you be a class tutor? What pastoral support will there be for you as a tutor?
- Will you have to teach personal and social education, or does a specialist teach that?
- Will you be offered the chance to come into school before starting work if you are successful?

EXAMPLE

One of the reasons for the smooth progress of my first few days at Stafford was the knowledge that I had gained during a number of visits to the school before the summer holiday. These proved to be invaluable, particularly as they allowed me to familiarize myself with the basic layout of the school, its routines and its policies and schemes of work. I was particularly pleased to have the opportunity to meet my future class and to discuss their progress with their present teacher. It was extremely reassuring to discover that they were not the class of horrors that I had dreamt of over the past few nights.

(Lee, NQT, East Sussex)

- What would your starting salary be (if this has not been made clear)?
- Would any pre-qualification employment be taken into consideration when you are placed on the salary scale?
- Is there an active parent–staff association?
- Do parents come into the school to help?
- Does the school put on any drama or music productions during the year?
- Is there information and communications technology (ICT) support for staff?
- What outings and visits do pupils go on?
- Have there been any other NQTs at this school recently? Did they successfully complete their induction periods?
- What are the main strengths of the induction programme here?
- Will there be consortium arrangements for the induction of NQTs (e.g. clusters of schools getting together to deliver support)?

It is always better to ask one utterly appropriate question than a flurry of non-specific ones, and it is perfectly acceptable not to ask any at all.

Out-of-school-hours learning activities are big now and very much a part of the extended schools agenda. Over two-thirds of schools have increased their provision of these activities in recent years to the extent that a typical primary pupil is now spending around two hours a week on out-of-school-hours activities and a typical secondary pupil around three hours a week. It would be shrewd to find out what activities are offered by the school so that you can determine whether or not you can offer an activity that has not been available at the school before.

Possible outcomes

You are offered the job

Congratulations! Make sure the offer is unambiguous – 'Are you in a position to accept this job?' does not constitute an offer. Providing you are happy to accept, some schools may want you to start before the end of term, even if only as supply teacher. If this offer is made, you would be wise to accept. It will make the start of term far less daunting. When your offer letter arrives, write a brief letter of thanks, confirming arrangements for your first day if appropriate.

You are unsuccessful

Although this is disappointing, it can be a blessing in disguise. You should be offered a debriefing that will be invaluable for future interviews. If you are turned down but desperately want to work there, it is worth sending a letter saying how much you enjoyed the interview, how impressed you were with the school and that you would like to be considered for future vacancies.

You are offered the job, but are not sure if you want to accept

One reason for this could be that you have another interview lined up in a school that you feel you would prefer. If this is the case, be honest with the panel and ask for 24 hours in which to make your decision. This should be granted, but any longer and the school may want to offer the job to the second choice. Difficult as it may seem, you may find yourself having to take a leap of faith in either rejecting the job in the hope of being offered the one that you would prefer, or accepting and resolving to make a go of it. Do not accept the job with the intention of pulling out should you be offered another in the future as you may find yourself in breach of contract, for which you could be sued, even if you only accept a verbal offer. Seek union advice urgently if you find yourself in this predicament.

If you verbally accept a job, make sure that it is subject to your acceptance of the written terms and conditions of the position. If you decide to pull out before accepting the post in writing, you may still be in breach of contract, but it would be unusual for this to be pursued by the school. Once you have accepted the job in writing, to withdraw may see you facing legal action. Don't do anything without seeking the advice of your union.

What if you're not successful?

If you don't manage to get a job to start in the September after you qualify, this will not necessarily affect your career prospects and is certainly nothing to be overly concerned about. It's a good idea to use the time to gain additional experience. Once your financial position is sorted out (you could get a temporary full- or part-time job, or sign on), you could organize some voluntary work in a local school if time allows. You could also look into special schools. Add any additional experience you gain while job seeking to your CV and Career Entry and Development Profile. When you do find a job and start mid-year, find out at the interview what the implications will be for your induction year – when will you be deemed to have started and completed your induction? Will you be given any additional support? Sometimes, delays in starting your teaching career can be a blessing in disguise. You may not be in full-time employment as a teacher, but what additional experience has it allowed you to get? You will probably find you will go for very different jobs as a result.

Key points about the interview process

Everything you do and say during an interview is about selling yourself. Every aspect of the process is relevant, so even when you think you are just chatting to a member of staff in the staffroom while waiting to be called in for your interview, what you say and how you come over will be fed back to the panel. You can't afford to be complacent at all on the day of an interview! It's essential to sell yourself. It's amazing how many NQTs let themselves down by appearing to fear talking about what they are good at. Interviews are not the time for misplaced modesty! And if you are asked whether you would accept the job if it was offered to you, say yes, unless you are certain that you wouldn't.

ACTION

Regardless of the outcome of your interview, take some time to evaluate what happened and your interview strengths and weaknesses. This will be useful to review before future interviews.

ABOUT THE CRIMINAL RECORDS BUREAU (CRB) CHECK

All teachers have to be checked by the Criminal Records Bureau (CRB) for previous convictions. This check can only be done after selection, rather than on all of the candidates for a job; therefore all verbal job offers are subject to this check. The purpose of this exercise is to protect children as far as possible from those unsuitable for the job.

It is vitally important to declare all convictions, cautions or bind-overs that you may have incurred, including any that would normally be regarded as 'spent'. Failure to do so could be interpreted as falsifying your application and could be grounds for instant dismissal. There is a Disclosure Service to use if you are in any doubt about this criminal record check (phone the helpline number on 0870 90 90 811 or check online at www.crb.gov.uk).

Your application will also be checked against what is known as *Information held under Section 142 of the Education Act 2002* (formerly known as List 99). This list contains details of people who are barred or restricted from working in schools by the Department of Children, Schools and Families (DCSF).

Moving to a new area

Any home move involves a tremendous amount of organization, and sometimes important tasks such as registering with a dentist and doctor are left until you are forced to act.

Registering with practitioners

Aim to get this sorted out before you start your first term at your new school. This will avoid any unnecessary delay in getting treatment when you need it.

Getting a GP

Every public library carries a list of GPs in the area. Use it to identify the practice nearest your new home. When you make an appointment to register with a new doctor, take into account any preferences you may have for either a male doctor or a female one, and any specialisms that the GPs at the practice may have.

Most GPs carry out a mini-medical as part of the registration process, including weight and blood-pressure checks and blood and urine tests, so be prepared for a slightly longer initial consultation.

Finding a dentist

Don't leave it until crippling toothache forces you into a dentist's chair before registering. Although few and far between, there are still some dentists taking on NHS dental work, which is by far the cheapest option for newly qualified teachers. Your GP's surgery should maintain a list of NHS dentists in your area, as should your local library. If you are not fortunate enough to get an NHS dentist, you may want to consider joining HSA, which is a mutual offering a choice of healthcare options including dental plans. By paying a monthly amount, you can claim back a percentage of the overall cost of treatments. See www.hsa.co.uk for further information.

Other healthcare providers

Many people now combine conventional medical treatment with complementary therapies. The availability of such therapies on the NHS is increasing rapidly as the medical profession embraces their success in treating many of today's common ailments. Ask your GP what complementary therapies are available on the NHS. Otherwise, your local health-food store or *Yellow Pages* will be sources of information on private practitioners. The professional body of a particular therapy can put you in touch with local practitioners and, as ever, personal recommendations are always valuable.

Arranging childcare

Arranging suitable childcare can be particularly difficult if you move to a new area. In the absence of personal recommendation, ChildcareLink will be a good place to go for information (call 0800 2 346346 or visit www.childcarelink.gov.uk). You can also get information on childcare issues from HM Revenue and Customs (www.hmrc.gov.uk/childcare).

Find out more . . .

Local authorities can be excellent sources of information on moving to the area. The Internet is also a valuable resource when researching schools and towns prior to interviews. The website www.teachingexpertise.com also carries advice on interviews, and the education press such as the *Times Educational Supplement* (www.tes.co.uk) and the education pages of BBC News Online (www.bbc.co.uk) will also offer up-to-the-minute information on the latest hot issues in education.

Chapter 3

All about induction

Experience: that most brutal of teachers. But you learn, my God do you learn.

(C S Lewis)

At the very core of your first year in the teaching profession (for those with full-time jobs at least) lies induction, by the end of which you will be meeting not only the Standards for the Award of Qualified Teacher Status but also the Core Professional Standards for teachers on the main scale. At least, that's the plan! This chapter takes you through all the 'need-to-know' essentials of this all-important period, including:

- QTS skills tests
- The Career Entry and Development Profile
- Induction
- Being mentored
- Learning styles
- Training for professional development
- Inspection and observation.

QTS skills tests

There are three skills tests that all trainee teachers must pass before they can be awarded QTS. These tests are in numeracy, literacy and ICT. If you are not awarded QTS because you have not passed the skills tests, you will not be able to start teaching (there may be some specific circumstances where this doesn't apply, but they would be incredibly rare).

Your training institution will be able to give you all the information you need on booking the tests, which are fully computerized. There is no limit to the amount of times you can sit the tests.

The literacy test requires you to show that you can:

- spell correctly, especially words from your professional vocabulary;

- punctuate texts with a professional content;
- understand and analyse the kind of texts that teachers encounter in their professional reading.

The literacy skills test is not about testing how you teach the national curriculum or your knowledge of English in the curriculum.

The ICT test requires you to show that you can carry out basic ICT tasks using the following applications:

- word processor;
- spreadsheet;
- database;
- presentation
- email; and
- browser.

The numeracy test requires you to show that you can:

- carry out mental calculations using time, fractions, percentages, measurements and conversions;
- interpret and use statistical information accurately;
- use and apply general arithmetic correctly.

Keep an eye on the TDA web site (www.tda.gov.uk) for the latest information on these skills tests as well as useful support materials.

The Career Entry and Development Profile (CEDP)

The Career Entry and Development Profile (along with the notes of guidance and standards) should accompany all NQTs with QTS to their first job. Designed by the TDA, the CEDP is a framework for target setting and action planning to enable your school to deliver to you the necessary support in a structured manner, based on your strengths and development needs.

It focuses on your professional development needs at three key transition points: as you approach the award of QTS, at the start of induction and towards the end of induction.

The three transition points are as follows:

Transition Point 1

This focuses on your reflections with your tutor as you approach the award of QTS. It asks several questions that are designed to get you thinking. You'll need to draw on evidence such as reports on your teaching, examples of your planning, course assignments or subject audits. You and your tutor will decide on how the Profile can be used in the most supportive way.

Transition Point 2

This focuses on the start of induction and your discussions with your induction tutor about your current development priorities and how these may differ from those identified at Transition Point 1. You'll need to draw on evidence such as your notes from Transition Point 1, the information you have about your school and any additional experience gained between gaining QTS and starting induction. Think of your notes for this transition point as being pointers to where evidence of your development can be found elsewhere. There's no need to repeat here what is recorded elsewhere.

Transition Point 3

This focuses on your reflections on your induction period as you reach its conclusion. You will 'take stock' and think about your progress and your aspirations for continuing professional development in your career. There is no need to write lengthy responses to the questions posed by the CEDP. This is all about the process of having discussions with colleagues about your progress, your priorities, your strengths and what you want to do next. Although these discussions should be recorded so that you can revisit that thinking, it's OK just to make notes, or gather together material that already exists. Ultimately, this process will help you to develop your analytical and reflective skills.

The purposes of the CEDP

According to the TDA, the purposes of the CEDP are:

- to help you make constructive connections between the initial teacher training, induction and later stages of your development as a teacher;
- to focus your reflection on your achievements and goals in the earliest stages of your teaching career;
- to guide the processes of reflection and collaborative discussion about your professional development needs which will take place as part of your initial teacher training and induction programmes.

The CEDP is not, however, the record of your progress towards meeting the QTS or Core Standards, a reference or testimonial, or an isolated document. Rather, it is part of your whole early professional development continuum but it cannot stand alone or achieve anything in its own right.

Primarily, the CEDP is just for you, as you will be at its centre, answering the questions it poses, in collaboration with your ITT tutor and with your induction tutor and other colleagues.

Who is responsible for the CEDP?

There are three main people with responsibilities for your Career Entry and Development Profile under the current induction arrangements:

- your headteacher, who will have to ensure that all the monitoring, support and assessment that you receive takes your Career Entry and Development Profile into account;
- your induction tutor, who will help to set up a suitable programme of monitoring, support and review that should be firmly based in your reflections as set out in your Career Entry and Development Profile;
- you yourself will be responsible, as you will be expected to work with your headteacher and induction tutor in target setting and generally be 'fully engaged' in your induction period.

What the CEDP does for you

The CEDP does actually allow you to take control of your career, providing it is treated as intended by your training institution and your school. You can identify aspects of your skills base that need improvement. Don't think of these aspects as weaknesses, but as areas that you would like to develop further. When you start your first teaching job, you are not expected to be an expert at everything – far from it. Most experienced teachers agree that it took them at least three years before they felt they had a strong understanding of what it meant to be a teacher, and even then they continued to learn. In order, moreover, to be in the position of taking up a teaching post, you have satisfied high standards of competence.

Think of the Career Entry and Development Profile as a way of helping to bridge the inevitable gap between training and working in post. The fact that there probably is a gap between training and working should not necessarily be considered as a shortcoming of your ITT provider – whatever the standard of your training, there will always be a period of transition at this time.

Maximizing the use of the CEDP

- Use it as evidence of progress. It can then serve as an excellent foundation for future professional development.
- Adapt it as necessary to take account of progress made in the early days and the context of your school. Don't consider it to be set in stone. Voice your needs if they change as a result of your first few weeks of teaching and talk about the possibility of accommodating them in your profile. What knowledge would make it easier for you to perform your job? Think of short-, medium- and long-term goals.
- Use it to support your induction programme at your new school – it should help you to receive the support you need rather than the help your school wants to give.

- Allow it to strengthen your bargaining position when it comes to further training. There should be a file of forthcoming training courses in your school. If not, ask the adviser with responsibilities for NQTs about what is coming up.
- Think of the processes by which you will achieve desired outcomes. Both process and outcome are relevant to your development. What do you want? How will you get it?
- Use it to establish sound reflective practices – vital for lifelong learning.

Induction

> Be aware of your own achievements.
>   (Dan Millman)

Not only is it vital that you receive induction into working at your new school, but you will also need inducting into the profession as a whole. In order to ensure that NQTs across the country receive equitable induction (as far as possible), a statutory induction period exists, which combines support, monitoring and assessment of your performance as an NQT.

The induction that you receive in your first year in the profession can really influence your attitude to, and opinion of, the teaching profession. For some, it is the main factor in whether they remain in teaching and it certainly forms the foundation of your further professional development.

For this reason, it is essential that you become familiar with the induction arrangements for NQTs. A good starting point is the Statutory Guidance on Induction for Newly Qualified Teachers in England (DCSF reference: 00364–2008). You can download this document from Teachernet (www.teachernet.gov.uk). It covers the induction process, the special circumstances (that naturally exist!), what happens in the event of making unsatisfactory progress, the appeals process, the roles and responsibilities of NQTs, headteachers, induction tutors, governing bodies, and others, as well as offering a very useful overview of the induction process and list of contacts and links. Make sure you print off a copy of this document and keep it somewhere readily accessible in case you need to refer to it. The TDA website has advice for NQTs too: www.tda.gov.uk.

The key features of induction

While there is no single model of induction, because each induction period must be individualized and specific to each NQT, there are certain key features to be aware of. The following is the minimum you can expect from your induction period:

- All teachers who gain QTS and who want to work in a maintained school or non-maintained special school must complete an induction period.

- The induction period to be served is the equivalent of one school year (three, four or five terms, depending on the system in place in your school), pro rata for part-time teachers.
- You must complete at least a term for that period to count towards your induction. This is particularly important to NQTs working as supply teachers in their first year. The headteacher will be able to tell you in advance if your time at his/her school can count towards your induction period. Induction cannot be done retrospectively.
- You will be given a reduced timetable, which will be no more than 90 per cent of the normal timetable for teachers at your school (this applies pro rata to part-time and supply NQTs). You are also entitled to a further reduced timetable for planning, preparation and assessment (PPA). If you are doing your induction in a sixth form or college of FE you should have a comparably reduced timetable.
- You will have at least three formal assessment meetings. These meetings normally take place towards the end of each term in a three-term year.
- At the end of your induction, your headteacher must write to the 'appropriate body' (usually your local authority) with his/her recommendation on whether you should pass or fail. The appropriate body will then inform you of the outcome of your induction (although this shouldn't be a surprise at this stage!).
- Your induction period may be extended if you miss a certain amount through absence.
- If you are deemed to have failed your induction period, you may appeal against the decision. The General Teaching Council for England deals with appeals and your union should support you through this process.

Who is responsible for your induction period?

Responsibility for your induction period is shared between you, your headteacher, your induction tutor/mentor, the 'appropriate body' and the governing body.

ABOUT WHERE YOU CAN DO YOUR INDUCTION

According to the Statutory Guidance on Induction for Newly Qualified Teachers in England (DCSF reference: 00364–2008), the induction period can be undertaken in the following institutions (under specific conditions – be sure to check with the Guidance mentioned above for the exact conditions that apply to each institution):

- maintained schools
- non-maintained special schools
- maintained nursery schools
- nurseries that form a part of a maintained school
- local authority maintained children's centre
- independent schools (including academies and city technology colleges)
- FE colleges
- sixth form colleges
- schools and colleges in Wales in which induction may be served under Welsh regulations

You may *not* serve your induction period in the following (again, specific conditions apply so be sure to read the above mentioned guidance for absolute clarity):

- pupil referral units
- secure training centres
- schools requiring special measures (there are some conditions in which this is acceptable)
- FE institutions which are deemed unsuitable by Ofsted
- independent schools which don't meet the conditions
- private nurseries and other early years settings that don't meet the conditions
- schools abroad including British schools

Remember, you are only legally able to start your induction period once you have been awarded Qualified Teacher Status by the General Teaching Council for England *wherever* you undertake it.

Your induction responsibilities

The responsibility for a successful induction is shared between certain key players such as you, the local authority and your school. What follows is what you should consider to be the minimum responsibilities that you have for your induction period:

- You must provide evidence that you have QTS before starting induction (the GTCE will tell you whether you have been awarded QTS).
- You must make your Career Entry and Development Profile available to your headteacher and induction tutor as early as possible and use it as a basis for planning your induction period.

- You should be actively involved in the planning of your monitoring and development programme, fully participating in it and taking increasing responsibility for your professional development as the induction period progresses.
- You must raise any concerns you have through the appropriate channels as soon as they arise. Failure to do so could mean that your chances of successfully completing your induction period are severely limited.
- You should keep copies of all induction reports and records of monitoring etc.
- You should agree with your induction tutor how to make best use of your reduced timetable.
- You should agree the start and end dates of your induction period with your induction tutor.
- You should monitor your progress against the Core Standards.

ABOUT RAISING CONCERNS

If you have any concerns about the way that your induction period is progressing, it is essential that you discuss these sooner rather than later. Your school must have an internal procedure set up for NQTs to raise concerns and it is best to use this first. If this route does not bring a satisfactory result, contact the named person at the appropriate body with responsibility for dealing with NQTs' concerns. This person should investigate your concerns fully as soon as possible so that they can be sure that your induction programme, post and responsibilities are suitable and fair and that you are being adequately supported. They will need to make sure that unreasonable demands are not being made of you. It would also be sensible to get advice from your union at this stage. Document all concerns that you have for your own reference. Include details of why you are concerned, who else is involved, what you have done to help the situation and what you consider may alleviate your concerns. Also keep a record of what your induction tutor/mentor and headteacher do to solve any problems you raise. Do not leave anything to drift in the hope that things will resolve themselves. It is not overdramatic to say that your future in the teaching profession could be at stake, and the Statutory Guidance on Induction places gives NQTs a responsibility for raising concerns.

Your headteacher's induction responsibilities include

- Your headteacher (along with the appropriate body) has overall responsibility for ensuring that the induction you receive is suitable and individualized.

- He/she will have to keep in close contact with the appropriate body regarding all aspects of your support, monitoring and assessment.
- He/she must liaise with other headteachers if you are completing your induction period in more than one school. When a teacher is doing induction in more than one school, only one headteacher can take the lead.
- He/she must ensure that NQTs teach a timetable that is 90 per cent of the normal teaching timetable in your school. The remaining 10 per cent of your timetable is for focused induction and development activities.
- He/she must keep copies of all induction reports and records of monitoring etc.
- Your headteacher will recommend whether you should pass or fail your induction period.

Your induction tutor's responsibilities include

- Your induction tutor/mentor is, in effect, your line manager as far as your induction goes and he/she must be fully aware of his/her duties.
- He/she must devise a suitable programme of induction for you that is individualized and will allow for fair and thorough assessment of your abilities as a teacher as well as suitable support including coaching and mentoring, and monitoring on a day-to-day basis.
- He/she must formally assess you at regular intervals and make fair and rigorous judgements about you. He/she must also do six reviews of your progress during induction.
- He/she must make recommendations to your headteacher on the outcome of your induction period.

The appropriate body's responsibilities include

- With your headteacher, the appropriate body is responsible for your training and supervision during your induction period.
- It is responsible for quality assurance of induction arrangements and may give guidance and assistance to schools and individuals.
- It must ensure that your headteacher and governing body are aware of what they should be doing and are doing it.
- It must make the final decision on whether you are deemed to have completed the induction period satisfactorily (in other words, whether you have met the Core Standards and continued to meet the Standards for QTS) based on your headteacher's recommendations.
- It must inform you and your headteacher of its decision.
- It must give the NQT at risk of failing additional support, and assure itself that the induction being offered is of the highest quality.
- It must ensure that there are no conflicts of interest arising from its duty to support an inductee at risk of failure and its responsibilities for making the final decision on satisfactory completion of induction.

- It must inform the General Teaching Council for England of its decision regarding your induction period. It will do this by supplying an electronic list of successful inductees and also those who fail induction or who have induction extended.

The governing body's responsibilities include

- The governing body must be fully aware of the implications of employing an NQT and ensure that the key personnel involved in the induction of NQTs are in a position to perform their duties to the highest standards. It must also make sure that the Statutory Guidance on Induction is complied with.

You can find out more about roles and responsibilities in the induction period from the Statutory Guidance on Induction for Newly Qualified Teachers in England (DCSF reference: 00364–2008).

What the induction period means for you

There are many distinct advantages for NQTs undergoing statutory induction, providing all concerned are aware of their responsibilities and are keen to maximize the benefits of the situation. For this reason, it is worth knowing these points at the very least:

- All concerned in your induction period must be conscious of its developmental purpose.
- You should be fully involved and actively participate in self-monitoring and assessment against the Standards for QTS (to ensure you are continuing to meet and build on them) and the Core Standards (see Appendices 4 and 5).
- You should be informed from the start of your responsibilities for your professional development.
- The induction that you receive should be equitable to induction received by NQTs in different schools, as the statutory arrangements and the monitoring procedures encourage national standards.
- Your induction should be individualized and well targeted rather than vaguely supportive. You should be told about institution-wide policies.
- You won't be expected simply to meet the Core Standards but to build on the Standards for QTS consistently and draw together your other skills and achievements as well.
- If your induction tutor is also your headteacher (be extremely wary of this set-up, although in some very small schools this may be unavoidable), a third party should also be involved at formal assessment meetings.

- Your teaching post should be one that does not require you to teach outside your age range and subject specialism, that means you teach the same classes regularly, that doesn't involve extra responsibilities (without preparation and support) and that does not present severe discipline challenges. However, there is nothing legally preventing you from teaching in primary or secondary phases, irrespective of the age range you studied during your training.

- Your timetable should be *no more than* 90 per cent of the usual timetable for main scale teachers at your school, and this must allow for targeted induction rather than extra preparation or non-contact time. The timetable reductions should be evenly distributed throughout your induction period. You should also receive time for planning, preparation and assessment (PPA).

- If your school is unable to provide induction of a high enough standard, your headteacher is responsible for arranging experience for you in another school. Be sure to talk to your induction tutor/mentor and named person at the appropriate body if you suspect this should be happening.

- You will be observed at least once in any six- to eight-week period and certainly within your first four weeks (and ideally in your first week). After these observations you should be given the opportunity to discuss the lesson and the conclusions your observer has reached.

- Assessment observations must be focused and a written record must be kept including details of any action needed as a result of the observations. Induction objectives can then be revised.

- You should have three formal assessment meetings with either your head or your induction tutor during the induction period. The third meeting will end your formal induction assessment and will be the basis of your head's recommendation to the Appropriate Body as to whether you have met the core standards or not.

- Your induction period must include the opportunity to observe experienced teachers. Each observation should have a focus.

ABOUT FOLLOW-UP DISCUSSIONS

It is really important that any discussions that you have with your induction tutor after an observation are focused and constructive. Although there may be time pressures for both of you, the benefits of talking through your collective impressions of what took place should far outweigh any inconveniences. These ideas may help you to make the most of your discussions:

- Make sure that all observations have an agreed focus so that the discussions afterwards have a relevant purpose.

- Aim to analyse the observed lesson and evaluate it for yourself before you discuss it with your induction tutor/mentor.
- Be honest about the positive points. Don't shy away from a bit of personal praise, but be sure to identify the evidence for your views.
- Likewise, ask for evidence to back up any statements that appear to be founded in opinion.
- Prioritize the points that you want to discuss in case time pressures prevail.
- Aim to identify through professional dialogue any future action that needs to be taken.
- Keep a written record of any post-observation discussions.

ABOUT FORMAL ASSESSMENT MEETINGS

The best way to view assessment meetings is as markers of your progress throughout your induction period. It is important that you feel free to discuss all your concerns, achievements and needs for further professional development. You should have at least three formal assessment meetings (i.e. one at the end of each term in a three-term year) with informal assessment meetings in between. At no point should you be surprised by any conclusion that has been reached on your work as, if everyone involved is performing their duties as they should, opinion on your progress should be made known to you throughout your induction period and not saved for formal assessment times.

These meetings should be informed by written reports from at least two observations and two progress review meetings that have taken place within the last term and any judgements must relate directly to the Standards for QTS and the Core Standards.

The first formal meeting will look at how consistently you are meeting the standards for QTS and beginning to meet the Core Standards, based on evidence from meetings and observations as well as your self-assessments, evaluations and lesson plans, etc.

The second formal meeting will look at how well you are meeting the Core Standards.

The third formal meeting is the final assessment of whether you are to be successful or not. If it is thought that you will be deemed to have passed your induction period, the meeting can also be used to discuss your development needs and to set objectives for the next academic year. For this reason, it is worth thinking about what these may be in advance.

You should be asked to sign the assessment forms, which will then be sent to the appropriate body within 10 working days of each assessment. You should also be given the opportunity to make your own comments on these forms and you should receive copies of every written report on you, which should be kept.

You can find out more from the Statutory Guidance on Induction for Newly Qualified Teachers in England (DCSF reference: 00364–2008).

ABOUT MAKING UNSATISFACTORY PROGRESS

The vast majority of NQTs will be successful in completing their induction period, especially as concerns on both sides can be raised very early on. You should be informed of any chance that you may not be successful as soon as concerns arise, and the summative assessment forms from your formal assessment meetings must record that you risk failing the induction period. Individual weaknesses must be identified and a structured plan of action to guide you towards success must be put in place. You must be told exactly why you are thought to be at risk of failing, and a third party (e.g. your headteacher) must observe your teaching. The appropriate body will be informed that you are considered to be at risk of failing the induction period and your headteacher should write to you about the improvements that you need to make in order to be successful. You must be told formally of the consequences of not making the necessary improvements.

If, at any stage of this process, you are unhappy with your treatment, talk to the named person at the appropriate body as soon as possible. Also seek advice from your union and the Statutory Guidance on Induction for Newly Qualified Teachers in England (DCSF reference: 00364–2008). Don't forget that you do have a right to appeal against a decision to fail you. This process, while ultimately designed to be supportive to NQTs, has certain key features that you should be aware of. It is really important not to attempt to navigate the appeals procedure without the professional support of your union.

Mentoring

The quality of the mentoring that you receive is central to your experience of induction and being aware of this can help you to ensure that you don't miss out.

Mentoring is no longer a new concept in the teaching profession and has been the subject of much research in recent years, perhaps reflecting the fact that the role involves far more than simply coordinating the support that you receive. There has to be a real partnership between you and your induction tutor and a culture of effective, challenging support for your induction period to be of value. It would not be unrealistic for you to have high expectations of the mentoring process. At the very least you can expect:

- a carefully selected induction tutor with excellent interpersonal skills who knows the exact details of his/her role;
- an induction tutor with sufficient time to devote to your induction period so that fair judgements can be made on your progress;
- a relationship with your induction tutor that can develop over the time of your induction, in response to your progress and changing needs, with support always remaining a constant.

Research from the United States suggests that the better the start you have in a profession, the greater are your chances of success. While mentoring and induction form only part of the picture, with conditions of service also playing a role in your levels of job satisfaction, it is important to be alert to the quality of mentoring that you are being offered and the impact it can have on this consequential year.

ABOUT POSSIBLE TOPICS FOR FOCUS

Throughout your induction period, there should be plenty of opportunity to focus on myriad topics. Your targets for development as set out in your CEDP will form the basis of many of your meetings, but you may also like to consider the following ideas (if they are not already targets). This book covers many of them and can be used as a basis of any such sessions:

- accidents;
- additional adults in your classroom;
- anger management;
- assemblies;
- assessment;
- behaviour management;
- body language;
- bullying (of adults and children);
- child safety/protection;
- circle time;
- citizenship;
- classroom atmosphere/organization;
- community involvement;

- cover lessons;
- curriculum issues;
- differentiation;
- effectiveness in the classroom;
- English as a second or other language;
- equal opportunities;
- Every Child Matters;
- extended schools;
- extra-curricular activities;
- first aid;
- governors and their roles;
- health and safety;
- homework;
- ICT across the curriculum;
- inspection;
- moderation of children's work;
- motivating children;
- multiple intelligences;
- parents' evenings;
- pensions;
- performance management;
- personalization;
- planning;
- prioritization;
- questioning skills;
- record keeping;
- refugee children;
- reports;
- rewards;
- rights and responsibilities;
- sanctions;
- school visits;
- self-evaluation;
- social, moral, spiritual and cultural education;
- special educational needs;
- stress;
- target setting;
- teaching styles;
- tutoring;
- voice protection and projection.

Your relationship with your induction tutor

While you should expect great things of your induction tutor, there is an obligation on NQTs to work at this relationship to help ensure that your induction period is an extremely positive springboard into the profession, allowing for your skills to be built on year after year.

If, for any reason, your relationship is not working effectively, make every effort to resolve this diplomatically within your school. If you are unsuccessful, the named person with responsibilities for NQTs at your local authority will almost certainly be able to help. Do keep records of your attempts to improve your situation. Usually, however, good communication skills will be sufficient in making your needs known.

What is known to be helpful

- The opportunity to visit your school and even take part in team teaching as much as possible before taking up your post.
- Early observations, particularly in your first two weeks at the school. These are helpful in identifying emerging issues.
- A relationship with your induction tutor that facilitates frank discussions. This should include having the opportunity to discuss your respective roles and share professional reflections.
- Frequent informal support from your induction tutor as well as other colleagues, perhaps through a 'buddy' system (where you are allocated a particular person, who does not have responsibilities for assessing you, in whom you may confide). This way, each meeting need only cover a few issues.
- An induction tutor trained in listening skills, and willing to question his/her own practice, while being competent and confident in his/her own understanding of teacher effectiveness.
- The opportunity to observe and then analyse with colleagues *why* a particular technique works.
- Support that covers curriculum issues as well as day-to-day job management.
- Encouragement when on a plateau, through a wide range of helping strategies so that consolidation does not turn into stagnation; pushing limits within safe boundaries.
- Coordinated approaches to mentoring rather than *ad hoc* arrangements.
- A school ethos of learning from mistakes.
- Asking for support before problems develop.
- Clearly focused observations with the opportunity for NQTs to discuss their rationale for the lesson content and their reflections following the event.
- Specific, timely guidance on problem areas identified by NQTs.
- Encouragement to take risks.
- Recognition and celebration of success.

However, there are some potential pitfalls to be aware of:

- If your induction tutor is not supported in his/her work, time constraints may mean that your induction depends heavily on the good will of colleagues.
- Your mentor may be untrained.
- Your reduced timetable may not be constructive if the time is frittered away through lack of planning.
- Your reduced timetable may be withdrawn part-way through the year (this is against schools' statutory duties).

If you suspect any of the above to be the case in your school, discuss your situation with your headteacher, induction tutor, your union or the named person at your local authority with responsibilities for NQTs.

ABOUT OBSERVING COLLEAGUES

When you observe colleagues as they teach, it can be easy to be swept along by the pace and content of the lesson without making clear sense of the 'how' and 'why'. Keep these questions in mind for discussion afterwards (to enable you both to deconstruct the lesson), and aim to spend most of your time experiencing the lesson and not taking notes!

'Why did you choose . . . activity?'
'Would the lesson have worked if . . .?'
'How could I employ . . . technique with my class(es)?'
'Will you explain why you introduced . . . when you did?'
'If I did . . . are there any pitfalls I should avoid?'
'How have these techniques developed over time?'
'What other methods of explanation do you use?'
You will undoubtedly have your own questions to add to this list.

ABOUT RECEIVING FEEDBACK

When your induction tutor has observed a lesson, he/she will have reached certain conclusions about your performance with reference to the Standards for QTS, the Core Standards and your agreed focus for the observation. These conclusions then have to be passed on to you in the form of constructive feedback.

The feedback that you are offered must take place in total privacy and certainly not within earshot of pupils. You should be given the opportunity to ask questions and seek clarification on what has been said if necessary. A written record should always be kept of any discussions that take place as a result of an observation for several reasons, the most important being that it can be extremely difficult to absorb all that is being fed back. A natural tendency is to latch on to the potentially negative and forget the positive.

When receiving feedback, it is helpful to consider whether you have any blocks to receiving feedback. Do you respect the person doing the observations? Are observations always undertaken to an agreed focus? Are you seeking praise or a critical assessment? An excellent working relationship with your induction tutor will be invaluable here to enable your personal needs (such as encouragement) and professional needs to be met.

If you feel that the feedback you have received is not as constructive as it should have been, you may have to employ the following strategy:

- Attempt to determine what the person debriefing you intends. For example, is there any positive intent, or does it appear to be purely negative (which would be extremely unusual)?
- Feedback should be objective. If you sense that it has become subjective, aim to discuss whether this has in fact happened. It would also be wise to ask for specific examples to illustrate the debriefing you are being given.
- Reflect back to the person debriefing you what you understand to be the key points from the feedback. Use constructive, positive language.
- Do be aware of the power of language. Could it be that you have been oversensitive in your interpretation of what has been said to you? Or do you genuinely feel that you have been treated unfairly?
- Always discuss any concerns you have about your relationship with your induction tutor with the named person within your local authority.

ABOUT ENCOURAGING EFFECTIVE MENTORING

There are certainly things that NQTs can do to encourage effective mentoring during the induction period. Use these points as starters:

- Get to know the Core Standards and Standards for the Award of Qualified Teacher Status thoroughly (see Appendices 4 and 5).
- Attend all the induction sessions that you are offered.
- Work hard at building a solid relationship with your induction tutor.

- Be aware of the time constraints that your induction tutor may be facing, but don't let that put you off asking any questions or raising any concerns.
- Be receptive to new ideas that may be different from those you have encountered in the past.
- Express your needs related to your workload as early as possible – be honest about this, as seemingly confident and capable NQTs can miss out on support.
- Put forward your ideas for your induction and think carefully about how challenging you want your targets to be.
- Get to know last year's NQTs and draw on them for additional support.
- Get to know the areas of expertise of your colleagues.
- Do regular evaluations of your work and acknowledge your progress. Keep records of incidents that have happened in your classroom to use as the basis of discussion.
- When possible and appropriate, give feedback on the quality of the mentoring you are receiving.
- Facilitate constructive discussions by displaying good listening skills and asking for clarification on anything that you don't understand or don't agree with.
- Aim to integrate what you learn from colleagues into your work on a daily basis.

Learning styles

A significant aspect of your induction year will be continuing professional development: in other words, continuing to learn. Having a clear understanding of the way in which you take in information has a profound impact upon the way you approach the lessons you learn as well as the way you approach teaching others. For this reason, it is well worth taking some time to identify, or at least consider, your preferred learning style(s).

A vast amount has been written about learning styles, and a quick search on the Internet will reveal thousands of relevant sites, all with a take on this important aspect of teaching. The often-quoted Kolb's Learning Cycle is an interesting place to start. This cycle identifies four phases of learning: experience, reflection, conceptualization and action. The likelihood is that, rather than moving through all four phases over time, learners in fact come to prefer one or two phases over the others.

Since Kolb's Learning Cycle, other thinkers have looked at learning styles in a different light. The work of Howard Gardner and his theory of multiple intelligences is an example (see www.howardgardner.com for more information).

Other training for professional development purposes

It can be easy to assume that everything you do in your first year of teaching must be based in your induction, and largely, this tends to be the case. However, there will be occasions when you receive training either as part of a whole school or as a department or in response to specific school needs.

Although this training would only be a small part of your overall induction, aim to cultivate a healthy attitude to it because there are undoubtedly benefits you can gather from attending.

The kind of training covers a wide variety of topics, from the generic, such as classroom management and assessment, to the specific, such as special educational needs or literacy at your school. It may be delivered by specialists from outside your school at a central location (such as a teachers' professional centre) or by colleagues in your school.

Maximizing the benefit of training

The best way to glean the most from any training you are offered is to make a conscious decision to gain from each session. Whether this is from the information that has been presented, teachers from other schools or inspiration for the formulation of an idea to incorporate in your teaching, there will always be something that you can leave the session with. Think about these points too:

- Before attending any training, be it in your school or provided externally, think about what the course is about and what you hope to gain from it.
- Plan some questions to ask those giving the training.
- Use the tutors/advisers as a resource – find out their specialisms and get names and numbers or their email addresses if you think they may be useful in the future.
- Take the opportunity to meet NQTs from other schools and perhaps build up your own support network for the exchange of resources.
- Tell training providers if there are any areas you think NQTs would benefit from covering – you could inspire a new course.

Using the information given

You may well leave a training session with a bundle of handouts and an array of ideas floating around your mind. As most teachers then return home with the usual demands on their time (marking, preparation, family etc.), it is no surprise that the information collected may never make it into everyday use.

- Keep a record of any training you attend that includes what was covered and how you can incorporate what you learnt into your work.

- Review these records regularly throughout each term. Even if this only takes a few minutes, you may be inspired by something you read at just the right moment.
- Photocopy any handouts that may be useful for colleagues at your school.
- Talk about the impact of training you have attended at meetings with your induction tutor.

About OFSTED inspections

A fact of teaching life is that you will almost certainly be inspected by OFSTED, the official body for inspecting schools, at some stage during your career and possibly even in your first year of teaching. As an NQT, a little knowledge about the inspection process and the reasons for inspection could help to alleviate any concerns that you may have about it.

The best place to start looking for information on inspection is the OFSTED website (www.ofsted.gov.uk). In particular, look at all the information under inspection of schools and notice the extent to which the Every Child Matters agenda informs what inspectors are looking for. In short, inspectors will report on:

- a description of the school
- the overall effectiveness of the school
    - effectiveness and efficiency of boarding provision
    - what the school should do to improve further
- achievement and standards
    - personal development and well-being
- the quality of provision
    - teaching and learning
    - curriculum and other activities
    - care, guidance and support
- leadership and management
- the extent to which schools enable learners to be healthy
- the extent to which providers ensure that they stay safe
- how well learners enjoy their education
- the extent to which learners make a positive contribution
- how well learners develop workplace and other skills that will contribute to their future economic wellbeing.

It is worth keeping these points in mind if you are inspected as an NQT:

- No allowances are made for the fact that you are an NQT. However, inspectors will not expect new entrants to the profession to be experts.

- You cannot be held responsible for what has happened in your school in the past.
- As someone in the first year of teaching, you are in an excellent position to develop your skills as a teacher using any conclusions from the inspection.
- Get support from other NQTs.

During an inspection:

- Don't change the way you teach; trying new things out for your audience is not a good idea. Don't worry that your lessons may seem unexciting. You should be given the opportunity to discuss with inspectors the context of the work you were observed doing and your rationale for it.
- One inspector compared inspection with the driving test. You know how to teach/drive, but you have to show the inspector/examiner that you do. There will be many aspects of your teaching/driving that you do subconsciously, but you must make sure that the inspector/examiner knows you are doing them. The best analogy for this is looking in the rear-view mirror during a driving test. If you don't physically move your head, the examiner may not realize you have performed this crucial task and fail you. Show or tell the inspector all aspects of your teaching, especially your attention to detail; make explicit the implicit.
- It will come as no surprise that drama teachers tend to do well in inspections. Being able to rise to the occasion with a little acting will certainly serve you well.
- If a lesson seems to fall apart, stop what you are doing and start another activity. You will then be able to demonstrate your flexibility and originality when it comes to problem solving.
- If you have any anxieties about the way that the inspection of your teaching is going, talk to your headteacher. He/she will be meeting the lead inspector on a daily basis and so will be able to raise your concerns.
- Make sure you indulge in some quality relaxation during inspection week, perhaps some early nights or a massage – whatever enhances your sense of relaxation.
- Try to enjoy the inspection!

Other observations

As an NQT, you will have other teachers observing your lessons as part of your induction. This can be daunting, but is mostly very constructive. However, in order for the observations to hold value for you, aim to:

- Spend time beforehand talking to your observer about the lesson you plan to teach, its place in the scheme of work and what it will lead on to.

- Give your observer all the necessary documents for the lesson, e.g. lesson plan (if applicable) and any worksheets or textbooks used.
- Decide where would be the best place for your observer to sit.
- Agree how much of the lesson will be observed.
- Arrange when you can meet to discuss the lesson and hear the feedback.
- Listen to the feedback carefully and accept any tips that may be offered while justifying your actions when appropriate.

Utilizing the feedback

It can be tiresome when you have completed your training, to listen to yet another review of your teaching skills. However, think of these positive aspects: your observer may not have seen you teach before so will be looking at you through fresh eyes; and you will be observed in the context of your school, and therefore feedback should be specific to your job.

After each observation, you should be given some constructive feedback. This should reflect on what happened in the lesson, what was learnt by the children and how effective your teaching appeared to be. There should be a dialogue. Don't feel you have to sit and listen to what your observer has to say without being able to interject and explain your actions and decisions.

You may want to amend your Career Entry and Development Profile. This will help you to glean the most from the observations, and to feel that you are not working alone, by involving your induction tutor. Try not to let any amendments be forgotten until the next observation when it is likely that the same points will be picked up. If the appropriate support is not forthcoming, talk to your induction tutor.

Find out more . . .

- All you need to know about the minutiae of induction can be found in the Statutory Guidance on Induction for Newly Qualified Teachers in England (DCSF reference: 00364–2008) downloadable from Teachernet: www.teachernet.gov.uk.
- There are useful publications and downloads for use to support induction and the CEDP. These are available from the Induction pages of the TDA website (www.tda.gov.uk, publications@tda.gov.uk) or from the TDA publications line (0845 6060 323).
- For more about OFSTED inspection, take a look at the OFSTED website (www.ofsted.gov.uk). *FAQs on School Inspection: Practical Advice and Working Solutions* (published by Routledge, ISBN 978–0–415–43263–4) also covers the experience of inspection in detail.
- Information on all aspects of induction and inspection can be found on the Teaching Expertise website (www.teachingexpertise.com).
- Information on mentoring and coaching can be found at the Centre for the Use of Research and Evidence in Education website www.curee-paccts.com

Chapter 4

Joining a school

A journey of a thousand miles must begin with a single step.
(Lao Tzu)

Becoming a part of a school or college for the first time as a qualified teacher is such a key transition in your career. There are numerous rights and responsibilities to juggle and considerations to make, quite apart from your work in the classroom, including how your school works with the community. This chapter takes an in-depth look at:

- Becoming a professional
- Establishing your position in the school
- Becoming part of a team
- Governing bodies
- The General Teaching Council for England
- Unions
- Parent/teacher associations.

Becoming a professional

Once you have gained QTS, you are no longer a student, and doing the job for real can be a frightening prospect.

ABOUT ACKNOWLEDGING YOUR NEW STATUS

You are now a qualified teacher, but don't be tempted to expect too much of yourself. David Berliner has identified four stages of teacher development: novice; advanced beginner; competent; proficient. It can be easy to expect yourself to sail from novice to proficient in the summer months between qualifying and starting your first job, but this would be an unrealistic pressure.

That said, your rate of growth throughout your first year of teaching will probably be rapid.

The Standards for the Award of Qualified Teacher Status and the Core Professional Standards for Teachers (see Appendices 4 and 5) clearly define what is expected of you and the way that you should work within the wider context of the school community. Make sure you are really familiar with these and get used to thinking about how they relate to your actual work in the classroom and school in general.

Establishing your position in the school

If you have joined a new school, you will have to start from scratch as far as establishing your position with staff and pupils is concerned. They will expect you to fit in and work with shared values and a corporate purpose, and may even look to you to convince them you should be respected. You will have to set up your own routines and expectations and, above all, be consistent at a time when many of your pupils will be more familiar with the working of the school than you are.

- Make sure that you have read and absorbed the appropriate staff handbooks and policies so that you know the professional procedures of the school, including information on special educational needs, sport and discipline. Also read other documentation relating to health and safety, resources, harassment, equal opportunities, child protection, first aid, emergency procedures, security (e.g. in the event of an assault or intruder), accident reporting and school visits.
- Make learning names (of both pupils and colleagues) a priority. Employ techniques such as making seating plans, spending time on name games and introductory sessions, handing out books yourself or taking pictures of your pupils to display on the wall of your classroom. Relating a piece of work to the image of a pupil is also effective.

EXAMPLE

NQT Richard knew how effective it had been to learn the names of his pupils on teaching practice and decided to ease this task once in post by taking a photograph of each pupil he taught. Using a digital camera helped to keep costs down and once he had printed the pictures he cut them up, stuck them to a piece of card and put the name of the child under each picture. He then had an excellent resource to use when marking work, allowing

> him to make direct connections with each child. Make sure you always speak to the Headteacher to get permission to take any photographs of children.

- Do all you can to become familiar with your pupils' personalities. Their abilities will flourish (and sometimes fluctuate) throughout the school year, so it is a good idea to avoid making rash judgements that pupils then have to live up (or down) to.
- Aim to build on what you have achieved in your training in the first crucial weeks. Do not try to 'build Rome in a day'.
- Be aware of your levels of self-confidence and how others might see you. Do not neglect your relationships with other members of staff. If you consider yourself to be fully immersed into the team so will they.

ABOUT VIEWING YOURSELF THROUGH THE EYES OF YOUR PUPILS AND COLLEAGUES

Everyone you meet, from pupils to fellow teachers to parents, will be aware of the fact that you are new. They will wonder what you are like. Are you strict or 'soft', funny or 'boring', better or worse than your predecessor? Most people will assess you in your first meeting and these impressions are hard to change. Bear this in mind as you meet new people, and try to view your classes and colleagues as groups of individuals that you will enjoy getting to know.

You should also consider that some members of the profession view NQTs with a sense of caution. The training that you have undergone and professional expectations that are made of NQTs are now very different from previous years. It is worth being aware that some colleagues may not be familiar with current terminology relating to new teachers and induction.

- Take opportunities to become involved in the whole of school life. For example, attend school concerts and plays, PTA fund-raisers and staff social events. If time permits, there are usually extra-curricular activities that you can contribute to.
- Be aware of the areas of school life where you will have to make your presence known. You will need to interact with many groups of people, so aim to build solid working relationships with each group.
- Aim to keep links with your ITT institution.

ABOUT BEING IN THE MINORITY

It is possible that you may experience additional difficulties settling in if the majority of staff members are of the opposite sex. This can happen to males, particularly in the primary sector, and both males and females in single-sex schools.

While what sex you are may not seem relevant when it is equally repre-sented on the staff, if you are the only male or only female, gender identity can suddenly take on new significance. Try these tips to prevent loneliness:

- Establish a class link with a teacher of the same sex from another school.
- Create friendships and links when on INSET courses.
- Encourage speakers of the same sex as you to visit your school. The pupils will also benefit from the attempt at gender balance.
- Keep discussions with colleagues open about the issues you face as a member of a gender minority. This may encourage sensitivity on the part of your co-workers.
- If you find yourself in a minority for another reason and you are not happy in your situation, talk to your induction tutor. Your union may also be able to offer support, and Internet staffroom forums on education web sites can be good ways of making links with other teachers in the same position as you.

But it's only me

Many new teachers go through a confidence crisis as they make the transi-tion from student to qualified teacher. It is common to wonder why classes should listen to you and pupils respect you. Never forget that there is a whole culture and tradition of education and teaching of which you are about to become a part and, to a certain extent, you can lean on that as you start your career.

When you take your first class as a qualified teacher, it is not 'only you'. It is you, the teacher, in whom many people – not least your tutors and the team of professionals who employed you – have a tremendous amount of faith.

EXAMPLE

In my first few weeks of term, I couldn't get over what a fine line there is between anarchy and order in schools. I felt that things could really get out of hand very easily and having sole responsibility for my classes suddenly felt like a massive challenge. It took me time to realize that what I felt inside wasn't how the kids saw me and that, even if I felt unsure about my place in the profession, to them I was a fully fledged teacher.

(Becky, languages teacher)

ACTION

Think about the reasons why you became a teacher. Now, think about how you can incorporate those ideals into your new post, using the opportunities that your job will give you. Allow yourself to indulge in a little positive thinking on how eminently suitable you are for the task that lies ahead of you.

Becoming part of a team

> None of us is as smart as all of us.
> (Japanese proverb)

As an NQT, you will be part of several teams, not least the team that makes up the staff at your school. Within the team(s) of which you are a part, it is essential that good relationships are created so that work can be completed, values shared and progress made. Good staff relations also have a knock-on effect throughout the school – a cohesive team will be less open to pupil manipulation ('I didn't do my homework because Miss Jones told me that if it was too difficult I should leave it') and more receptive to the dissemination of good practice. They also allow a sense of collective worth and direction to be felt by all staff members.

Ask yourself how effective you are as a team member:

- Do you listen well to others?
- Do you contribute your ideas in good time?
- Do you fulfil your share of the tasks?
- Are you aware of the balance of the distribution of tasks?
- Do you accept assistance from other members of the team?
- Do you offer assistance when you can?
- Are you able to assert your own needs as an NQT? For example, you may have a slightly reduced burden of work within the team because of your other commitments.

Too often, teachers are working hard at creating resources that may be improved by a little collective creativity. There is no doubt that this is the most effective way of coping with the rapidly shifting ground on which teachers work. Effective teams don't carry dead weight in the form of teachers who are not willing to share.

Your responsibilities and rights

Any form of employment involves obligations and duties on the side of both employer and employee. The difficulties related to understanding this in the teaching profession are that a teacher's responsibilities are outlined in several separate documents. This means that you will have to read around to ensure that you know the particular responsibilities and rights associated with your post.

The following documents will be invaluable:

- your contract and job description, which may not be given to you before you begin work;
- the *Standards for the Award of Qualified Teacher Status*, available on the TDA website (see www.tda.gov.uk) and in Appendix 4;
- the *Core Professional Standards for Teachers*, available on the TDA website (see www.tda.gov.uk) and in Appendix 5;
- the latest Teachers' Pay and Conditions Document, available on Teachernet (see www.teachernet.gov.uk).

It is also worth keeping up-to-date with developments regarding teachers' responsibilities on websites such as www.schoolsweb.gov.uk, www.teachernet.gov.uk and www.teachingexpertise.com.

ABOUT UNDERSTANDING YOUR RESPONSIBILITIES AND RIGHTS

It may seem as though you are wasting valuable time by even thinking about your legal liabilities, and a chat with a fellow teacher may reveal that he/she has never bothered looking into this area of employment. However, knowing what you are obliged to do gives you an understanding of what you should not be doing, and will minimize the chances of you becoming involved in a dispute related to your employment. Spend a little time now browsing some of the relevant documents and websites for added peace of mind in the classroom.

Staff conduct

The conduct expected of you should have been made clear when you were employed by your school. It is the governing body of maintained schools that has overall responsibility for regulating teachers' conduct and there should be reasonable and non-discriminatory disciplinary rules and procedures made known to all staff. Grievance procedures should also be made known to staff.

ABOUT 'DISOBEDIENCE'

Your conditions of service will oblige you to obey the 'reasonable directions of the head', be they spoken or written in the various policies of the school. In extreme cases, 'disobedience' could be interpreted as a breach of contract, whether or not you verbally express, or simply demonstrate through your actions, your 'disobedience'. As disciplinary action and, worse, dismissal can follow, it is always essential to discuss with your headteacher any legitimate reasons you may have for not being willing to carry out his/her instructions.

Common-law duty of care

All teachers have what is called a 'common-law duty of care', although precisely what this means is not properly defined. Consequently, any judgements made regarding the duty of care are based on case law.

As an NQT, you should understand the 'common-law duty of care' to mean that you will do 'what is reasonably practicable' when caring for pupils. This means that carrying out ongoing risk assessment is probably wise so as to minimize the number of potential hazards. At the very least, teachers should bear the following factors in mind when assessing risk:

- the hazards and who would be affected by them;
- the safety measures needed to ensure an acceptable level of risk;
- the cognitive development and skill acquisition of pupils (including their motor skills);
- pupils' physical strength, size and shape;
- the school environment.

As long as you demonstrate reasonably careful standards while at work, you should not bear any liability for accidents.

Safeguarding or promoting children's welfare

Every child has the right to protection from abuse and exploitation, and to have enquiries made to safeguard his or her welfare. Although responsibility for investigating child abuse rests outside schools, there may be occasions when you and members of the pastoral team in your school will have to liaise with social services departments over the possible abuse that one of your pupils may be suffering. This is an extremely problematic area for teachers and, as an NQT, you should always talk to the member of the pastoral team who has been designated as the receiver of information about possible abuse as soon as you suspect neglect or any form of abuse. Under no circumstances should you wait to gather more evidence, or talk to the child about your suspicions, before voicing your concerns to the appropriate person.

Your school will have set procedures for dealing with suspected abuse and will pass any information on to the social services department. Only then can investigations begin, which will probably require the cooperation of the school. For this reason, it is vital that you keep a record of every conversation you have regarding the possible abuse of a child, including details of whom you spoke to, what was said, what was decided and the date/time. You should also receive training in child protection issues during your induction period.

ABOUT RECORDING YOUR CONCERNS

Protecting children from abuse is a teacher's legal obligation, and part of that duty must be to protect yourself from allegations of negligence in the future. Always document every conversation you have about suspected abuse. You could also keep a diary in which you keep track of the development of your concerns. Such information can be invaluable at a later stage, especially if there are court proceedings. Remember to record:

- whom you spoke to;
- what was said;
- what was decided;
- the date and time.

Above all, make sure anything you commit to paper is strictly confidential and cannot be accessed by any child or adult other than the person in your school designated to deal with suspected abuse.

ABOUT APPROPRIATE PHYSICAL CONTACT WITH PUPILS

Issues regarding appropriate physical contact with pupils and the physical restraint of pupils are potentially fraught with difficulties. While certain laws and guidance documents do cover this important area, there is, naturally, room for interpretation, which is why it is essential to follow your school's guidance on this. If you are in any doubt about what might be construed as being 'appropriate' and what might be 'inappropriate', talk to your headteacher as soon as possible. You can also get guidance on this from your union, but it is essential for peace of mind to abide by your school's guidelines.

Personal property

> Opportunity makes a thief.
> (Francis Bacon)

All teachers take personal property to school with them, which may or may not be valuable. An item such as a handbag, containing money and credit/debit cards as well as keys, mobile phone and an iPod etc., will be extremely tempting to some pupils. To a certain extent, you should consider that it is your responsibility to avoid placing pupils in positions of temptation, however much you feel you can trust them. This approach usually guards against potentially unpleasant situations arising. For this reason, schools should ensure that teachers have somewhere to secure valuables, such as a lockable desk drawer or a locker. Some teachers prefer to keep their valuables with them all the time.

- Find out what insurance cover you have for loss of, or damage to, personal items. Check your own home contents insurance and any cover your union that may provide. It may seem unfair, but your school and local authority have no legal obligation to protect your property.
- In the event of loss or damage, report the incident to your headteacher and ask what can be done about it. You could also approach your local authority's education human resources department and your union, depending on the seriousness of the loss.
- If ever you suspect that something has been stolen, don't deal with the situation alone. Ask for assistance from your line manager. Never accuse a pupil, however sure you may be; for many people, a false accusation will seem a worse crime than the theft itself.
- If there is a reason for you to look after a pupil's personal property, do so as though it was your own – lock it away. Always return the property personally. Don't give it to another child to pass on, or give your keys to the child so that they may help themselves. However, children should be discouraged from bringing valuables of any kind to school.

Your rights

This is a far more difficult area to quantify. It's not that you do not have any rights as an NQT, far from it, but the rights you have are, in the main, moral rights, such as the right to dignity at work, which is open to varied interpretations.

What follows is what NQTs can consider to be the minimum in terms of rights at work. It is not intended to be definitive and you should refer to your own conditions of employment documents and local practices for more details of your specific situation. Rights associated with induction and professional advice from outside your school are dealt with elsewhere in this book.

The right to correct pay

The governing body of a school commonly has the responsibility for developing a school pay policy and reviewing teachers' salaries annually. The local authority then has the duty to act on the decisions made by the governing body and arrange for payments to be made to the teachers of the school.

The main pay scale that was introduced in September 2002 has six points, from M1 to M6. The minimum starting point for NQTs is M1.

There are separate salaries and allowances for teachers working in inner London, outer London and the fringe areas.

Check with your union and local authority education human resources office that you have been placed on the correct point with the appropriate allowances. From that starting position, every teacher must have an annual salary assessment by the school's governing body and be given a formal statement explaining what his/ her salary is and how it has been arrived at. Salary assessments should also be made whenever the need arises throughout the year, for example if you take on an additional responsibility mid-year.

Unless your local authority or governing body decides that your teaching experience has been insufficient, or you have been employed for fewer than 26 weeks in any one year (not necessarily in the same school or consecutively), you are entitled to an additional full point every year (to a limit – your union can advise on this).

If your performance has been unsatisfactory for any reason, you must be told in good time (in writing) if one of these experience points is going to be withheld. It would be most unusual for a point to be withheld without incompetency procedures being followed. You must also be given suitable help and additional training to help improve performance and, as soon as it is deemed to be adequate, the additional point should be awarded, regardless of when this is in the school year.

Not only are you entitled to correct pay, but also to being paid on time. This is usually the responsibility of your local authority's payroll department. Do be aware that the day you receive your payslip may not be the day that you can start to draw on the money.

The right to equal opportunities

While issues relating to equal opportunities will need to be addressed in your teaching, you also have entitlements as an employee. Most local authorities have their own equal opportunities statements. These will aim to ensure equality of opportunity for all employees on the grounds of:

- gender;
- race;
- religion or creed;
- colour;
- disabilities and medical conditions;
- nationality;
- ethnic origin;
- marital status;
- sexual orientation;
- social class;
- living with HIV and AIDS;
- political belief;
- age;
- dependants;
- trade union membership and affiliation.

This usually entails a commitment on the part of employers to review selection criteria and procedures so that those who can best perform the duties of the job fill vacancies. That way, the focus can remain on abilities and merits as opposed to anything else. This could mean that, in order to remain true to an equal opportunities policy, you may be entitled to extra training so that professional progress can be made.

ABOUT AFFIRMING YOUR RIGHTS TO EQUAL OPPORTUNITIES

Part of an effective equal opportunities policy must be the provision of facilities for complaint and appeal for all employees who feel they have been treated without due regard for the policy. Make sure that you know what the procedures are for lodging a complaint about unfair treatment under your school's equal opportunities policy. To ease the process, document any situations that you feel flout the standards set out in the policy, and talk to a trusted colleague or mentor and a representative from your union about your experiences before making a complaint. Input from others helps you to retain perspective.

The right to take leave

There could be many situations when you may need to take leave. The most common reason is for ill health, but you may also need maternity/paternity or compassionate leave. The exact arrangements and entitlements for leave vary from authority to authority, but there are some minimum standards that you can expect. Your union will be able to inform you about your specific rights regarding leave (those for sick leave, for example, depend on your length of service).

> ### *ABOUT* COMPASSIONATE/EMERGENCY LEAVE
>
> You do not have an automatic right to paid compassionate leave, but, on the whole, employers understand the occasional need of employees to take compassionate leave in the event of the death of a close family member or friend. If you require compassionate leave, speak to your headteacher as soon as possible. Your union will also be able to advise you at this time too. These points will help:
>
> - You will need to keep your school informed of your requirements at such a time, and under no circumstances should you feel guilty about taking time off.
> - Your GP will be able to sign you off sick if you both decide you should have some more time after your compassionate leave ends. As soon as your compassionate leave turns into sick leave, your sick leave entitlements kick in.
> - Compassionate leave is extended in some areas to allow for a day for moving house. Obviously, at such a stressful and busy time, you need to be aware of easing your situation. Moving on a Friday or even in the holidays would be the ideal, but clearly this is not always possible.
> - Other reasons for taking leave may include weddings, christenings, funerals etc. There will be local arrangements, which your union and local authority can inform you of, and it is likely that your school's governors will have devised a policy covering such occasions. These rites of passage can be incredibly important, so don't assume that you won't be able to take time off. It could be that you only need a half-day, which may well be accommodated, but may not be paid.

The right to knowledge of agreed duties and codes of conduct

You have a right to be fully informed of your duties before you begin work at a school. This should include every aspect of the expectations that will be made of you. If you have not been told fully what your duties and obligations entail, you cannot be held responsible for their non-fulfilment.

You are also entitled to be told of the individual codes of conduct at your school, so that you do not have to suffer embarrassment should you inadvertently break one.

The right to be treated in accordance with the law

Although this should be assumed, it is surprising how often teachers find themselves victims of treatment that is either not in accordance with correct procedure, or it is only just within the legal framework when interpreted literally. Advice from your union and your local authority will be useful here.

The right to knowledge of a clear line of authority

You have entitlement to guidance on the power structure in your school and your position therein. This should include information on which personnel you should consult under which circumstances, for example in the event of discipline problems. Much of this will be covered in the early days of induction. Without such knowledge, you may be in danger of ignoring the lines of authority that are already established in your school.

The right to knowledge of disciplinary and appeal procedures

Before any disciplinary action needs to be taken, you should be informed as to where you can find details of disciplinary and appeal procedures. The chances are you will never need to refer to such information, but you do need to be in a position of knowledge.

Such procedures are usually a matter of local agreements, and your governing body or local authority should give you a copy of them. If ever you are involved in a disciplinary matter, it is essential that you consult your union. There are usually informal and formal ways of addressing disciplinary matters. If formal procedures are invoked, you have the right to representation, full information as to the timing and schedule of the process and protection from unnecessary delays.

ABOUT REDUNDANCY

If there is a need to make you redundant on the grounds that your post will cease or significantly diminish, governors should:

- give as much warning as possible;

- consult your unions to seek agreement on the criteria for selection of staff for redundancy;
- ensure that the criteria are reasonably objective;
- consider any representations by union reps;
- consider whether alternative work can be offered.

If ever you are told that there is a possibility that you will be made redundant, or even if rumours start to circulate about imminent redundancies, be sure to consult your union at the earliest stage.

The right to dignity at work

Dignity at work covers many different areas, but holds equal importance to other rights you have. Some of these rights to dignity at work stem from written laws; others are moral rights that you are entitled to assert in a civilized society; for example:

- the right to work in a safe environment with due recognition of health and safety legislation – this includes all safety at work issues and the right to appropriate medical assistance if/when needed;
- the right to work in a clean environment – this especially covers the state of your immediate workspace as well as staff kitchen areas and toilets;
- the right to appropriate treatment from peers and superiors without harassment or bullying.

The governing body

Every school has a governing body. In the maintained sector, governing bodies have far-reaching powers and responsibilities. Their nature varies from school to school; some governors are rarely seen in the building between meetings, yet others are fully integrated in the work of the school, often helping in classes and with school events. Most schools welcome the help and support that is freely given by those governors who are generous with their time and skills.

Governors are volunteers and are responsible for a school's budget. They are central to the running of your school, and must steer it through all eventualities in accordance with the law, the school's articles of government and the policies of the local authority (in community schools).

A school's governing body consists of appointed and elected governors. There are eight different types of governor including local authority, community, associate, foundation, parent, sponsor, partnership and staff governors. The size of the governing body is dependent on the size of the school it serves, but it will usually number between 9 and 20, and it runs on the basis of collective responsibility.

The role of governing bodies

- The main role of governing bodies is to aid in the raising of standards in a school, including creating plans for the school's development. This entails ensuring that pupils at the school are offered the best education possible, through effective leadership and management and correct delivery of the National Curriculum and religious education, assessments and target setting.
- Governors must also ensure that the school has a character in line with its ethos and mission, particularly in voluntary-aided schools. To do this, they must determine the aims of the school as well as the conduct, and appoint, promote, support and discipline staff (including headteachers and deputies) as appropriate. They also set the times of the school day, and the governors in foundation and voluntary schools can set term dates as well.
- Governors have a role in deciding how best the school can promote the spiritual, moral, social and cultural development of pupils.
- Governors must manage the school's budget in accordance with current education law. For example, the Financial Management Standard in Schools (FMSiS) is a requirement that demonstrates that a school is well managed so that the best use of resources is made.

When these roles are considered (among others), it is essential that the governing body and the senior management/leadership team have a good working relationship. The decisions that a governing body has to make are far-reaching, but as long as they act in good faith and stay within education law they are protected from financial liability. The strength of a governing body comes from the ability of its members to work as a team, using the resources and skills at their disposal.

ABOUT WORKING WITH YOUR GOVERNORS

Your governing body must meet at least once a term. Between meetings, the headteacher of your school will keep governors informed of curriculum matters and anything else that is relevant, and there should always be a continuous dialogue between these two aspects of leadership. The agenda, minutes and related papers from governors' meetings must be available for staff to read. Staff governors or the Clerk to the Governors are usually the ones to ensure that this is done.

- Get to know the staff governors in your school. They are the conduits of information between staff and governors, although they are not the delegates of the staff body. You may pass on your views to staff governors but they don't necessarily have to be represented at meetings.

- Find out who the parent governors are at your school. This is particularly important if you teach their children.

- If a governor visits you, find the time to talk about the issues that are facing you in your classroom.

- Try to think of the governors at your school as 'critical friends' as well as nurturers and supporters of your work. Allow (or ask!) them to motivate and inspire you.

- Use governors as a valuable resource.

- When a vacancy arises for a staff governor in your school, consider applying (although ideally not in your first year in the profession).

- Governing bodies must establish a complaints procedure and make it public to all it concerns. If you have a grievance with your governing body, you should seek advice from your headteacher and your union and, (if you work in a faith school), your diocese. If you work in a community school, you can also seek advice from your local authority. Governing bodies have a duty to deal with grievances fairly and promptly.

The General Teaching Council for England (GTCE)

The General Teaching Council is the professional body for teachers in England. It was established on 1 September 2000 and the register of teachers was established on 1 June 2001. The GTCE is an independent body and is not answerable to government.

The *Teaching and Higher Education Act 1998* set out the GTCE's main aims, which can be summarized as follows: to contribute to improving the standards of teaching and the quality of learning; and to maintain and improve standards of professional conduct among teachers.

It also has a statutory duty to provide advice to the government and other bodies on education policy, including the recruitment and supply of new teachers, ITT and induction, professional development, medical fitness to teach and professional conduct. Within these aims lie the priorities to listen to and work for teachers, to raise the status of the profession, to provide a professional voice for teachers and to guarantee high standards. The GTCE's Corporate Plan sets out the Council's work programme for the coming year. For the latest plan, visit the website (www.gtce.org.uk).

The GTCE is not a union – it has no role to play in pay and conditions of employment – so it is advisable for all new teachers to join a union as well as registering with the GTCE.

The GTCE's register of teachers with QTS records current employment, qualifications and entitlement to teach, as well as names and addresses. The law requires all qualified teachers currently teaching in maintained schools or non-maintained special schools to be registered. The GTCE has the power to register and deregister individuals. Those in the independent sector and further education are encouraged, but not required, to register, as are all those with QTS, as holding a place on the register guarantees each teacher's qualifications and fitness to teach.

The GTCE provides information, services and support for teachers as well as putting them in touch with professional networks and assessing professional development opportunities.

Through the GTCE, teachers are regulating their own profession, and helping to safeguard its own standards. This is in line with other professions such as medicine, law and nursing. Council members hear cases referred to them by employers of alleged unacceptable professional conduct or serious professional incompetence. Such hearings could ultimately mean removal from the register, although this would be a final resort.

To date, the GTCE has had a significant impact on entitlement to continuing professional development as well as influencing debate on accountability and inspection, and teacher qualifications and professional standards.

For more information on the GTCE, take a look at www.gtce.org.uk or telephone 0870 001 0308. There are also General Teaching Councils for Wales, Scotland and Northern Ireland. Information on the General Teaching Council for Wales can be found at www.gtcw.org.uk, for Scotland at www.gtcs.org.uk and for Northern Ireland at www.gtcni.org.uk.

The school and the community

The school in which you teach is not isolated. It forms part of the complex structure of society in which many institutions are co-dependent. Schools are crucial in the preparation of the community's young for adult life, and the many institutions and organizations that will either employ them or educate them when they leave your school seem to be playing an increasing part in the education these children receive. For this reason, NQTs should look to the community in which they are working for ways of involving the many agencies that can add to the education they offer.

Utilizing connections

Your school may already have well-established links with schools, businesses and other organizations in the community. Ask your induction tutor or headteacher for details of such links so that you may benefit from them. There is much to be gained here, such as:

- the possible sharing of resources between schools;
- cooperation on major projects such as school plays, concerts and sometimes even residential trips;
- input from specialists who may not be on the school's staff;
- support for the needs of the school – many businesses are happy to supply equipment if it means good publicity;
- opportunities for work experience for pupils, and for them to gain greater economic awareness;
- the chance for teachers to update their knowledge of the world outside education and what will be required of their pupils.

Links with other schools

This is where you can really benefit from sharing resources and ideas with colleagues from outside your own school. The value of developing strong working relationships with other schools cannot be overestimated. On a professional level, such links will ensure that your teaching and resources enjoy regular injections of added inspiration and, on a personal level, they put you in a better position for retaining your perspective.

ABOUT UTILIZING CONNECTIONS

If your school does have well-established links with other schools and businesses, aim to make use of them where possible. Think of ways in which you can supplement your lessons, thereby adding an extra dimension as well as easing your own pressures. Always explain to your classes the relevance of any visitors and try to devise follow-up work that will record the event in some way.

Ways of creating links with other schools

- Use training courses and other professional development opportunities to strike up friendships with your counterparts in other schools. With your headteacher's consent, liaise with another school over a particular project by way of experiment. If it works, the road is open for future collaboration.
- Ask any local authority advisers you meet if they can put you in touch with suitable colleagues in local schools. Advisers are in the position of knowing a wide selection of schools and the strengths and weaknesses of individual teachers. They also have an overall view of the work in progress in their subject area across a range of schools.

Links with businesses and public services

There is so much scope for combining education and the world of employment. It may take a little time to set up useful links, but you could find that it's time well spent. The choice of possible visitors is vast, from police, local religious groups, the medical profession and civil servants to all levels of business, retail and charity personnel. There is, therefore, bound to be someone who could add a dimension to a scheme of work in some way. It is also worth considering that it is generally lessons that outsiders have attended that pupils remember well.

Ways of creating links with businesses and public services

- Ask your headteacher about links that currently exist, and get permission to create your own as appropriate.
- Read the local press, flick through the *Yellow Pages* and listen to local commercial radio to gain ideas and information on businesses and public services in your area.
- Find out if there are any parents and governors at your school who might be useful to you. You could also involve any family and friends who may be able to contribute to a lesson.
- When contacting appropriate businesses, find out if there is an education officer. These people will be in the best position to arrange what you require.

Public relations

There are few professions so much in the public domain as teaching. It sometimes seems that the only qualification needed to pass judgement on the state of education today is attendance at school yourself! For this reason, it is particularly important to appreciate that the extra roles related to teaching that you may not have been informed about include marketing and public relations for your school.

Before you open your classroom up to visitors, consider these points:

- Cast an eye over the appearance of pupils before they meet outsiders. Deal with any obvious grime and untidiness discreetly.
- Think about how your class will greet a visitor.
- Make sure that your classroom is tidy and that wall displays look neat and up-to-date.
- Your headteacher may want to meet any visitors personally. Arrange beforehand the best time to do this so you don't have to drag your guest around the school on a hunt for him or her.

- Spend time creating a congenial atmosphere in the class before visitors arrive. Deal with questions such as 'What's this got to do with anything?' in good time.
- Encourage your pupils to interact freely with visitors and talk about the processes they have used in their work related to the visit.
- Plan questions in advance with your pupils that they may want to ask the guest. Prompt individuals if necessary.
- Take any opportunities to demonstrate good achievement and progress.
- Involve the local media (and national educational press if appropriate). Favourable reporting will undoubtedly impress the governors.

ABOUT INVOLVING OUTSIDERS

It seems today that it's not only teachers who are pushed for time. Many of the people that you need to contact when creating and utilizing links with outsiders will be giving up time in order to help you out Follow these points to help ensure everything goes smoothly:

- Think about which aspects of the curriculum you teach could benefit from outside input before contacting anyone. You will probably need to explain your ideas to your head of department and headteacher, so make sure the visits are relevant to the curriculum and make sure you have identified clear learning intentions that would not be possible without the input of the outsider.
- Decide what level of input you would like – information and free items such as posters etc., someone to visit the school or a chance to take your class out into the community.
- Follow your school's guidelines on visitors. It is extremely important that anyone you involve is suitable for the task, and under no circumstances should you leave your visitor alone with pupils.
- Try to greet your visitor personally and make him/her feel at ease. The last time he/she visited a school could have been as a pupil.
- Be respectful of your visitor's time. Tell your visitor exactly when he/she is needed.
- Arrange for your visitor to be offered at least a drink.
- Always involve the class in thanking outsiders, whether visitors or contributors, for their input. This will make the people more likely to help again in the future.
- Be aware of any biases that may be presented. These can then be discussed with your class as appropriate.

- Share your contacts with colleagues. You may want to invite other classes to listen to outside speakers.

ACTION

Make a list of any local businesses or services that may be able to support your teaching. Keep a keen eye on any organizations that are in the local news or that seem to be raising their public profile. Perhaps these are the ones to approach when you want to involve outsiders.

Unions

Without wanting to sound alarmist, the importance of membership of a professional association or union cannot be overstressed for new teachers. You may have joined a union while you were still training but, if you haven't, join one now. Don't leave it to chance that you will not be involved in any number of the many disputes that arise between teachers, employers, parents and pupils.

The benefits of membership

Unions perform many functions for their members, but for NQTs these are the most useful:

- They give advice over work-related matters.
- They represent members at many levels of discussions with employers.
- They provide welfare benefits, personal legal help, professional insurance and financial services.
- They offer confidential crisis support.

On a more general level, your membership will enable unions to continue their work towards improving pay and working conditions for teachers everywhere in the country and give you national representation.

ABOUT UNION MEMBERSHIP

Although the 'beer and sandwiches' days of the government/union relationships are certainly over, there are many issues today that unions can use to gain ground lost previously. A good way to contribute to change in teachers' pay and conditions is to be part of a union from your first day of teaching. However, choose wisely and question thoroughly.

Questions to ask before joining a union

Think carefully before you decide what union to join. Unions are usually under the impression that, once a new member has joined, they can count on that membership for life, so they always covet NQTs. The assumption is that NQTs have their whole career ahead of them – a career during which they will perhaps encourage others to join the same union they did.

The services offered by teaching unions vary little from union to union. The difference lies in the way these services are delivered, the extent of the support offered and the amount of time it takes to receive appropriate help.

Resist the wooing, and obtain answers to these questions before making your decision:

- 'If I am involved in a disciplinary matter, will you supply a legally qualified representative to defend me?' (Some unions don't consult a solicitor – who may or may not be an education or employment law specialist – until after dismissal, preferring regional representatives to deal with hearings.)
- 'Will you ensure that any case in which I am involved will be passed on to a suitably qualified person at an appropriate stage?' (You don't want representatives to struggle at a local level if someone higher up the union ladder will be able to settle the dispute sooner.)
- 'What responsibility do you take for the advice you give me?' (If union advice causes you to lose a case, or significantly disadvantages you, will you have recourse to redress?)
- 'If I choose not to follow your advice or want a second opinion, will you still represent me?' (You don't want your case to be dropped with this excuse.)

Being aware of these issues will ensure that you can glean maximum advantage from the fees that you will pay throughout the course of your career.

Regardless of which union you join, do take out your own professional insurance as extra protection. It is inexpensive, and can usually be added to your car or house contents insurance. Make sure that the policy allows you to choose your own legal representative and covers you for at least £50,000 legal expenses.

ABOUT SEEKING PROFESSIONAL ADVICE

If you find yourself needing professional advice, do remember that you should remain at the centre of the way in which your case is handled. Your permission should be sought at each stage of the proceedings and, if you feel a particular route should be taken, throw in your suggestion. Seek second and third opinions about what you can do to move towards a resolution and never absolve yourself of the responsibility to stay in control.

Parent–teacher associations

Most schools run a parent–teacher association (PTA), which usually has responsibilities for raising funds for the school to be spent on items not allowed for in the school's budget. It may be a registered charity and/or affiliated to the National Confederation of Parent Teacher Associations (NCPTA).

Their value to the school

Given that PTAs raise money (that all-too-rare resource), they are generally of great value to the school that they serve. If it were not for the PTA in some schools, it would be impossible to provide equipment such as mini-buses, sports and additional computer equipment or to pay for end-of-term celebrations such as a Christmas meal for staff and pupils.

In addition to the funds that PTAs can raise, they also offer the opportunity for parents to become more directly involved in the work of the school, without taking on the responsibilities of governorship. A well-functioning PTA draws from the parent, teacher and pupil communities of a school and therefore can consider itself, in many ways, at the hub of school life.

The pros and cons of membership

As an NQT, you will have the opportunity to become involved in your school's PTA at some level. Before deciding how much commitment you would like to make to the PTA, you should consider the pros and cons.

Pros are:

- Membership gives you the opportunity to influence the decisions of the PTA, for example the way funds are spent.
- Membership gives you the chance to contribute to constructive ways of improving the teaching and learning environment in your school.
- You can become known to a significantly involved group of parents in a relatively relaxed atmosphere.

- Membership gives you contacts for use in your lessons. Many parents are able to make valid contributions to the curriculum.

Cons are:

- Some schools see PTA membership as a burden and 'nominate' the newest member of staff to join.
- Being a member will commit you to evening meetings at times when you may prefer to be preparing, marking or relaxing.
- You may end up being committed to turning up early on Saturday mornings to prepare for car boot and jumble sales.
- If membership becomes a 'duty', your enjoyment will be seriously affected.

Find out more . . .

The 'need-to-know' basics of joining a school are what you'll pick up through-out your first few weeks and months anyway, but being mindful that there is a bigger picture around your employment is always best. Spend some time browsing the sites that have been set up for teachers to make sure you're not in the dark about any aspect of the job:

- Teachernet: www.teachernet.gov.uk
- Schoolsweb: www.schoolsweb.gov.uk
- The General Teaching Council for England: www.gtce.org.uk (and for the rest of the UK as appropriate)
- The Training and Development Agency for Schools: www.tda.gov.uk

Don't forget, too, that it's wise to keep up with the education press such as the *Times Educational Supplement* (www.tes.co.uk) and BBC Education News Online Education (www.bbc.co.uk), and Teaching Expertise (www.teachingexpertise.com).

Chapter 5

Behaviour management

> If people are good only because they fear punishment, and hope for reward, then we are a sorry lot indeed.
>
> (Albert Einstein)

In spite of the fact that this book contains a whole chapter on behaviour management, there is actually only one thing, and one thing only, that you need to take on board: behaviour management is all about relationships. Once you appreciate that, and allow relationship building to permeate every aspect of your work in the classroom and at school in general, you'll deal effectively with every (or nearly every!) situation you encounter. With this in mind, this chapter looks at:

- The basic features of behaviour management
- Learning styles and behaviour management
- Classroom rules and routines
- Being slick
- Motivating pupils
- Rewards and sanctions
- Classroom folklore
- Pupil-teacher confrontations
- 'Difficult' children
- Attention Deficit Hyperactivity Disorder (ADHD)
- Classroom body language
- Using humour in the classroom.

Not surprisingly, one of the areas of greatest concern for new teachers is behaviour management. The need for this is certainly not a recent development; pupils have been misbehaving since schools began and people have been devising methods of managing misbehaviour for just as long. Yet teachers appear to be experiencing a worsening in pupil behaviour, and this has been recognized at the highest levels. Whether this is real, or a symptom of reduced tolerance because of the other demands of teaching, remains to be seen. Nevertheless, these views of teachers need to be addressed.

The following section draws on commonly accepted good practice and cannot be attributed to any one behaviour management method. The first thing to remember when thinking about behaviour management is that you are human. For all the rules you may devise with your classes and all your good intentions, there will be some days when they are harder to implement than others. This is natural, so don't give yourself a hard time. Also, it is not violence and serious confrontation that cause the most problems in schools, but the persistent interruptions of chatterers and comedians. This relatively low-level misbehaviour is what is most likely to stress (negatively) new and established teachers. Being aware of this can help you protect yourself from the harm that such antagonisms cause.

The basic features of behaviour management

When thinking about your own model for behaviour management (for that is, in effect, what will emerge – teachers may use a model as a base, but the reality is that only you can develop systems that work with the dynamics between you and your classes), find out how much freedom you have in this area. If your school has set discipline procedures, you will have to follow them but, to a certain extent, within your own room, you are free. It hardly needs to be said that any behaviour that contravenes the school's code on equal opportunities and discrimination needs to be dealt with promptly and severely.

It does seem to be the case that classes behave best when teachers are working in a style most natural to them. If you like order and calm, you are never going to be happy with the apparent 'chaos' of the teacher who likes to work less formally. Do also be aware of the fine line between order and anarchy. Good behaviour can be dependent to some extent on the good will and acceptance of pupils, which is why every minute spent on nurturing good relationships is time well invested.

Here are some more points to consider:

- Anger is often at the heart of a child's misbehaviour. Be aware of the many battles that the child may have already fought that day before he/she started messing around in your class. Don't greet a child's anger with your own. Remember what it was like being the age of the children you teach.
- Think about how you have behaved in lectures, seminars and meetings. Can you honestly say that you have never talked when someone else is speaking, or looked bored, or yawned?
- Don't think of discipline as a means of control, but accept that everyone needs discipline for a variety of reasons, not least security and protection.

- Plan your ideas around the rewarding of success.
- Think about how children gain your attention in your lessons – is it through good or bad behaviour?
- Are there any changes you could make to the way you teach in order to minimize the need to correct behaviour?
- When implementing a behaviour management plan, never give up on your expectations. It may be a long (continuous) haul, but you cannot plant seeds today and pick flowers tomorrow.

Eight points to remember about managing behaviour:

- Don't speak too fast or too loudly and try not to blush; all these reactions can be interpreted as weakness.
- Give known troublemakers a responsibility that involves an element of trust. This is a good way to make your 'worst nightmare' your 'best friend'.
- Explain the stages of your displeasure. Never go straight from cold to hot, as you will only confuse the folk you are trying to nurture.
- Don't look as though you are expecting trouble, even when faced with the toughest of classes.
- Address your displeasure specifically, not to the whole class, and avoid public reprimands, as these are always counter-productive.
- Time your interventions carefully. Does every misdemeanour need correction? Can you express the point (for example, about dropping litter) without falling into a confrontation?
- Frequently convey to your pupils how much you enjoy your job and what specific aspects you like.
- Don't take on the world single-handed. Get support from your induction tutor or head of department. These people should be involved in rewards and sanctions anyway.

Above all, never resort to saying, 'This couldn't work with my classes.' Something certainly will, so what aspects can you modify for your own use?

Learning styles and behaviour management

Loosely linked in to the literature on the theories of multiple intelligence are theories on the learning styles of children. It can be particularly useful to attempt to ascertain the learning style of any pupils giving you particular difficulties. Don't, however, attempt to do this yourself. The special needs coordinator at your school should be able to provide you with the means of achieving this and there may well be some simple diagnostic tests available for teachers in your school to use. Failing that, a search on the Internet will reveal the extent of information out there on this approach to teaching.

One theory of learning styles, which is useful to start with, has the premise that children are either visual learners, auditory learners or kinaesthetic learners.

Visual learners

These learners learn through seeing. They observe body language, facial expressions, visual displays, illustrations, diagrams and so on. They often like to be seated at the front of the room where they can enjoy a clear view of what is going on, and tend to think in terms of pictures rather than text. Spoken instructions can be difficult for visual learners to understand as they may have a tendency to misinterpret words. These learners often have a strong sense of colour and its uses.

Visual learners are helped by:

- colour diagrams and graphics etc.;
- written instructions;
- the opportunity to create visual prompts and learning aids such as flow diagrams, flash cards and written brainstorms.

Auditory learners

These learners learn through listening. They like to talk to others and listen to what they have to say while paying particular attention to the tone and speed of voice etc. Such learners will become frustrated if the atmosphere in your classroom is such that it becomes difficult for them to have the quiet they need in order to hear.

Auditory learners are helped by:

- having written instructions read out to them;
- having the opportunity to talk through what they have learnt and verbally answer questions;
- listening to key concepts from each lesson, preferably several times, rather than reading from a book, board or worksheet.

Kinaesthetic learners

These learners learn through doing and touching. They are the children eager to get out on the field to get on with the lesson, or to get their hands on the equipment so that they can conduct their own experiments. Sitting still and listening are not what these folk like to do!

Kinaesthetic learners are helped by:

- the opportunity for experiential learning;

- brain breaks;
- being prompted to think, review and revise while doing.

To find out more about learning styles, start by asking your colleagues what they know and what information is available in your school. You may also want to search for relevant books on a site such as Amazon, and a search on learning styles on a search engine such as Google will come up with over 1,800,000 sites!

Classroom rules and routines

The only reason to have classroom rules and routines is to make life easier and safer, so improving the quality of learning that takes place in your room. By articulating the behaviour you expect through rules and routines, you are specifically organizing your expectations of pupils. The act of making explicit what may be implicit in the way that you teach helps to create further security for your pupils by removing uncertainty about what is expected of them. Appropriate rules and routines also help to steer pupils towards effective learning, and you towards effective teaching.

This book cannot provide a list of rules and routines for you to adopt because they must be specific to you, your pupils and the subject(s) you teach. However, you may like to think about devising rules around these areas, but be aware that they can at best provide a framework on which to develop your learning relationships with pupils further:

- the way pupils speak to each other and to you;
- the way pupils listen to each other and to you;
- pupils' attitudes to homework and classwork;
- pupils' attitudes to time management and the completion of work;
- the way pupils sit and move around the room;
- eating and drinking in the classroom;
- the beginnings and endings of lessons;
- the handing in (and out) of work.

Many teachers like to devise rules with the help of pupils. This serves to emphasize the fact that behaviour management is a continuous dialogue between pupils and teachers, with commitments on both sides. When you actually write the rules with your pupils, keep them positive. 'In this room, we sit in silence when Mr Brown is talking to us' is infinitely better than 'Don't chatter when Mr Brown is talking'. Certainly don't create rules that put ideas into pupils' minds. Just think about the consequences of 'Don't throw chewing gum at teachers'. Does such a rule actually need to be written?

Here are some hints for using rules:

- Make sure your rules reflect the ethos of the school.
- Don't relax your rules or expectations, however familiar you become with pupils; they will appreciate the stability and security that your lessons give them.
- Think about ways of using peer mediation/pressure to ensure your rules are met.
- Build on respect for the right to learn and to teach and pupil accountability. Forget any desires for popularity; respect will serve you far better.
- Once you have devised your rules and routines, stick to them, use them, refer to them and discuss any changes with pupils.
- Use the rules that you devise with your class(es) to build on a sense of community in your classroom.
- Don't just aim to be 'captain of the ship'. You also want a happy crew. Ask your pupils what it is about your lessons that helps them to learn, and what hinders their learning.

ABOUT UNDERSTANDING THE CLASSROOM

In his Association of Teachers and Lecturers document, *Managing Classroom Behaviour* (available to members and non-members – see www.askatl.org.uk for further details), Chris Watkins identifies five key features of the classroom situation:

1. Classrooms are busy places – apparently, teachers engage in 1,000 interactions a day!
2. Classrooms are public places – the behaviour of teachers and pupils is visible to everyone in the room.
3. Classroom events are multidimensional – personal-social aspects of pupils' and teachers' lives are always affecting classroom life.
4. Classroom events are simultaneous – they do not occur on a step-by-step basis.
5. Classroom events are unpredictable – despite the development of routines, no one can predict events with complete accuracy.

Keeping these factors in mind when thinking about what happens in your classroom can help you to develop and retain perspective about your expectations of yourself and your pupils.

Being slick

Behaviour management is not about fighting every battle. If you do, your lessons will become far too stilted and pupils will become desensitized to your rules. The key is to be slick and deft, brisk and businesslike in your behaviour management from the very first second of a lesson:

- Start work promptly. If pupils are taking a while to settle, give them a task to do in limited time. Make this first task simple, straightforward and achievable.
- Identify the cause of a disruption. Is it due to boredom, peer pressure, inappropriately pitched work or concentration difficulties?
- Use these three steps with any child who seems to be unfocused:

  - *Anticipate* bad behaviour. This is much easier when you know your pupils well.
  - *Distract* with simple instructions for work. Try written and verbal instructions to cover most learning styles.
  - *Praise* as soon as you can.

- Don't get into a dialogue about behaviour while the lesson is going on; this is unfair on the rest of the class and wastes valuable time.
- Go to where pupils are sitting rather than the other way round. This prevents the need for crowd control around your desk or chair.
- Don't be afraid to scan the room and say 'That's good, Ben', 'I don't like that behaviour, Angie', 'Nice work, Mustapha', 'That's better, Annie.' Quick-fire feedback can whip a class into shape with speed.

EXAMPLE

I was getting increasingly incensed by a year 9 boy who was clearly passing something around the room. Instead of responding calmly, I shouted, 'What are you doing?' I was really embarrassed when the boy said that he was passing a Christmas card for me round for the class to sign. I'd lost my temper when I could have dealt with it earlier and minimized the disruption to the lesson.

(Second-year teacher, West Sussex)

ABOUT DEALING WITH INTERRUPTIONS

The best way of dealing with interruptions is to pre-empt them. Explain, in your first lesson and every lesson that follows, that you will allow plenty of time for questions so interruptions aren't necessary. Respond to all interruptions firmly – they are a huge source of stress for teachers and there is no harm in telling pupils how infuriating it is to have someone talk when you are trying to explain something, not to mention the violation of the most fundamental classroom rule.

Always give jobs to interrupters, such as tidying the room at the end of the lesson or picking up litter; and connect the sanction to the interrupting. If you are able to anticipate an interruption, block the offender by raising your voice slightly, or move towards where he/she is sitting, which sends the signal that you will not be stopped from finishing. Other non-verbal cues include making eye contact and subtly shaking your head, or dropping a card saying 'Listen, please' on his/her desk without interrupting your flow.

Motivating pupils

> You can discover more about a person in an hour of play than in a year of conversation.
>
> (Plato)

The development of natural internal motivators must be at the heart of all behaviour management. This is an ongoing task for teachers that cannot ever be forgotten. Motivated pupils have no time to misbehave.

In order to motivate your class, you need to know what their general mood is. Are pupils buoyant, mad, angry, petulant, playful, tired or slothful? You can use the time while they are settling to assess this and it may be necessary to adapt your lesson plan. A series of very short tasks may be more suitable than a longer project. This doesn't mean rewriting your plan, but it may mean changing the way you deliver it.

If pupils appear to be angry, it can be worth sacrificing some of your lesson to establish what the problem may be. Spend some time talking about it and focusing on solutions before attempting to start your lesson. This is more likely to result in receptive students and you have shown yourself to be aware of the greater picture of their school experience.

EXAMPLE

I had one year 9 class all through my NQT year that seemed to really drain me. Individually, I liked the pupils, but together they were awful! The start of every lesson was a battle and I never felt I had them on side. I decided to follow this advice and at the start of one lesson I asked them what I could do to make the lesson more enticing for them. I didn't intend that the discussion should take all the lesson, but it did in the end. We got loads out in the open – I learnt so much about them all in that one lesson. It didn't solve all my problems with them, but it did more than any other technique. Best of all, they now see me as someone who will listen to them, and even those that I had thought really weren't interested in learning have shown me that they want to know that I'm interested in them. It's been a big lesson in understanding that delivery of a subject has to come second to creating an environment for learning.

(Secondary NQT, Cumbria)

Man is so made, that whenever anything fires his soul . . . impossibilities vanish.

(La Fontaine)

Try some of these ideas to help motivate your classes:

- Keeping personalisation in mind, give pupils the chance to plan part of a lesson. Ask them how they want to do something and allow them to create their own conditions (within your parameters, of course). You could then ask them to assess the lesson.
- A step up from this is to allow children to teach part of a lesson. This shares the 'power' and allows you to take a back seat (literally).
- Time tasks throughout the lesson. This is a great motivator and also teaches time management. Do be flexible though. You want to motivate, not stress.
- Think of ways of teaching through the interests of your pupils. If a particular craze is sweeping your class, how can that be incorporated into your lessons?
- Shun labels. Some children (and whole classes) get inextricably attached to a label they may have been given in the past, for example 'I'm thick, sir – got anything else for me to do?' or 'We're the bottom set, miss'. You could reply by saying 'You can't be. I don't teach thick kids [or trouble-makers, lazy tykes etc.]', and move quickly on to a positive aspect of the group or child.

Creating the habit of work

If, lesson after lesson, you allow time at the beginning and end that does not have a constructive purpose, pupils will certainly learn one thing – that work is not the habit in your room. Your starting work cues need to be totally understood and respected, and your expectations for good behaviour high. If you know that what you are teaching is useful, that you would want to learn it and that it has an immediate application for pupils, you can easily create a sense of urgency to start work.

You could also think about how to use the peace of silence in your lessons. It can give children a boost, as it offers temporary respite from having to respond to the many stimuli around them. Silence also creates a sense of common purpose – everyone is working under the same conditions.

Why not ask pupils if there is anything you can do to improve their work habits? You may be pleasantly surprised by the suggestions of even the most demotivated of classes.

ACTION

Think about an occasion when a lesson has gone really well with little or no misbehaviour: What characterized that lesson? Can you harness those factors for future use?

Rewards

> There is no such whetstone, to sharpen a good wit and encourage a will to learning, as is praise.
>
> (Roger Ascham)

This is where your ingenuity can really shine. The more original and inspiring your rewards, the more likely pupils are to want them. Use these general ideas as a basis for any reward structure that you may devise:

- Follow school policy. There may be an existing house points or merits scheme or perhaps letters can be sent home detailing achievement. This still leaves you free to introduce some of your own incentives in your lessons.
- Think about power differentials when you praise a child. For example, are you communicating with your heads at the same height? This can make all the difference.
- Can you celebrate achievement in public? Do remember though, that this may seem more like a punishment for some pupils!
- Do your pupils have any preferred activities as a reward, such as being allowed extra time on a computer, being able to play a game in class or being given an edible treat? Discuss this with them, and remember that these activities may well change. What's popular this week may be out next.
- Your rewards should be worth the effort and certainly not too easily attained. You want them to be held in high esteem by pupils and for them to know that you will be consistent.

ABOUT APPROPRIATE AND EQUITABLE REWARDS

There is nothing more annoying to staff trying to build up respect amongst pupils for a system of reward than a maverick teacher dishing out praise lavishly and indiscriminately. The danger here is the slippery slope to piling on the praise because a child hasn't done something (e.g. hit his/her neighbour) rather than has done something (e.g. listened attentively and contributed to the lesson when usually this is not the case). Those members of the class who do not require this 'encouragement' will see this as grossly unfair.

Do also be aware of the many stages of praise before you reach for the high-prestige rewards. For example, a positive comment written in a book, a memo sent to the form tutor, etc. could be more appropriate than a merit.

Sanctions

> It is better that ten guilty persons escape than one innocent suffer.
> (William Blackstone)

Schools vary tremendously in their attitudes to sanctions and it is essential that you absorb school policy. The hints on sanctions below will provide additional support.

ACTION

Whenever you have to deal with indiscipline, ask yourself how many pupils it involves. This will help you to see that the 'subversiveness' is not that extensive.

EXAMPLE

My tutor told me a great analogy to remember . . . A retail manager does not discipline his shop. He manages it. He does not wait for problems to occur and then wonder what to do about them. He has a plan in place.

(Primary NQT, London)

Hints on sanctions

Do:

- Avoid sanctions that simply reiterate what the rules are, such as repeatedly copying out the school code. They know them; that's why they broke them! Aim to teach through sanctions, preferably about emotional intelligence, awareness of others and citizenship.
- Be courteous to pupils when punishing them. Always offer a good example and explain exactly what you believe to be right and wrong in the situation. Be sure to convey the fact that your preference would be to reward them for deserving achievement rather than punish for indiscipline.
- Be extremely wary of detaining a child other than in a formal school detention. Laws apply regarding a school's right to detain a child (see your school's policy on detention for further information) and a notice period must be given. In addition, detention is rarely considered by pupils to be anything more serious than a nuisance.
- Listen to a child if he/she offers an explanation or an apology.
- Address problems and administer sanctions after the lesson. You will not gain the respect of the child through humiliating him/her in public.

Don't:

- React impulsively to a 'crime'. Think about an appropriate sanction – perhaps have some ready-prepared. Instant reactions will not lead to consistency.
- Expect pupils to be in the right frame of mind for listening to your reasoned arguments. They may need time to calm down and reading has been shown to be an excellent way of bringing children out of anger and impulsivity and into (or at least towards) a space of calm and reason.
- Threaten punishment and not follow through precisely.
- Be alone with pupils when reprimanding them. Always ask for another member of staff to be present to witness what happens.
- Refer to siblings. The child may have had a lifetime of listening to cries of how well behaved his/her brothers and sisters are.
- Give collective punishments. Have you ever taught a class in which every child deserves exactly the same level of punishment?

Avoiding punishing yourself

> A smooth sea never made a skilful mariner.
> (Anon)

Think about these questions:

- Do you respond and punish automatically? Could you halve the amount of sanctions you deliver?
- Do you talk to pupils about their behaviour at a time that is convenient to you, when you have cooled off?
- Do you take misbehaviour as a personal insult? (It is extremely rare for this to be the case. There are always other factors affecting a person's behaviour and there is no harm in letting pupils know that you are not the cause of their anger on this occasion.)

If you have a really bad day, when you feel as though all you have done is respond to poor behaviour, use this recovery plan:

- Put the day in perspective. Was it the whole day that went wrong or just part of it?
- Identify what went wrong and who contributed.
- Resolve to talk to the pupils and/or staff who contributed to your bad day before you go home if possible.
- Write down two things that you can do to prevent the same circumstances occurring again.
- Ask yourself why you expect to have perfect lessons and great days every day. Does it really matter if you don't?
- Give yourself an evening off – no marking, no preparation. What is not done now can wait. Don't even take work home; you need the break.
- Treat yourself to whatever makes you feel good, e.g. nice food for dinner, some flowers, a novel or a bottle of wine, etc.
- Book something enjoyable for the near future – cinema tickets, a night out or even just some time with a loved one.

ABOUT CONFISCATING PROPERTY

This is a potentially problematic area that is best avoided. If a pupil has an illegal item in his/her possession, a member of the senior management team should be dealing with the situation and your role is to pass on any information you have as soon as possible. If you want to remove any other item from a child's possession, make sure that you have given the opportunity for the child to put the item away, that the child knows exactly why it is being removed and when and from whom (perhaps the pastoral head) the child can retrieve the item. Never seize something or force yourself into a corner by saying 'Give me that now.' You could easily be met with refusal. If something (e.g. a note) is being passed around the room, don't destroy it yourself – ask a pupil to. Take the dustbin to the child to minimize disruption.

Classroom folklore

There is no particular order to this list; just look through it for inspiration to perhaps trigger you own ideas. Teachers of pupils of a variety of age groups and subjects have implemented these ideas, so they can work:

- Give older students a short break mid-lesson. This gives them a chance to chat briefly and can result in everyone feeling refreshed.
- Do simple stretching exercises with young children (year 6 and below) mid-session. This can help to prevent fidgeting especially in those who cannot sit still for long. When the children are standing, ask them to stretch up as high as they can from toes to fingertips, and then flop over and slowly come up again. This can be invigorating for the teacher too.

ABOUT 'SMART MOVES'

Learning is experience. Everything else is just information.
(Albert Einstein)

There is a good deal being written now on what have become known as 'brain-gym activities'. Much of what is seeping into schools now (under various 'schemes' and 'approaches') has roots in the work of Carla Hannaford, a neuro-physiologist and educator. Her book, *Smart Moves: Why learning is not all in your head* (1995), explores the body's role in thinking and learning, and how movement can lead to enhanced performance.

Simple activities can improve fine and large motor movement, laterality and generally wake up the mind/body system. While you can find endless lists of such activities to try with your class in several popular texts for teachers, it will be most useful to you to explore a book such as Hannaford's for a solid background and explanations of the relatively few key moves that will improve learning most effectively in your classroom.

- Be spontaneous. This worked well for the teacher of a year 10 boy who was being particularly disruptive. She was working with a child at the back of the room when there was a sudden outburst of laughter. The boy was trying on her jumper that she had left at the front of the room. She laughed spontaneously simply because he looked so ridiculous and after a while everyone got back to work without the need for the teacher to say anything. Her relationship with the boy was much improved afterwards, as she had shown that she was human and able to overlook some aspects of his behaviour.

- Ask a child who has misbehaved to help you through part of your lunch break. You could use the opportunity to get a job done, as well as chat to the child about aspects of his/her behaviour. This helps to minimize the chances of either party seeking to dominate and can work with all age groups. Don't do this too often – working through a break is not a good habit.

- Introduce a 'stop' law. If anyone does anything that adversely affects another, anyone can say 'Stop.' This can create a very safe environment and, if managed well, with clear consequences for violation of the law, empowers everyone in the room.

- Offer the opportunity for pupils to visualize the way they would like others to behave towards them. Link this in with their understanding of the way they behave towards others.

- Keep a marble jar. When someone in the class does something good, put a marble in the jar. When the jar is full, give the class a treat. Don't take marbles out of the jar if someone misbehaves. You don't want to punish the whole class.

- Give out a token (e.g. a plastic disc or a raffle ticket etc.) for good behaviour. At the end of the day/week/term, pupils can purchase treats with the tokens. For example, 10 tokens might mean they can buy the choice of an end-of-term DVD, two tokens might pay for some sweets etc. Build up your own 'shop'.

- Offer the best worker the choice of what song you listen to when you pack away. You could play CDs through a PC, laptop with speakers or a portable CD player.

ABOUT BEHAVIOUR MANAGEMENT MODELS

There are many models for behaviour management; most with their own ideas on why children misbehave. Many of these draw from existing good practice and require whole-school approaches for their effectiveness. However, there is only one behaviour management model that will truly work for you and that is the one you develop for yourself throughout the course of your career. Behaviour management is such an individual thing.

ABOUT CIRCLE TIME

Circle time is talked about with zeal in some schools and the idea can certainly work with pupils of all ages, and adults too. There is nothing new about the concept of circle time. Some tribes and cultures have long used such a system for discussion and, as a tool for educational purposes, it is thought to date back to Sweden at the turn of the last century.

Much of the literature on circle time draws heavily on the original research of Ballard (see, for example, Ballard, J (1982) *Circlebook*, Irvington Inc, New York) and his work is the best place to start for the underlying principles of circle time. You might also like to consider two points.

Firstly, circle time should not be associated with discipline or problem solving. 'Issues' should not be brought to a circle. Rather, it is a tool for developing self-awareness, self-image and group awareness. Acceptance of each other must be unconditional.

Secondly, it is possible to use circle time to teach pupils that we all have feelings that need to be expressed, that we need to be able to respond constructively to the feelings of others and that from this starting point we can express ourselves without fear of criticism or judgement.

Pupil–teacher confrontations

> Time cools, time clarifies; no mood can be maintained quite unaltered through the course of hours.
>
> (Thomas Mann)

Regardless of how well you establish routines and explain your expectations, there will inevitably be occasions when pupils cross the boundaries of acceptable behaviour.

However you decide to approach these confrontations, you should aim to do it rationally and honestly. These solutions should perhaps be avoided:

- sarcasm – some bright teenagers may understand sarcasm but generally it is lost and only serves to frustrate the teacher;
- humiliating pupils – this is unproductive and certainly not supportive of pupils' welfare;
- losing your temper – this is rarely beneficial, especially if it happens in front of the whole class for the sake of one pupil.

Serious misdemeanours need to be dealt with immediately in accordance with the established policies in your school. The most effective method is to remove the offending pupil from the room and deal with the problem after a 'cooling-off' period. Asking a trusted pupil to get a member of the senior management team to come to your class to collect the child is effective. This sends clear signals to the rest of the class that boundaries have been crossed and that teachers are united. It also ensures that you don't have to face the public humiliation of having your requests for a pupil to leave the room ignored.

> **ABOUT** BEING ASSAULTED AT WORK
>
> If a colleague, pupil or parent assaults you at school, you will need to record the incident with your headteacher (who may need to report it to the Health and Safety Executive). Also talk to your union and seek medical advice. Such a situation needs to be treated most seriously.

When you do face the child to resolve the situation, remember these points:

- Explain quietly, clearly and calmly (with 'soft words and hard arguments') what it is about his/her behaviour you cannot tolerate and why. Avoid ranting 'How dare you . . .', as this simply shows you have lost your cool and makes it very hard to bring the conversation to a constructive conclusion.
- Calmly insist on eye contact and general respect. Pupils should look at you when you talk to them and you may want to ensure that they don't slouch or overtly show that they simply aren't bothered. Pupils should always listen without interrupting.
- Don't exaggerate the behaviour. You can expect pupils to see that you are not unreasonable without the need to embellish.
- Aim to establish what the pupil got out of the misdemeanour; was it a win/win situation for him/her? Does the pupil think what he/she did was a good idea? The response will almost certainly be negative.
- Avoid raising your voice during a one-to-one as this is always counterproductive:
  - there is no physical need;
  - you will alienate the pupil you are trying to encourage to see reason;
  - you will raise your blood pressure unnecessarily;
  - you risk losing reason and saying something offensive – 'How can I get this into your (thick) head?';
  - you will earn a reputation for losing your temper;
  - you will disturb classes trying to work in the vicinity.

- Aim to understand how you feel about the situation. A teacher trainer in the US 50 years ago suggested that teachers should consider whether they are irritated, challenged or hurt by a child's behaviour. His theory was that, if you are irritated, the child is likely to be an attention seeker, so good behaviour should be reinforced. If you feel challenged, the child may be a power seeker. This is more difficult to handle, but not impossible. Restate rules and expectations as frequently as necessary. If you feel hurt, the child may be a revenge seeker. In each situation, it can be helpful to explain to the child what you think is happening. However, dealing with these character types is complex and your response is bound to change from day to day. Seek the advice of your induction tutor, as it may be time to set up a meeting with the child and his/her carers.

- Initially, don't spend a long time trying to sort out the problem. Once you have explained why you have had to reprimand the pupil, dispense your punishment and leave it at that. However, you should arrange a mutually agreeable time when you can discuss both the child's behaviour and ways of enabling him/her to improve. Be sure to explore how the pupil views his/her behaviour as well as the view the pupil has of him or herself. This stage is vital in this process and allows you both to talk rationally while sufficiently distanced from the original misdemeanour. Your aim is to reach an understanding of each other's needs and a commitment to improving your relationship.

This whole process may take a long time. Some pupils may be resistant to your methods and it is important to persevere. You're not going to succeed with all pupils all the time, but calm determination can go a long way. Be consistent in your expectations and praise any subsequent improvement in behaviour. Never give up on a pupil.

'Difficult' children

Unless children's crimes are so heinous as to warrant exclusion, you are going to have to exist in the same institution with children who have behaved unacceptably towards you. Whatever methods you adopt to deal with the situation, keep this in mind. It is not enough to agree to disagree or to write a relationship off. Go for peaceful, constructive resolutions even if they take a term or year to achieve, or if they result in you having to face your own role in the situation's demise (if you had one).

ABOUT CONFRONTING CHILDREN

When you are confronting children with your disappointment and anger at their poor behaviour, always keep in the forefront of your mind what the best possible outcome would be. How do you want the situation resolved? Visualize your perfect scenario. There is no harm in telling children the hopes you have for an improvement and involving them in creating some appropriate criteria by which you can both assess whether progress has been made. This approach can be taken with whole classes as well, and some teachers periodically set aside a part or whole lesson to discuss behaviour and attitude. It is extremely difficult for even the most deviant of pupils to completely ignore such reason from a teacher.

- When it looks as though a relationship with a child is beyond repair, you need, initially, to go for damage limitation.
- Think of examples when the child has worked well for you. Is there a common theme here? Tell the child what you have liked about him/her in the past.
- Seek advice from colleagues who teach the child, including the form tutor, or colleagues who have had success in dealing with 'difficult' children.
- Don't get into power games – you are the teacher and therefore always 'in charge'. However, that should be taken as read, so don't humiliate yourself by reiterating it in front of pupils.
- Avoid saying things like 'When you're away, the class works really well'. The child may already be battling with feelings of rejection to be misbehaving, so adding to these will do nothing for your relationship.
- Aim to reach an understanding of each other's needs and be prepared to concede something to the child.

ABOUT YOUR PERSPECTIVE ON 'DIFFICULT' CHILDREN

When you feel you are spending disproportionate amounts of time on certain pupils, it is easy to start viewing the whole class as being difficult. This is very rarely the case and it is important to retain a sense of perspective. You may find teaching a particular class difficult because of the actions of one or two pupils – don't let that taint your enjoyment of the group.

Changing your perspective

It is very easy to make judgements of pupils that are extremely hard to remove or change. Sometimes it is appropriate to review your perspective of a child and situation:

- Do you really need to fight every battle? Perhaps some situations can be overlooked in order to preserve the overall ambience of a lesson. The fact that Johnny is doodling this week may be a huge improvement on his previous behaviour. You should have high expectations of all your pupils, but the reality of teaching means that you are sometimes going to have to ask yourself 'Does it matter? Is it worth it?'

- Be prepared to question your own attitudes. Do you find that pupils' behaviour is much worse on days when you are tired or angry at some aspect of your life? Be aware of fluctuations in your levels of tolerance.
- Try to find out as much as possible about children who you consider are being 'difficult'. There will be something that you have in common and you may be able to build on that as a basis for a better working relationship.

An often-used quote from Lord Elton is worth keeping in mind when thinking about behaviour and discipline:

> Members of staff who treat their pupils with discourtesy, impatience or contempt, or are late for those from whom they demand punctuality, who scribble illegibly on words which they insist must be impeccably clear and tidy, who will not listen to those from whom they demand absolute attention, who bawl their heads off at those from whom they demand soft and respectful speech, who hold up to ridicule those whom they instruct to treat all men with respect, or who treat any of their own colleagues with anything but courtesy and respect in the presence of any of the pupils, are suffering a painful and obvious discontinuity of logic.

Attention Deficit Hyperactivity Disorder (ADHD)

This condition, known as ADHD, is being diagnosed with increasing frequency in school-age children. It is believed that the condition is caused by a minor brain dysfunction affecting the part that deals with behaviour inhibition, perhaps due to an imbalance of neurotransmitters. The condition affects more boys than girls; the ratio is about 6:1.

Stimulant medications can be used to try to correct imbalances, but recent research has shown that fatty acid supplements can lead to significant improvements for children with ADHD.

Symptoms of ADHD include impulsiveness, overactivity, clumsiness, dis-organization and an inability to sustain attention. In the classroom, this may manifest itself as fidgeting, being easily distracted, being forgetful, being disrespectful of authority, interrupting others, having difficulty listening, talking incessantly and being incapable of following instructions.

This can all be incredibly frustrating for a teacher (as well as for the pupil). You should have been told about any sufferers in your classes, and given management strategies for their particular learning difficulties, but there may be some others who are undiagnosed for various reasons. If you suspect that a child you teach may be suffering from ADHD, talk to your SEN coordinator.

Bear these general points in mind when teaching ADHD sufferers:

- Many children who have been diagnosed with ADHD suffer from poor self-esteem. They may be aware of their shortcomings, probably from years of criticism before their condition was diagnosed, but are somehow unable to remedy them. Use techniques to boost esteem as frequently as possible. Any behaviour that could warrant positive reinforcement should be praised.
- Children with ADHD may be very impatient and might use waiting time destructively. Try to avoid this situation by making sure they are occupied, even if this means dealing with them first within the class.
- Many ADHD children respond well to routines. Try to make your classroom routines consistent from the start, including the sufferer's seating arrangements, and explain any changes clearly and in good time wherever possible.

ABOUT OTHER EDUCATIONAL AND MEDICAL NEEDS

There will be a wide variety of conditions and circumstances affecting children's learning in your classes. While it would be ideal if you could find out all about the conditions suffered by the children you teach, that is quite impractical. If you get a chance, read about Asperger's syndrome, dyspraxia and autism, and lean on your SEN coordinator for ideas and guidance on educating children with additional needs.

Management strategies

When teaching pupils who appear to have ADHD, or who have been diagnosed as such, these tips will be useful:

- Make sure the child sits as close to you as possible and away from distraction (e.g. windows and doors). Seat some positive role models nearby.
- When talking to the pupil, maintain eye contact for as long as possible.
- Encourage the child to use tools to structure his/her day, for example timetables, daybooks, diaries, etc. These all help to create routines.
- Break any tasks down into timed sections. Aim to do this surreptitiously so that the child does not feel different. Avoid giving multiple commands and make sure the child has understood the instructions before beginning the task. You should already have a culture of tolerance in your group for children who feel the need to clarify and question.
- Make sure that when you explain tasks the child is listening and not holding, touching or fiddling with anything.

- Calmly insist on consistent rules for politeness in the classroom. For example, no child should call out or interrupt another person. You may need to spend time teaching and reteaching the child these rules.
- Work with your SEN department to modify work as necessary. You may agree that child with ADHD should have more time to complete certain tasks.
- Think about the way ICT can be used in your lessons, as this can help to focus a child.
- Be aware of the amount of stimuli surrounding a sufferer. Is there anything you can do to reduce this?
- Be prepared to adjust your expectations of the child in terms of self-responsibility. There may be days when you have to explain tasks calmly several times and monitor each stage religiously. Perhaps these are the days when frequent rewards would provide the incentive for the child to carry on.
- Stress and fatigue can affect these children more profoundly than other children. Be sensitive to their personal circumstances and try to avoid overload.
- As soon as behaviour starts to deteriorate, use distraction strategies. Point out good work and behaviour and as far as possible ignore the child's challenges to your expectations. However, if other children are distracted then you will have to correct his or her behaviour. Aim to reward more frequently than you punish and, instead of focusing on the negative, express the positive, e.g. 'Sit still please' rather than 'Stop fidgeting'.
- Discuss the consequences of misbehaviour.
- Utilize the concept of breaks during lessons by giving the child a 'job' to do. This gives the child temporary respite from classwork and also serves to boost self-esteem, as the child feels trusted.
- Encourage the child to reward him or herself. Teach him/her methods of positive self-talk. For example, when you praise good work, ask the child what his/her opinion is. Try to draw out of the child the aspects that he/she is particularly pleased with. The aim is to get the child to say 'I'm pleased with my work' or 'I did that well' or 'This is good'.
- The therapeutic value of play has been shown to be great for children with these symptoms. Apparently, the more play you have as a child the more rational and less impulsive you are as an adult. Avoid restricting opportunities for play. This is most clearly illustrated by the stresses of teaching a class that has been prevented from playing because of a wet break – they all seem to have ADHD then!

EXAMPLE

For me personally, what helped was to be told exactly what to do stage by stage. If I was given something to do and told to go away and do it then I struggled, but if I was given a task at a time I could go away and complete that, and then go back to the teacher for the next task. I found it very difficult working for myself. It helped when the teacher outlined specifically what I had to do but not when he or she made a big deal of it in front of the class because it just made me feel stupid and inferior.

(Alex, diagnosed ADHD)

ABOUT MEDICATION FOR ADHD

Medication for ADHD is still highly controversial. Some teachers fear that it is being used to calm disruptive children and there has been a steep rise in prescriptions for drugs used to control the condition and other similar ones.

Medication cannot cure ADHD but, used in carefully controlled conditions, it is thought by some to moderate its effects. However, this can only be successful as part of a package of help – medication cannot teach and encourage, nurture and support, but may provide a backdrop against which help can be absorbed by the child.

Classroom body language

There is no doubt that the non-verbal communications that we give convey messages more efficiently than the spoken word. For no profession is this more the case than teaching. When your greatest weapon in the battle for control is sheer force of character, your body language can serve as an excellent reinforcement.

There is an element of acting in all teaching, and attention to body language and posture is a quick way into character. Exponents of the Alexander Technique know clearly the extent to which the way we use posture affects physical and mental health.

ACTION

Before focusing on your own body language, observe colleagues in action. How does their body language and posture change to deal with different situations? Now turn your attention to yourself. What posture do you adopt when talking to the whole class, talking to individuals, reprimanding, praising and joking? Do you stand defensively (abdomen and chin pointing outwards) or protectively (shoulders rounded and pelvis tipped back)?

In order to achieve 'free' posture, whereby your body is able to function efficiently, you need to pay attention to your body's extremities – your head and your feet.

Imagine that your head is filled with helium, eager to float upwards. Notice the immediate lengthening effect on your spine, while your shoulders fall naturally into place.

Now focus on your feet, making sure that when you stand they take your weight evenly and that when you sit both feet are placed comfortably on the ground (crossing your legs does nothing for circulation).

By remembering these simple ideas, your basic posture will not only be physically correct, but will also have a positive effect on your mental state.

Subtleties for the classroom

Consciously using body language in the classroom can be an excellent way of correcting or recognizing behaviour without speaking or interrupting the flow of your lesson. Do try to be aware of habits that may be annoying to pupils as these can totally dominate their concentration. Think back to your own schooldays – did you ever do something like count the number of times a teacher said a certain phrase or touched his beard?

Do:

- Smile. Forget the old-fashioned notion that no teacher should smile before Christmas! You're a human, not a robot, and showing that to pupils can only strengthen their respect for you.
- Use eye contact. Make a direct link with a pupil when you talk to him/her to encourage the pupil to feel that he/she has your undivided attention.
- Look at the class when you talk. Some teachers don't bother to look up from what they are doing to issue further instructions to a class, or continue to speak when facing the board and writing.
- Use hand and arm gestures to illustrate points. This will help to guard against stagnation in the delivery of your lessons.

- Use professional touch. For example, a hand on a pupil's shoulder can give reassurance or positive reinforcement.
- Observe the body language of pupils for signs of boredom. This will help you to pace your lessons.
- Listen actively. This conveys a sense of the importance you are attaching to what is being said.
- Lean or walk towards a child who is talking. Again, this is a way to engage directly in what is being said.
- Use encouraging gestures to help a child to continue talking if he/she is stumbling when answering a question.

Don't:

- Point at pupils. Always use names, even when trying to correct behaviour. Pointing can be perceived as far too aggressive for the classroom.
- Frown. It can be easy to hide behind a permanent frown, which forces you to tense your facial muscles. Reserve frowns to indicate displeasure at a specific individual or incident.
- Cry. As an expression of emotion, crying is fine, but you will save yourself unnecessary embarrassment if you can hold back the tears until there are no pupils around. However honest it may be to cry in front of children, there will be some who will only remember the loss of control.
- Clench your jaw or fists. Pupils will spot the rising tension before you do and may play on your stress.
- Habitually touch parts of your head or face. This can be associated with insecurity.
- Invade a pupil's personal space. Allow the pupil some territory. This is perhaps more important for older pupils.
- Adopt a 'hands on hips' posture. This is negative body language.
- Move around the room in a manic fashion. Gently paced movements will help to set the tone of lessons.
- Make unnecessary sound to get attention, such as banging on desks etc. The noise is unsettling in itself, not to mention what it does to your own stress levels.

What to wear

Gone are the days when teachers paraded in gowns, although some schools do still use them for assemblies and similar occasions. This, in one way, is a pity; at least the problem of what to wear would not be so profound for some teachers!

You will need to find out what the dress code is for your school by asking colleagues if you are not formally told. It is pretty unusual for suits to be compulsory now – most schools allow teachers to be smartly comfortable:

- Respect the dress standards your school is trying to achieve.
- Don't use clothing as a way of expressing discontent.
- Think about the image you portray through your clothing.
- Aim to blend in with staff rather than stand out dramatically. Perhaps confine flamboyance to the weekends.
- Wear stimulating reds and oranges with caution and go easy with accessories.
- Aim to throw out any shoes or clothes that are beyond repair. This may be difficult considering the immense financial pressures NQTs are under, but there's no doubt that your self-image is reflected in your outer appearance.
- Build up a wardrobe of clothes that 'work'. A few good-quality, coordinating items will be most useful.
- Think about whether you need to dress for occasions such as meeting parents or visitors. Perhaps dressing up a little may boost your confidence.
- Whatever guidelines you have to follow when working out what to wear to school, do remember that it is still possible to convey individuality within the tightest of restrictions and extremism is rarely constructive.

Using humour in the classroom

> The most wasted of all days is that on which one has not laughed.
> (Nicholas Chamfort)

The physical benefits of laughter are well documented and such that most teachers would do well actively to seek amusement on a daily basis. It is infectious, relaxing and an excellent reliever of tension, exercising hundreds of muscles in the face and neck.

We don't know for certain why laughter evolved, but, from a behaviourist viewpoint, it is clear that it is a social signal. Research has shown that we are 30 times more likely to laugh in social settings that when we are alone. We use laughter to strengthen bonds and show that we are willing to be free and open. Therefore, say researchers, the more laughter there is within a group of people, the closer the bonds are likely to be.

Laughter is a disarming mechanism: a universally understood signal of trust. When we laugh, physiological responses take place within our bodies, such that it is impossible to suffer the effects of negative stress at the point of laughing. In addition:

- Immune function is enhanced.

- The fight or flight response is inhibited (leading to a reduction of stress hormones).
- The diaphragm receives a workout.
- The effects of pain can be less pronounced.
- Muscles relax.
- Intellectual performance is boosted through increased flow of oxygen round the body.

Psychologists also believe that humour helps individuals to confront personal problems in a more relaxed and creative state, generating heightened flexibility of thought.

You don't have to earn yourself the reputation of the one who tells terrible jokes all the time in order to employ a little humour in your lessons. There is no government circular stating that classrooms must be devoid of laughter and, in fact, some teachers work laughter breaks into their lesson plans.

Don't worry about overexciting children and not being able to bring them down again. They will soon get used to your routines and quirks, and you will work out the best time to employ a little humour. If you fear an inappropriate response from your pupils at any time, leave the humour for another day. The key here is balance. Use too much humour and you risk appearing to need adulation and affection from your pupils. Aim to throw in occasional high points of humour. But:

- Be sure not to waste time.
- Be aware that any jokes or funny tales you tell will be repeated outside the classroom.
- Never employ humour at the expense of a pupil, however well you know that pupil. This could easily be misunderstood.

ABOUT HUMOUR AT SCHOOL

You only have to glance through a newspaper and see all the cartoons and humour-based columns, or look through TV listings, to see the amount of humour that surrounds us. There is nothing wrong with injecting some light-heartedness into school life. Some schools have humour boards in staffrooms so that staff can read them for light relief. Perhaps establish one in your school, or dedicate a small area of your room (perhaps a cupboard door) to appropriate humour.

Find out more . . .

You can explore more ideas about behaviour management on the Teaching Expertise website (www.teachingexpertise.com).

Chapter 6

Being an effective teacher

Confine yourself to the present.
(Marcus Aurelius)

The effectiveness of teachers is naturally a concern for all involved in education, from parents to policy makers, professional associations to general teaching councils, employers to teachers themselves. But what, exactly, does effectiveness mean? This chapter looks at:

- What makes lessons effective?
- Tips on effectiveness
- Lesson evaluation
- Peer observations
- Spiritual, moral, social and cultural education
- Homework strategies
- Your domain – the classroom
- Emotional intelligence/literacy.

What makes lessons effective?

The most effective kind of education is that a child should play amongst lovely things.

(Plato)

Thousands of lessons are taught across the country every day, the effectiveness of which varies tremendously. Effective teaching is not something that can be taught, understood and regurgitated consistently; the effectiveness of your lessons is bound to fluctuate, but one thing is certain – if you have the skills to respond to the dynamics of the moment, the overall value of your lessons will be great.

During an effective lesson, experienced teachers perform with a degree of intuitiveness. They make decisions about the pace and content of a lesson with ease and there is almost subconscious use of established routines to ensure that the lesson flows smoothly and effortlessly.

As an NQT, don't place such expectations on yourself. Allow time to develop your own skills of effectiveness and don't expect everything to work all the time. Use your experiences to propel you towards the goal of effectiveness through regular evaluation and analysis of your lessons.

ABOUT EFFECTIVENESS

What does 'effective' mean? If you consider effectiveness to mean having 100 per cent of pupils on task 100 per cent of the time, then no lesson that has ever been (or will ever be) taught can be thought to be effective! However, if learning has taken place, you can consider the lesson to have been effective on some level. Even the teacher who abandons a planned lesson to respond to the behavioural needs of a class sets standards for future lessons and so facilitates effectiveness. The perfectly effective lesson is something that good teachers continue to strive for throughout their careers.

Useful tips on effectiveness

Get into the habit of sticking to certain routines that keep your lessons moving and minimize the opportunity for misbehaviour (good behaviour is a cornerstone of effectiveness in the classroom). The emphasis is on pace and rhythm.

ACTION

Think about what it would be like to experience one of your lessons. Would you feel safe enough to take part and offer your ideas, feel stretched but not rushed, and at peace in your environment? 'Be' one of your pupils for a moment. What image of you as the teacher do you see? Are you stimulated, inspired and motivated by what is being said? Is the presentation filled with vitality? Do you understand the purpose of the work you are given?

Before a lesson

Once in the flow of the first term, effective lessons presuppose good relationships with the pupils, adept group management and slick organization of resources. These are all aspects to work on from day one until retirement!

- Make sure your planning is sound. Know what you want to teach and how. Do you know how the group is organized? Is it streamed, set or banded? Is the group 'mixed-ability'?

ABOUT THE HAY McBER MODEL OF TEACHER EFFECTIVENESS

In June 2000, Hay McBer published a model of teacher effectiveness, which is still relevant today. The descriptions were based on research into what it is that effective teachers do in practice. There is not the space here to cover the minutiae of the report (which can be downloaded from www.teachernet.gov.uk) but, in brief, it supports the often-held view that it is a combination of interconnected factors (teaching skills, professional characteristics and classroom climate) that contributes to overall effectiveness.

The report identifies a 'Dictionary of Characteristics' for main-scale teachers, teachers at the threshold and outstanding teachers. These characteristics have been summarized below:

- professionalism:
  - challenge and support;
  - confidence;
  - creating trust;
  - respect for others;

- thinking:
  - analytical thinking;
  - conceptual thinking;

- planning and setting expectations:
  - drive for improvement;
  - information seeking;
  - initiative;

- leading:
  - flexibility;
  - holding people accountable;
  - managing pupils;
  - passion for learning;

- relating to others:

—   impact and influence;
—   teamworking;
—   understanding others.

Do get a copy of this report, as it will not only be helpful in focusing on your own effectiveness in the classroom but could serve as a basis for many a discussion with your induction tutor/mentor. You can also use your experience of teaching to add to the characteristics of effective teachers identified in the Hay McBer model.

- Don't aim to plan too far ahead, especially if you are teaching a topic that is unfamiliar. You can't be an expert in everything.
- Check any equipment that you plan to use to make sure it works properly. Do all you can to avoid pupils having to share resources. If you prepare any of your own resources (and most teachers do), guard master copies closely.
- Prepare your room as much as possible, including the board. Be creative with your board space, be it black, white or interactive! Think of board routines you can teach your class. Perhaps put directions in boxes and questions in bubbles. Once you have created your own formula, stick with it. Use the board as a way of presenting the lesson – a valuable resource. Some teachers write statements about what the lesson is about on the board, for example 'Today we will explore the causes of World War I'.
- Whenever possible, be waiting for your class to arrive, even if that means missing a few minutes of your break. You can, perhaps, ask pupils to line up quietly (or in silence) outside if space permits, before they enter your room. Reiterate your need for pupils to enter quietly and calmly.
- Welcome pupils with confidence. The first two or three minutes of a lesson are crucial.
- Allow some time for pupils to unpack and settle and again insist on silence before beginning the lesson. Give a clear signal when the lesson is to begin. Be consistent so that pupils learn your cues.

During a lesson

- Introduce each lesson or session.
- Link each lesson to the previous one through the use of questions and answers. It is essential that pupils see how the work they do is related. Aim to build on existing knowledge and offer the opportunity for your pupils to demonstrate what they know. Aim for information to be conveyed to pupils personally rather than by relying on 'third party'

materials such as books and worksheets. The connection is between you and the pupils, not the pupils and a book.

- Think about when you want to hand out books, paper and materials – before your introduction or after? Try to hand out work yourself and comment on the quality of it. Avoid broad generalizations.

ABOUT LESSON PLANNING

Effective lesson plans contain certain key features, including:

- learning objectives that are clear, evident, well timed and that link in to activities;
- details of how staff in the room are to be deployed, including relevant briefing notes;
- details on resources needed;
- explanations of differentiation and details of assessment for learning;
- evaluation notes.

You may be involved in the development of individual education plans (IEPs) for your pupils. These plans must be achievable and measurable with a long-term vision if they are to be of value to both pupil and teacher. With specific targets, precisely worded, children can recognize when they are achieving and begin to move themselves forward. If would be useful to discuss IEPs with the SENCO and with your induction tutor. You can find out more about IEPs from www.schoolsweb.gov.uk

- Don't let latecomers disrupt the lesson. Deal with them at an appropriate time during the lesson or at the end.
- State the lesson's subject, context and purpose in a relevant way for the children you teach. Pupils should always know what will be expected of them, how and why. What is the key competency they will be learning? How can they apply it to real life? Use analogies and examples as much as possible.
- Announce activities in advance if appropriate, for example 'In five minutes we will move on to role-playing'.
- Use examples that your pupils can directly relate to. Clarify points throughout. Find the simple starting point and develop it. This helps to bring the distant within easy reach.
- Keep the lesson bubbling. Be enthusiastic about what you are teaching and, if you can introduce a 'wow' factor, all the better.

- Encourage enthusiasm for related learning, for example through visits to the library, museums, further reading, visits from experts and the use of ICT (including video, radio, TV, etc.). Make lessons interesting and dynamic through the use of themes. Guide each child's discovery. This encourages children to take responsibility for their learning and helps to facilitate personalisation.
- Be flexible and adaptable. Abandon your lesson plan if necessary. Be a 'leader' in your classroom.
- Vary the timed activities you give children. Keep individual abilities constantly in your mind and draw on the practical, intellectual, oral and written. Can pupils keep track of their progress and take part in target setting? Are they surprised by the activities or can they predict them?
- Allow only minor digressions before pulling the group back to the topic. Minimize blocks to learning. Catch pupils doing things right rather than wrong.
- Think of ways you can draw key concepts from pupils. Are you appealing to their curiosity and encouraging them to respond creatively? Anecdotal input from teachers can have a profound effect on the learning environment that is created.
- Allow time to recognize and celebrate attainment in your lessons.
- Give pupils the opportunity to develop skills in your lessons by allowing them to apply intellectual, physical and creative effort to the work you set. Nurture imaginative thinking and encourage problem solving.
- Be sure to include memory aids in your lessons, for example mnemonics, prompt cards, bulleted summary sheets and so on.
- Allow plenty of time to set homework and check that all pupils know exactly what they have to do. You could ask specific questions such as 'Annie, when is the homework due in?', 'William, where will you find the information you need?', 'Kuldeep, what page are the questions on?' etc.
- Allow time to clear away before recapping and reflecting on the lesson. Connect the threads of new learning with past and future learning.
- Dismiss the class clearly, perhaps a few at a time. Don't allow them simply to wander out.

EXAMPLE

As a student, Amanda, a secondary teacher in Greenwich, had to teach a class after the sudden death of a pupil had been announced. She had to abandon the lesson she had planned and simply respond to the children's reactions.

ABOUT MIXED-ABILITY CLASSES

The notion of streamed classes as an alternative to mixed-ability classes is a little nonsensical. All groups are of mixed abilities and for this reason you will need to take into consideration the ability of each child in every class you teach. This approach supports personalised learning too.

Most schools have some mixed-ability classes, but not necessarily mixed-ability teaching. A skill all teachers need is in finding the optimum level of differentiation needed – too much and you launch yourself into a planning nightmare while too little means that it's unlikely that you will stretch any child.

True mixed-ability teaching involves enabling children to work independently. Make sure that you always have supplementary materials for the faster and slower learners and be aware that pupils' abilities will appear to change, depending on how inspired they are by the topic. Underachievement is to be avoided at all costs and at all levels of ability. Watch out for pupils who:

- occasionally offer flashes of brilliance in their work;
- may seem permanently distracted;
- lack confidence in the classroom;
- overcriticize their own efforts;
- apply creativity and originality to problem solving;
- ask probing questions;
- show you extra work that they have done in their own time.

Gently raise your expectations of such pupils, praising and nurturing at every stage.

You can find out more about personalised learning from www.schoolsweb.gov.uk

ABOUT EXPLAINING

> The mediocre teacher tells. The good teacher explains. The superior teacher demonstrates. The great teacher inspires.
>
> (William Arthur Ward)

Whatever you teach, the basis of all lessons will be explanations. The universal law here is pace, although it is surprisingly difficult to assess this objectively.

Think about the speed at which you talk. Are you too fast or too slow? Too loud or too quiet? Do you vary the tone, volume and speed of your speech?

Start with the real basics – you can't begin too simply. From this point, you can always build on the complexity:

- Make good use of key terms and phrases in appropriate language. Use a natural, logical progression of concepts and repeat, repeat, repeat.
- Ask pupils to demonstrate their understanding of your explanation. Look out for misinterpretations.
- Remember to vary the way you deliver explanations to accommodate the ways different children learn (e.g. verbal definitions, hands-on experience and so on).

After the lesson

> Only the mediocre are always at their best.
> (Jean Giraudoux)

- Insist on an orderly exit from your room or to another area of your teaching space.
- Clean your board for the next lesson.
- Be available to talk to pupils between lessons. Even a chat in the corridor can keep a pupil's enthusiasm bubbling.
- Evaluate the lesson and resources you used – even if only mentally.
- Be realistic about what you first think to be a disastrous lesson. Was it really? What can you change for the future? Don't expect to sparkle all the time and don't dwell on mistakes. There isn't an advanced skills teacher in the country who doesn't make mistakes – and learn from them.
- Praise yourself!

ABOUT GROUPWORK

Many teachers like to set group tasks for pupils to offer the opportunity for collaborative learning. If you choose to use groupwork in your lessons, these ideas may help:

- Think about how you will group your pupils. Common choices are by friendship, by ability (either deliberately mixed or streamed) or by location in the room. You will also need to consider the size of each group. If it is too large, there may not be enough work to go round.

- Plan each stage of the groupwork carefully, with the emphasis on cooperation and interdependence. There would be little point in pupils working independently within their group.

- Make sure that your pupils know exactly why they will be working in the groups you have chosen, and how you intend to assess them. Emphasize the relevance of what you have asked them to do.

- If your pupils are not used to groupwork, they may need to be given skills to make the situation work For. example, can they fairly divide labour? Do they know how to keep a group together?

- Help each group to get started and to plan the work they have ahead of them.

- Encourage the groups to deal with their own problems. Only step in if absolutely necessary. That said, you will need to keep a close eye on what is happening in each group.

- Don't let the task pass by without giving pupils the opportunity to evaluate how well they worked in the group and to consider what would make things easier in the future. This needs careful management on your part so that such evaluations don't degenerate into finger-pointing sessions.

ABOUT QUESTIONING

> I was gratified to be able to answer promptly. I said, 'I don't know.'
>
> (Mark Twain)

- Announce questions in advance if appropriate, for example 'I'm going to be asking you about ocean trenches in a few minutes'. This provides pupils with a little advance processing time.

- Aim questions at particular pupils and don't favour the reliable few. Adapt questions to individuals.

- Asking questions to the whole class can prove to be a discipline debacle as some patiently put hands up and others yell out the first thought that comes to mind.

- Word questions carefully – you may be asking for a witty or glib answer.

- Aim to draw knowledge rather than a one-syllable grunt. Get pupils to analyse and synthesize in their answering. Higher-order questions will do this. Avoid lower-order questions such as basic comprehension, as it is possible to answer these without any knowledge at all.

- Allow sufficient time for the pupil to think of an answer. Encourage through non-verbal cues.
- Select something positive about a wrong answer.
- Ask the same question to different pupils for variety in response.
- Repeat answers for the benefit of the class – they may not all have heard.
- Encourage pupils to ask you questions, and be honest if you don't know the answer. Do, however, make a note to find the answer to tell pupils the next time you see them.

Use questioning to intervene when a child's understanding is off target. Think of an appropriate tactic, such as posing a question that contains a clue to the answer, and be sure to take a step back when understanding has taken place: you don't want to fire developmental questions immediately, but should seek to consolidate what the child has achieved.

Lesson evaluation

For a lesson to be effective, you need to plan, deliver and evaluate it. Your training probably saw you furiously writing out an evaluation for every lesson that you delivered, as well as every resource you created. If it didn't, start evaluating now.

Keeping up good habits

It would be ridiculous to expect new teachers to fill in a pro forma after every lesson, documenting how it went, what resources were used, what worked and what failed, whether pupils were challenged and how you could improve things in the future. However, if you don't spend time reflecting on the lessons you deliver and your teaching, you are unlikely to be able to give effective lessons in which your skills as a teacher continue to develop.

Even if you consider the lessons you have taught during a day for a few minutes only, you will get into the habit of being a reflective practitioner, ever open to learning and improving. If you can get into the habit of jotting your thoughts down, all the better. A small resource evaluation notebook will enable you to keep track of improvements you can make and successes you've had. It can make great reading on a bad day!

Ask yourself:

- Did pupils achieve my learning intentions?

- Has learning actually taken place?
- Did pupils participate?
- Can I assess what pupils have achieved? (Think about qualitative and quantitative assessment.)
- Did I enjoy the lesson?

You could even ask your pupils at the end of a lesson what they learnt. Did they enjoy the lesson? Would they like to do it again?

EXAMPLE

For Sam, the evaluation process was much more natural once he was in his first job. It became an automatic mental assessment of what was achieved and learnt: a running commentary.

A group of West Sussex teachers developed the checklist below for use in lesson evaluation and it can easily be adapted for use with classes of all ages.

Checklist for lesson evaluation

Did I:

• introduce the lesson?	YES/NO
• put the lesson in context?	YES/NO
• make sure the pupils listened in silence?	YES/NO
• introduce the key words to be used?	YES/NO

Did I:

• maintain the pace of the lesson?	YES/NO
• maintain high expectations?	YES/NO
• differentiate the tasks appropriately?	YES/NO
• regularly interact with the pupils?	YES/NO

Were the pupils:

• on task?	YES/NO
• actively engaged in their learning?	YES/NO
• aware of when they could talk and when they should remain silent?	YES/NO

Did I:

• respond to the previous homework?	YES/NO
• set homework?	YES/NO
• make sure that the homework task was clearly understood?	YES/NO
• make sure that all pupils entered the task into their organizers?	YES/NO
• set a deadline for completion?	YES/NO
• provide differentiated opportunities?	YES/NO

Finally, did I:

• restate the learning intentions?	YES/NO
• summarize what had been achieved?	YES/NO
• explain the intentions for the next lesson?	YES/NO
• ensure that pupils were focused and listening in silence?	YES/NO

Peer observations

An excellent way of helping you to improve the effectiveness of your lessons is to observe colleagues in action from all areas of the school's curriculum. This can give you good ideas to utilize yourself and bad ideas to avoid at all costs.

Before you observe a colleague, discuss why you want to watch him/her teach. Keep in mind that it can be intimidating to have a new teacher fresh from training in your class. Make sure that your colleague is in full agreement that you should be there. This process can help to create some strong, trusting relationships. Ask in advance if your colleague minds you taking notes or moving around the room at appropriate times.

Learning from colleagues

- How did the teacher gain the attention of the pupils?
- How was the lesson introduced?
- What motivated the pupils?
- How were resources used?
- How did the teacher employ questions?
- How was the lesson paced?
- Did the teacher respond to the needs of the pupils with flexibility? What links were made to previous and future lessons?
- Was there an air of enthusiasm from both teacher and class?
- What would you have done differently? Why?

Aim to have a specific focus for your observations.

Spiritual, moral, social and cultural education

The spiritual, moral, social and cultural (SMSC) aspects of learning in the classroom are incredibly important and ideally need to be fully integrated in what you do as a teacher. Don't leave SMSC education to chance; pupils cannot be relied upon to catch the knowledge they need in this respect.

Think about how you can make SMSC education specific and identifiable in your lessons. These ideas may help, but are by no means definitive:

- Is pride in achievement something that you encourage?
- Do your pupils display a 'have-a-go' mentality?
- Is creativity nurtured in each child?
- Do you encourage courtesy and trustworthiness in your pupils?
- Do you offer them the opportunity to work collaboratively and to develop skills of cooperation?
- Do your pupils form constructive relationships with one another and with teachers and other adults?
- Do your pupils work in an atmosphere free from oppressive behaviour, such as bullying, sexism and racism?
- Do you actively promote equal opportunities in your classroom?
- Do your pupils reflect on what they do and understand the impact they have on others?
- Do you appreciate the role of emotion in your classroom? Are you an emotional coach?
- Do you encourage your pupils to respect other people's differences, particularly their feelings, values and beliefs?
- Do you encourage initiative in your pupils?
- Do you encourage a sense of awe and wonder in pupils at their existence and what surrounds them?
- Are all aspects of human existence celebrated as welcome and valid experiences?
- Can the natural environment be brought into your teaching?
  You can find out more about SMSC values in schools from SMSC Online (see www.smsc.org.uk).

Homework strategies

Your school should have a clear homework policy outlining how much homework should be given to each class and how frequently it should be given. At best, this will be written into schemes of work and planning, making the setting of homework relatively painless for new teachers. At worst, common practice in your school will be to yell out the homework at the backs of departing pupils as they rapidly disappear into the corridor!

The notion of homework suffers from the hugely differing interpretations of what constitutes good practice. The line from the DCSF is that homework is not an 'optional extra', but is an 'essential' part of a child's work. There is more on this to be found at www.teachernet.gov.uk.

If you do have an element of freedom in the way you set homework, it is worth regularly affirming to pupils and parents your commitment to setting meaningful tasks. This tends to create a positive homework ethos that you can build on.

ABOUT SETTING APPROPRIATE HOMEWORK

Ask yourself these questions when you are planning and setting homework:

- Does it have a place in my scheme of work and planning?
- Can pupils make use of libraries and study centres?
- Is it fair in length and context?
- Have I differentiated?
- Does the task discriminate in any way?
- Does the homework vary in length and nature?
- Does the class have access to the relevant information?
- Can the homework lead to pupil achievement?
- Am I encouraging motivation in pupils?
- Can pupils derive from the work set what I want them to?
- Do pupils know what my learning intentions and assessment criteria are?
- Can my pupils value the work set?
- Am I forging links between school and home?
- Can I ascertain whether the homework has been completed?
- Do pupils know that I will follow homework up?
- Is my focus on quality (as it should be) or quantity?

When OFSTED inspectors visit your school, they will look at how homework is used as an effective part of your lessons. While the actual work you set is important, you also need to consider such issues as how you will collect in the work. Establish firm routines with your classes so that everyone knows your arrangements (which, incidentally, should be mutually helpful).

Getting what you want from a task

Homework that is hastily set is unlikely to produce the results you want. If you have placed the task within a scheme of work and your pupils know the context of what they have been asked to do, the chances of getting what you want from a particular task are much greater. Basically, the only way to get what you want is to know what you want:

- Have homework tasks pre-prepared on sheets of paper or written on the board/screen.
- Allow plenty of time at the end of a lesson to explain the homework. You need to make sure that pupils have written down the details of the task, when it is due in and how it should be completed.
- Never explain the task while pupils are copying into their books. Wait until they have all finished reading and writing and then explain.
- Ask pupils to explain to you what their task is.
- Make sure every child has the resources to complete the task. Ask your SEN department to help you to differentiate the work you want to set.

Utilizing the homework notion

The best way to ensure that your classes actually complete the homework tasks you set is regularly to reiterate the value of independent study at home. You could also explain to your classes a few general tasks that they could do as homework in the event of your absence. Make sure that you keep a stock of such tasks and that pupils know the circumstances in which they should complete them. They could even have them written down in the back of their exercise books or homework diaries and you could nominate someone from the class to inform the cover teacher which task should be done. Although it is harder to place such tasks in the context of current work, this does give pupils an element of choice and responsibility over their work. Tell other members of staff about your system. They will know what to expect if they have to cover your classes and may even want to adopt your idea.

Homework is another opportunity to do some positive PR for your school. View the tasks you set through the eyes of parents. Are they varied and relevant? Are the books that go home in good condition? Can parents easily discern the purpose of a task?

Avoid giving homework tasks connected to your subject or classwork as a punishment. You run the risk of putting the child off your subject for ever. Punitive tasks should be complete in their own right.

Be reasonable in your homework expectations. Just like you, your pupils have lives outside school.

Marking strategies

The whole point of homework is that pupils work independently at home, or at least outside school hours. An unfortunate by-product of this arrangement is the amount of marking that this can generate for teachers. There are a number of strategies that you can employ to cope with the burden:

- Make sure that you know how you will assess each piece of homework and what the purpose of this assessment is (for example, is the assessment to be formative or summative, objective or subjective and so on).
- Create tasks that can be self-marked or peer-marked in class.
- Set some non-written homework.
- Pace your homework setting so that you don't have hundreds of projects to mark at the same time. It can take a while to get into the rhythm of a term but homework is one area of teaching that you can control.
- Plan homework setting to complement your energy levels. There's little point in arranging piles of marking when you know you are coming down with a cold.
- Think about how you can create tasks requiring short answers. Some subjects lend themselves to this more easily than others. However, you should not rely on short-answer questions too heavily in any subject.
- Have your marking criteria and the task set in front of you as you work through the books, for quick reference.
- Set a time limit for marking a set of work and stick to it. Minimize distractions and focus. Perhaps introduce an element of surprise by using different coloured inks – do you always want to use red?
- Find out if there are any possibilities of help with marking from your department or year colleagues.

ABOUT GATHERING GOOD IDEAS

Keep a record of all the homework tasks that you have set for each scheme of work. These will probably be suitable for future use and you can adapt them on the basis of previous evaluations on their effectiveness. You could even ask pupils what homework tasks they have enjoyed and have found inspiring.

ABOUT EXCUSES

Throughout the course of your career you will hear some of the most amazing excuses for non-completion of homework. Make your homework tasks excuse proof by following these ideas:

- Be consistent with your sanctions for homework not completed. Giving the benefit of the doubt once is just about permissible but certainly no more. It would be a good idea to discuss with the pupil what the problems may be.

- Explain tasks carefully and slowly and offer your class the opportunity to talk to you about the task at a later stage if necessary.
- Create routines for the setting and collection of homework for each class. Have homework days.
- Make the reason for the homework clear. If pupils know the relevance of what they have to do they are more likely to do it.
- Where appropriate, explain to pupils the assessment criteria you will use.
- Think of how tutors can help you create good attitudes towards homework in pupils.
- You will need to discuss with persistent offenders exactly what the problems may be. Explain what your expectations are and what the shortfall is. It may be appropriate to adapt homework tasks or to work with the child after school for a while.

Your domain: the classroom

Whether you work in a classroom or an open-plan environment, the area in which you teach is your domain. The changes you make to this space can greatly affect the organization and ambience of your lessons, and the effectiveness of your teaching.

Before you go ahead and redecorate, do check with your line manager and induction tutor what house rules there are regarding classrooms and displays and always follow the guidelines given.

Creating the environment you want

If you are fortunate enough to have a room assigned to you, without having to share, you can start your interior design from scratch. While the amount of work you do in any holiday should be kept to an absolute minimum, preparation before the start of a term can help to give you an empty space in which to create the environment you want; a learning environment.

- Throw out any clutter from previous years as well as anything that does not serve a purpose.
- Aim to zone your room – primary classrooms are usually organized in this way anyway, but the idea works in secondary classrooms too. Zoning helps to establish order and routines in your space.
- Brighten dingy corners with plants. You could involve pupils in their care.
- Think about creating a 'peaceful' corner. Look out for pictures of natural scenes and place them where you can see them when addressing the class.

If possible, swathe the background of this corner with paper or fabric in a shade of blue or green.

- If space permits, allow your class or tutor group to decorate a small area of your room.
- Be aware of the light in your classroom. Try not to let the room get too dark, as this will make for gloomy lessons and gloomy pupils.
- Keep the air in your room circulating; have a window open all the time. Anyone who has walked into a room after 35 sweaty adolescents have just vacated it will know exactly how important fresh air is – and infants can be just as fragrant!
- Watch the heating levels – too cold and your pupils will grumble, too hot and you'll all become sleepy. Either extreme can lead to negative stress.
- Keep your room tidy and safe on a day-to-day basis. Don't wait until the end of term for a tidying blitz because the chances are you won't want to be bothered then. Utilize storage drawers and cupboards and avoid using your own unique filing systems. Label everything so that anyone can use your room and understand your systems. This will also encourage others to keep your space tidy.
- Think about the use of colour in your room. You may not be able to do anything about the colour of the walls, but most teachers are free to choose what colour they use as a background to wall-mounted work. Reds and oranges are said to be stimulating while greens and blues are relaxing. Black can be a stunning base for mounted work. Be aware of the way colour affects your classes both in the classroom surroundings and in the clothes you wear – do you want unnecessarily to stimulate your pupils?
- Explore the possibilities of using music in your room. The use of appropriate sound can have a positive effect on learning situations (Plato considered it to be 'a potent instrument for learning') and some teachers consider it as an additional resource, particularly for art and history (as well as music) lessons. Some teachers use music to signal cues for learning such as marking the start of a lesson, or when pupils are to be on task. There is also research to suggest that knowledge gained when listening to music is easier to retrieve. For further information, look at the work of Don Campbell of 'Mozart Effect' fame (see www.mozarteffect.com). Do, however, be aware of the effect that time signatures and numbers of beats per minute in a piece of music can have on pupils. Music can entrain the body, regulating brain, breathing and heart rhythms. For this reason, it is best to go for music that has 60–70 beats per minute as that is the rate at which the heart beats when relaxed.
- Wipe your board clean/clear your screen as soon as you have finished with the work. This will help to keep lessons flowing smoothly, as you won't have to waste time with chores like this when you really want to be writing on it.

- Keep a stock of tissues and paper towels in your room. This will help in the event of spillages and will also prevent requests to go to the toilet for a tissue.

Getting the most from your space

Work on the assumption that change and movement are more advantageous than stagnation. Make sure, though, that you can always see all the pupils, that they can see you and any materials you use, and that you can see the door if you have one.

- Try different seating arrangements. Horizontal rows, vertical rows, conference style, grouped tables – all are useful for different purposes and it may be appropriate to change the furniture around at regular intervals. You could ask pupils to create seating plans.
- Alter the position in the room from which you function.
- Change displays regularly, making sure they are clearly labelled.
- You don't have to do everything in one go – altering displays on a rotation basis is fine. Aim to change at least one aspect of your room once every half-term.
- Make sure that everything in your room is functioning as it should. This includes such things as power points, windows and blinds.

ACTION

Contact one museum, one publisher and one bookshop to ask for display materials for your classroom. You may be pleasantly surprised by the selection you receive.

ABOUT ADVERTISING

Be aware that you may be advertising certain products and places inadvertently through the resources you use to decorate your classroom. Advertising in schools is at the discretion of the headteacher and the governing body, so it might be best to check first if anything you want to use bears a brand name.

Every now and then, it is worth reassessing the environment in your classroom. Think about how you would describe:

- the atmosphere you have created;
- the noise that your pupils make whilst on and off task;
- the effectiveness of the communication in your classroom;
- the way your pupils relate to you and vice versa;
- the degree to which your classroom rules and routines are adhered to.

Are there any changes you would like to make? It can be helpful to discuss these with your induction tutor/mentor.

Emotional intelligence/literacy

> We are being judged by a new yardstick: not just how smart we are, but also by how well we handle ourselves and each other.
>
> (Daniel Goleman, 1998)

Emotional intelligence (sometimes known as emotional literacy) is now quite firmly embedded as a priority in many schools. There is a vast amount of literature available on this most crucial aspect of teaching, with organizations such as Antidote (www.antidote.org.uk) producing particularly relevant and useful information for teachers.

Emotional intelligence has many definitions, but can broadly be taken to mean the ability to recognize the role that our feelings have in the way we live our lives and interact with others. It is thought that there are emotional intelligence competencies. These comprise:

- self-awareness:
    - emotional self-awareness;
    - accurate self-assessment;
    - self-confidence;
- self-management:
    - self-control;

- – trustworthiness;
- – conscientiousness;
- – achievement orientation;
- – initiative;

- social awareness:

  - – empathy;
  - – organizational awareness;
  - – service orientation;

- social skills:

  - – developing others;
  - – leadership;
  - – influence;
  - – communication;
  - – change catalyst;
  - – conflict management;
  - – building bonds;
  - – teamwork and collaboration.

Websites worth browsing for ideas on how emotional intelligence/literacy can be incorporated into your teaching include:

- www.antidote.org.uk (Antidote);
- www.nelig.com (National Emotional Literacy Interest Group – NELIG);
- www.eiconsortium.org (Consortium for Research on Emotional Intelligence in Organizations);
- www.casel.org (the Collaborative for the Advancement of Social and Emotional Learning);
- www.esrnational.org (Educators for Social Responsibility).

Daniel Goleman's books are also well worth reading: *Emotional Intelligence* and *Working with Emotional Intelligence* are both published by Bloomsbury.

ABOUT The SEAL materials

The SEAL materials (SEAL stands for Social and Emotional Aspects of Learning) have been designed to help teachers to develop social and emotional skills in their pupils. Primary SEAL is organized into seven themes, which can be covered within a school year:

- New beginnings

- Getting on and falling out
- Say no to bullying
- Going for goals
- Good to be me
- Relationships
- Changes

Secondary SEAL promotes the social and emotional skills that underpin effective learning, positive behaviour, regular attendance, staff effectiveness and the health and well-being of all who learn and work in schools.

You can find out more about the SEAL materials from Teachernet (see www.teachernet.gov.uk).

Find out more . . .

Effectiveness as a concept is incredibly broad. In the context of teaching, you may also want to explore the notions of mentoring and coaching as ways of boosting your effectiveness and there is much out there to inspire (for example the website of the Centre for the Use of Research and Evidence in Education: www.curee-paccts.com). Spend some time browsing the Internet for ideas, and don't forget to delve into the realms of effectiveness in the broader sense in your life. Stephen Covey's books remain relevant starting points for this.

Chapter 7

Work/life balance

The greatest wealth is health.
(Virgil)

Life in the teaching profession is many things. It's invigorating, exciting, challenging, rewarding and sometimes exhausting. How to establish and maintain a work/life balance is arguably the most useful skill that you will acquire throughout your teaching career, so this chapter explores how best to do this so that you thrive in both your personal and working lives. You'll find out about:

- Coping with meetings
- Time management
- Managing your preparation and planning
- Balancing work with your home life
- Stress busting
- Looking after health and lifestyle.

Coping with meetings

Part of life in the teaching profession is attending numerous meetings. In fact, the end of your teaching day is only half the story for most teachers, not least NQTs.

You may be asked to attend any or all of the following:

- full staff meetings;
- induction meetings;
- year or department meetings;
- union meetings/briefings;
- planning meetings;
- SEN meetings;
- ICT meetings;
- PTA meetings;

- special events meetings;
- meetings with parents.

You will (should) also have informal meetings about your day-to-day planning and progress. For some, this could amount to many meetings (both 'official' and 'unofficial') each week, requiring preparation and follow-up.

ABOUT REMODELLING

Over recent years, there has been a strong focus on teacher workload and the bureaucratic burden facing teachers. Several initiatives and documents have been produced by the DCSF (in its previous incarnations) in order to assist schools in protecting teachers' work/life balance. To find out more about these, visit www.teachernet.gov.uk/remodelling for all the latest relevant documents and information on the subject.

Meetings, particularly those which are well-run, are essential in schools, so we'll never reach a time when they don't take place in one form or another. As schools differ so greatly in their organization and administration, NQTs can have very different experiences of meetings. In order to maximize their use, consider these points:

- If you are unable to discern the relevance of a meeting, ask its organizer if you need to attend. If you can't contribute to or learn from a meeting, there is little point in attending.
- Make sure that you know the purpose of the meeting.
- Send your apologies if you are unable to attend.
- Be particularly aware of any items on the agenda that directly relate to you or your classes.
- Ask for clarification on any aspect of the meeting that you don't understand, although the chair should have ensured that there was no possibility for confusion. If you allow jargon to whizz over your head, the crux of the discussion could pass you by.
- Plan in advance any input you would like to have. Perhaps you could prepare some questions to ask or comments to refer to. Be clear and succinct in your speech and make sure you stick to the point. Try not to feel intimidated and don't be put off asking questions; it's only by questioning that progress through dogma can be made.
- If you feel the chair is being manipulative or dominating, keep your tone of voice consistent and maintain eye contact with calm assertion.

Organizing the information you need

Attending meetings invariably means gathering a small forest's worth of paper. Avoid information overload by:

- assessing what is relevant to you while you are in the meeting;
- using highlighter pens to colour-code what needs immediate action, what can wait and what can be thrown away;
- sticking to a rigid filing system. For each piece of paper that comes into your possession, you have only three options: file immediately for future reference, act on it immediately or destroy it;
- creating a 'recycle bin' for documents you cannot bring yourself to file or destroy – make sure you empty this bin regularly.

If a meeting results in you having a task to do, make sure you have been given the means by which to achieve it – in other words, time and/or resources. Any deadlines must be realistic.

Minutes

You should be given the minutes a few days after the meeting (although do be aware that not all meetings will involve an agenda and minutes). Once you have read them, mention anything you disagree with to the person who produced them. Be especially vigilant if you are quoted. If you feel that an important matter has been omitted from the minutes, raise this as soon as possible. If necessary, you can have it recorded that you disagree with the minutes when they are discussed at the next meeting.

If you would like to have something included on the next agenda, ask the chair of the meeting. You may not be successful, but your request should at least be heard and discussed.

ABOUT RECYCLING

Schools use a tremendous amount of paper and consequently generate piles of paper waste. Unless your school makes the effort to recycle this waste paper, most of it will end up in a landfill site. Britain falls way behind other European nations in its attitude to recycling and this is now beginning to pose real threats to the environment and to health, with some areas of the country having only very limited landfill space left. Recycling is now an urgent necessity, not a new age fad. The order of preference for waste management is to reduce consumption (use less paper), reuse (as scrap) and recycle (anything that cannot be reused):

- Keep paper use to a minimum.
- Organize your waste so that paper can be easily recycled. Even if paper is not collected for recycling, most municipal tips offer paper-recycling facilities.
- Encourage classes to adhere to your systems of waste management and make sure they understand why this is important.
- Suggest a whole-school approach to recycling if there is not one in place already.

However, it is also important to be aware of confidentiality issues and the need to shred certain types of document. You school will give you guidance on this.

- For information on recycling take a look at: www.recycle-more.co.uk/
- EnCams is an environmental charity, which runs the Keep Britain Tidy campaign. For further information, visit www.encams.org
- Friends of the Earth also has details of waste reduction strategies (call 020 7490 1555 or see www.foe.org.uk).

Time management

> If it weren't for the last minute, nothing would get done.
> (Anonymous)

Few professions rely on effective time management and awareness quite as much as teaching. As an NQT, it would be helpful to think of effective time management as a way of enabling you to live a full life outside your work – a life that allows for relaxation and rest as well as hobbies and relationships. It is not a way of creating time to do more work or of managing crises.

ACTION

Think about your relationship with time. Do you have enough time to complete the tasks you want to complete, or are you always running against the clock? Are you in control, or does time control you?

In order to develop time management skills, you need to become *aware* of time. Teachers often suffer from time 'poverty' – too much to do in the time available. Added to this is the fact that, as an NQT, you are less likely to be in a position to delegate your tasks and, often, jobs will be delegated to you.

Pacing yourself

Working in such a structured environment, it is important for teachers to pace themselves, not only on a daily basis but on a termly and yearly basis as well. Just as each day has its own rhythm, so does each term and year. Therefore, your targets for a day, term and year need to be realistic and take into account rhythms and fluctuations. If you tend to collapse after pressured times with exhaustion or some other ailment (and many of us do!), you are clearly not pacing yourself.

- First, look at the calendar for the whole year and write down anything that applies to you, for example parents' evenings, reports, school plays and so on. This will give you an initial picture of the busiest times of the year.
- Then look at the term – where do your biggest commitments fall? Do you have extra departmental or curriculum work, for example writing exams or schemes of work to do? This will give you the basic shape of the term. Pinpoint the very busy times when other aspects of your job like marking and preparation will have to be minimized. Aim to ease your workload at these times. Lean on pre-prepared work and take opportunities for pupils to self-assess.
- Next, look at the rhythms of your week. Do you have any nightmarish days? Where are your opportunities to catch up on administration and marking?
- Throughout each day, get to know the times when you work most efficiently. If you suffer from a 4 pm low, don't attempt to work. The aim is to maximize productivity at your most productive times. It is simply a waste of time to attempt to work at the same pace all through the day. It is better to rest, or turn your attentions to other things, rather than work unproductively.

Once you have established the rhythm of your days, aim to give yourself treats at low points of the day, term or year. Perhaps plan a weekend away mid-term or spend some time indulging your interests. Planning is an essential part of this process, as anticipation and excitement are part of the enjoyment:

- When you are working slowly, don't punish yourself. Recognize it as a part of your natural rhythms and energy levels.
- Taking on piles of work will not add to your feelings of self-worth and esteem, but will add to your stress and anxiety levels.
- When you feel yourself working at a pace that is uncomfortable, slow down, regardless of any deadlines.

- Learn to know when to stop working on a project. There will be an optimum time to let it go.

Prioritizing

Rather than attempting to work through each task as it comes to you, manage the time you have by prioritizing. This means allowing yourself the time to think before launching into work. For every job, ask yourself does this need to be done? If the answer is yes, assess its importance as being:

- high
- moderate
- low.

Another question to ask is 'Will this make life easier?' For example, spending time sorting through a pile of papers may be beneficial if it means you are now more organized. It is worth accepting at the start of your career that reaching the end of your list is highly unlikely!

It is best to go through the prioritizing process as soon as you can so that jobs don't pile up. Once you have done this, you have created a 'to do' list that takes account of any deadlines and can be worked through systematically. If you find yourself getting behind, either knock something off your list or seek help. This is sensible and, at times, vital. Aim to empty your pigeon-hole/inbox daily and respond to emails, memos or phone calls as soon as possible.

Prioritizing should not just be done in relation to work. Sometimes, you will have to put your private life above work if you are to remain an effective teacher. In his book *Time Shifting* (1996), Stephan Rechtschaffen writes about the 'trickle-down' approach to time. He explains that, generally, we place our work first, followed by our primary relationship/family, then our everyday chores, then social life and finally ourselves – if there is any time left. We tend to neglect the bottom of the list upwards so, if you find you're neglecting your social life, alarm bells should be sounding. If you find it hard to devote time to your primary relationships, your work really is dominating beyond reason.

Managing your preparation and planning

Preparation and planning, in combination with the resulting marking, make huge demands on your time and, while you will have time specifically for this purpose, it is still important to start your career with good habits. Try these ideas:

- Take as much help as possible. If your department has a successful scheme of work for a topic, use it. If a textbook or website covers a topic well, use it rather than create your own. Be sure to familiarize yourself with the schemes of work available on the Standards site (www.standards.dfes.gov.uk/schemes3/). There are also schemes and lesson plans to be found on Teachernet: (www.teachernet.gov.uk).

- Don't feel inadequate if you are only one step ahead of the class – it doesn't matter. However, if you can get a little ahead of yourself, you will relieve some of the pressure to plan every night. Ask colleagues to help you with this.
- When you are planning for one lesson, see if there are ways of planning for two, three or four lessons at the same time. Block planning in this way helps to relieve pressure.
- Talk to colleagues and your induction tutor/mentor about your preparation and marking. Are you overdoing it? Do they know any short cuts that you could be taking? Do you know when to stop?
- If, through your experience this year, you can see ways of saving time next time you have to plan and teach a topic, write them down.
- Keep good records of all your planning and preparation for the next time you cover the topic.

Working at optimum levels

> Some people can stay longer in one hour than others can in one week.
> (William Dean Howells)

Beware the law of diminishing returns. You will have an optimum level at which you can work effectively. Go beyond that level and you risk wasting your time and wearing yourself out. If your working hours are so long that you have to force yourself out of bed in the mornings, ask yourself what it is that you hope to teach your pupils. If you feel depressed about your work, it is likely that you are not working at an optimal level and it is essential that you reduce the hours you work before you burn out.

Working fewer hours does not mean that you get less done; it just means that the time you spend working is probably more productive. When you decide to work, focus on what you are doing. Minimize all distractions; better to do that for one hour and complete your task than spend three hours unfocused and still not finish what you have to do.

- Establish what it is you like to do and aim to spend time on that. For example, if you enjoy designing worksheets, create that job for yourself. Perhaps others in your department will tackle some of the tasks you don't relish.
- Take opportunities throughout the day to get work done. Your class may be needed for sport or music practice etc.
- Delegate as much as possible. Fully utilize support staff (within reason!).

- Time your tasks, but be realistic with your deadlines. Giving yourself a specific time limit to complete a task is far more likely to result in success.
- Try to avoid feeling pressurized into working at the perceived pace of others around you.
- Do you have time-wasting habits or inefficiencies? Try to develop a conscious awareness when you work and assess how efficient you are.
- Take regular breaks from intense work like exam marking.
- Buddhists practise 'mindfulness'. This means being aware of the present moment, of what you are doing and how you are doing it. This is quite the opposite of doing A while thinking of B and C. Practising mindfulness tends to have the effect of apparently expanding time.

ABOUT ENCOURAGING YOURSELF TO WORK AT YOUR OPTIMUM LEVEL

If you suspect you are not working at a pace that is good for you, think about these questions:

- Do I avoid beginning tasks because it all seems like too much?
- Do I allow myself time to plan what needs to be done?
- Do I spend time on tasks that are not essential?
- Do I allow myself to be interrupted by colleagues and pupils?
- Do I help others to achieve tasks at the expense of my own work?
- Do I view deadlines as constructive encouragement or a source of unparalleled stress?
- Do I struggle with tasks that could or should be done by someone else?
- Do I underestimate how long something will take me?

If you answered yes to some or all of these questions, take the opportunity to discuss time management and awareness with your induction tutor/mentor at your next meeting. It may be a gradual process, but time management will get easier as your confidence and experience grow. Don't, however, give yourself a hard time!

Balancing work with your home life

> The intellect of man is forced to choose
> Perfection of the life, or of the work.
> (W B Yeats)

> Personal relations are the important thing for ever and ever, and not this outer life of telegrams and anger.
>
> (E M Forster)

Balancing work and home life is an extremely difficult skill, and one that many teachers never quite learn. This is mostly due to the extent to which schoolwork encroaches on the evening. The irony is that evidence seems to suggest that teachers who can maintain a work/life balance tend to be more effective in the classroom, not to mention more enthusiastic about their job. Teachers most profoundly affected tend to be those who live alone, as there is no one to say 'Stop working now; it's 11.30 – why don't you relax for a while?' or 'Can I help you with anything?'.

The key word is 'flexibility'. It would be ideal if you were more than a day ahead of yourself, as this would enable you to take an evening off at short notice. However, the teacher who can avoid working at home at all is rarer than a heatwave at Christmas!

That said, there are going to be times when you will have to focus more intently on work after school – perhaps just before an inspection or at report time – and therefore need flexibility from those you live with.

- Always be aware that you need to maintain good relationships outside work. If you find yourself cancelling arrangements, ask yourself why. Are you over-committed to your work?
- Allocate some time for nothing and everything – whatever you most feel like doing. Keep spontaneity alive in your life.
- Make sure that at least 75 per cent of your holidays are work-free. If you do have to do some work, do it at the start of the break so you can then enjoy uninterrupted free time.
- Instead of thinking about how much time you spend working, calculate how much time you spend not working. How much of the time available to you do you have control over? Work/life balance can only be established when we seek out where our control lies.

Keeping your identity

It can be easy to work yourself into the belief that you are a teacher and only a teacher. Use time management and awareness to free up space when you can nurture neglected needs.

- Are there hobbies that you would like to pursue but don't because of work?
- Have any aspects of your character changed since you started work?
- Are you forgetting birthdays and other events that you would normally remember or paying more attention to the finer details of schoolwork rather than the finer details of your life?

- If you had to stop teaching, where would that leave you? Would you be at a total loss as to what to do?
- Have you had more or less fun in your life since you began teaching?

Help yourself maintain balance by the following:

- Spend time on indulging yourself. Whether you enjoy sport, going to the theatre or cinema, going out with friends or pursuing your favourite hobby, ring-fence time when you can do these things without feeling guilty.
- Have at least one evening a week totally devoted to relaxation.
- Allocate time to keep in touch with friends and family. Make phone calls, write letters or send email – take an interest in the lives of those around you.
- Spend some time each day simply focusing on you. Some people meditate, others go for a walk, listen to music or take a long bubble bath. Whatever works for you, do it! Those you live with will soon learn that this time is sacrosanct to you, and that to allow you uninterrupted space makes you easier to live with.
- If necessary, take a sick day *for the benefit of your mental health* if nothing else. You would not be the first (or the last) teacher to take a day for resting.

Stress busting

> The universe is transformation; our life is what our thoughts make it.
> (Marcus Aurelius)

The degree of negative stress experienced by members of the same profession varies tremendously from individual to individual, but it is fair to say that workplace stress does appear to be on the increase. Negative stress is not to be ignored. Its effects are far-reaching and can lead to life-threatening conditions.

The *New Oxford Dictionary of English* defines stress as 'a state of mental or emotional strain or tension resulting from adverse or very demanding circumstances'. There is nothing intrinsically wrong with being stressed; it is virtually impossible to avoid being stressed at times and can lead to the necessary stimulation required to complete a task. It is when stress continues beyond the event for which you were preparing, or the interview etc., that you should start to take evasive action before mental, physical and emotional symptoms occur and the stress becomes negative.

Recognizing the symptoms of negative stress

Negative stress can be hard to identify, despite the fact that it can cause your body to present a wide variety of behavioural, physical and emotional symptoms. If you think that you may be suffering from negative stress, consider these questions:

- What do others say about you? How are you described?
- How do you interact with others? Are you patient and attentive or snappy and distracted?
- Are you less confident than you used to be? Are you shyer and more introspective?
- Is your mood stable and balanced or do you find yourself swinging from contentment to distress in one go?
- Is decision making more difficult than it used to be and concentration a thing of the past?
- Are your thoughts generally positive or negative? Do you have any thoughts of impending doom?
- Do you rely on stimulants more than usual? Has the occasional drink become a daily necessity?
- Has work taken over where leisure once reigned? Once you have completed your work, do you have the energy for a full social life?
- What are your energy levels like? Do you experience the highs and lows of adrenalin 'dependence'?

Recognizing the symptoms of negative stress requires self-observance and honesty. Denial of stress-related problems compounds the situation and prolongs recovery time.

The causes of stress in teaching

It is impossible to identify the exact causes of stress in teaching, especially when you consider that one person's stress is another's motivation. However, these factors do seem to have some responsibility for negative stress amongst teachers:

- *time:* feeling unable to perform the required tasks in the time available;
- *control:* not being in control of the number of tasks that have to be completed or of external pressures;
- *information:* having to keep up with a rapid pace of change and feeling ill-informed about the latest situation, with ever-increasing expectations;
- *workload:* having to complete work at home in order to keep up-to-date; cope with sometimes unrealistic expectations and possible inequality in work distribution; and also the tremendously diverse nature of the job;

- *indiscipline:* having to control unruly pupils and deal with constant inter-ruptions on a daily basis;
- *deadlines:* facing many deadlines each day as work must be prepared and books marked for each class or part of the day;
- *personality overload:* depending on what age group you teach, you could interact with over 100 different personalities each day;
- *fear:* about accountability, inspections, job insecurity and so on;
- *resource limitations:* having to prepare resources to supplement material in the school and for differentiation purposes, and coping with the poor condition of some classrooms;
- *aggression:* the potential threat from pupils and parents as well as possible bullying from staff members.

ACTION

Think about areas of possible stress in your job. Are you able to identify clear factors that contribute to the pressures you face? Do any of these seem to be intractable? Talk about the stresses you have identified with your induction tutor/mentor and read on for further advice. What action can you take to reduce your stress?

Stress-busting skills

Begging your doctor for tranquillizers to calm your mind and ease your day is probably not a good idea without adopting some stress-busting techniques. However, stress is now thought to be a contributory factor in many diseases and it is well worth talking to your healthcare provider about any negative stress you feel.

Managing through a crisis

Whether you are experiencing the sudden symptoms of feeling overwhelmed or, worse, a panic attack, take these steps:

- Stop. There isn't anything that cannot be dropped, even if you are in the middle of a lesson. Someone will be free to take over from you.
- Focus on your breathing. Count slowly as you breathe in through your nose and out through your mouth, until a sense of calm gradually pervades you body and mind. The more you practise this when you are already calm, the easier it will be to do in a crisis.
- Look at ways of immediately reducing your workload. Go home if necessary.

- Talk to someone about your feelings before leaving school. Take support from senior colleagues and any stress counsellors your school or LEA may have. Don't worry about admitting your anxiety to a senior member of staff. Other members of staff would be lying if they said they hadn't suffered in the same way at some point in their careers!
- Release the stress of the day when you get home. Talk, cry, shout, exercise or go for a walk – whatever works for you.
- Commit yourself to undertaking some of the maintenance tips that follow. For example, book a massage. Now!
- Compose an affirmation that you can use the next day.
- Visit your doctor or other healthcare provider if you feel that stress is piling up. It may be best for you and the school to take some time out.

ABOUT THE PHYSICAL SYMPTOMS OF STRESS

A number of changes take place in the body when it is working under too much stress:

- The blood supply to muscles is increased.
- The adrenal glands produce more adrenalin.
- Pupils become dilated.
- The heart rate increases.
- Blood pressure can rise.
- The sweat glands produce more sweat.
- Breathing becomes more rapid.
- The menstrual cycle can become disturbed.
- The digestive system can become upset.
- The immune system becomes less effective.
- Skin problems can develop.

It is important to consult your GP or other healthcare provider sooner rather than later if you find yourself suffering from any of the above. It is easier to correct minor health disturbances than major ones.

ABOUT THE TEACHER SUPPORT LINE: 08000 562 561

The Teacher Support Line is a free national information, support and counselling service for all teachers. It is open 24 hours a day, every day, as a resource for teachers with problems, be they personal or professional, in school or out.

The Teacher Support Line is being widely used to discuss stress, anxiety and depression, and conflicts with managers or colleagues, among other issues. All of the Teacher Support Line's fully qualified counsellors have worked in or with the teaching profession.

According to the Teacher Support Line, NQTs are contacting them with issues concerning stress and isolation, as well as concerns over poor induction, conflicts with induction tutors/mentors and financial problems.

Ringing a helpline such as the Teacher Support Line is by no means an admission of failure. By seeking help and advice, you are taking important steps to reaching solutions that will enable you to continue your career with less stress and increased satisfaction.

Learn this number! 08000 562 561.

For more information, take a look at their website (www.teachersupport.info).

Managing day-to-day

> Sometimes a scream is better than a thesis.
> (Ralph Waldo Emerson)

- Develop a flexible attitude to your work. Detachment can sometimes be necessary as the path of least resistance affords some freedom from stress.
- Adopt the 80 per cent philosophy. Drop your need for perfection; you can still get an 'A' grade with 80 per cent!
- Have at least one evening a week and one full day at the weekend off. Even if you are tempted to work, don't.
- Don't expect yourself to be on task 100 per cent of the time. Daydreaming is good for you.
- Be aware of times when you can still your mind throughout the day, even if it is during assembly or in the toilet!
- Stay in the present. Avoid thinking about what you have to do in the future and what you've done in the past. Give all your attention to the task in hand – divided attention leads to tension.
- Set realistic goals for yourself.
- Prepare your room for the next day the night before.
- Take any opportunities to share the burden of your work. For example, a classroom assistant may offer to put up a wall display, or the SEN department may want to develop some differentiated work for a child.
- Identify the value of the tasks you have to perform. If you cannot discern the value of a task, speak to your induction tutor/mentor; perhaps it needn't be performed in the future.

- Break each project down into manageable chunks.
- Aim to inject more humour into your life. Laughter is a tremendous stress releaser.

ACTION

Using an A4 sheet of paper, write down all the things you like to do, places you like to go and friends you like to see when you are not pressured by work. Keep the sheet in a place where you will see it frequently and be sure to make the commitment of doing at least one thing on the list every week. Even if this treat is as small as browsing round your favourite shop or buying your favourite magazine, be sure to do it so that you send self-nurturing signals to yourself.

ABOUT USING AFFIRMATIONS

An affirmation is an often-repeated phrase that focuses on something positive. Affirmations are an excellent way of managing negativity, but there are some important points to remember when constructing them:

- Always use positive statements. Say 'My work is enjoyable and manageable' rather than 'I am not stressed about my work'.
- Use present rather than future statements. 'I am calm and relaxed' is better than 'I will be calm and relaxed'.
- Visualize your ideal scenario while you use affirmations. Believe that you can create the situations that you want to create.
- Repeat your affirmations often throughout the day. Research suggests that the mind needs to hear an affirmation at least six times before positive benefits can be achieved.

Maintenance tips

The long-term management of stress requires you (and those you work with) to be ever vigilant. Ignoring negative stress in schools is costly and short-sighted.

- In his book *Calm at Work* (1997), Paul Wilson writes that deciding to become calm is the first step in being calm. Analyse how much your attitude is responsible for the degree of negative stress you experience.
- Work with colleagues to encourage stress-reducing practices that can be

adopted. Even the development of a forum for the discussion of negative stress would be helpful.

- Once you are in the habit of dealing with stress on a daily basis, you can resolve to learn from the experience rather than let negative stresses accumulate unaddressed.
- Keep an ongoing list of what triggers the symptoms of stress in you. This will probably need to be updated regularly as your proficiencies develop.
- Keep a running list of everything that calms and relaxes you: perhaps a book, a person or a place – anything that makes you feel good. You could even include photographs of yourself when you are relaxed and happy. Refer to the list whenever the ill effects of stress start to develop.
- Maintain a positive attitude about the work that you do. If talking to certain people results in you feeling down, avoid them.
- Pursue a hobby – something you have always wanted to do. If it increases physical activity, even better. Outside interests often serve to balance your working life.
- If massage, reflexology or some other relaxing experience works for you, book a session regularly.

Looking after health and lifestyle

Good health is not a foregone conclusion for any of us, yet so often we can find excuses not to undertake health-improving pursuits. However, a little effort can reap great rewards in terms of increasing vitality and enjoyment of life. Teachers have the responsibility to give themselves a chance. Sit on early warning signs of health problems and you are nurturing a certain crisis.

The advice given here is intended to provide ideas on how health and lifestyle might be improved. Your healthcare practitioner should check out persistent health problems.

Diet and exercise

In order to operate, we have to feed and move our bodies. Without good food and exercise, we cannot function at optimum levels. This has tremendous implications for work performance and stress levels, and consequently enjoyment of the job could be much diminished.

Eating for health

> It's not the horse that draws the cart, but the oats.
> (Russian proverb)

Erratic eating patterns and a deficient diet are increasingly being held responsible for many symptoms of ill health. There are several ways that teachers can use food to create health, providing these rules are followed:

- Always ensure you have at least 20 minutes in which to consume your lunch uninterrupted.
- Never eat while emotionally upset.

Despite the plethora of healthy eating books on the market, there are only three basic tenets of a good diet and health, which are easy to remember:

- Eat plenty of fresh, raw fruits and vegetables (at least five helpings a day).
- Avoid potentially harmful substances such as sugar, artificial sweeteners, caffeine, cocoa, alcohol, tobacco and recreational drugs.
- Moderation can be good enough. Remember the 80 per cent rule.

While you can increase your intake of fruits and vegetables immediately, it is important to wean yourself off harmful substances slowly. For example, if you consume caffeine in the form of tea, coffee, chocolate or fizzy drinks, reduce your intake by one cup a day, every day, until you are no longer reliant on the boost it gives you. By reducing gradually, you should avoid the withdrawal symptoms associated with addiction.

Replace caffeinated drinks with fresh, diluted fruit juices, filtered tap water or fruit/herb teas. Once you have cleared your body of caffeine, you will not want to go back to being dependent on it.

A varied diet is important. Go for unprocessed wholefoods as often as possible and avoid eating combinations of white flour, sugar and fat (for example, processed cakes and biscuits).

ACTION

Spend time at least one day a week preparing a really fantastic meal including plenty of fresh produce. Sit at a properly laid table, even if you are eating alone. You could invite some friends to share your meal but, if they are teachers, avoid school talk!

In his book *The Vitamin Bible* (1985), Earl Mindell suggests that teachers should take supplements of vitamin B-complex, vitamin C with bioflavonoids and good-quality multi-vitamin and mineral tablets, to help replenish the nutrients used up during the teaching day (refer to *The Vitamin Bible* for exact details). Always go for natural supplements, and buy them from your local health food shop rather than a supermarket if you want advice and a wide range of brands to choose from.

It is relatively easy to ensure an intake of at least five fruits and vegetables a day. Try these suggestions:

- Buy them! This may sound obvious, but if you are not in the habit of buying fresh fruit and vegetables, it will be easy to sail past the section in the supermarket.
- Drink pure (diluted) fruit juices. Make sure, however, they don't contain hidden sugars and other additives.
- Add fruit to breakfast cereals or porridge and main-course dishes.
- Prepare a fresh salad to eat with your evening meal.
- Add salad vegetables to sandwiches.
- Make a batch of home-made soup and freeze it in portions. Eat it as a starter or main course.

This is not about being a food fanatic, but it is about treating foods that drain energy and vitality with caution.

Moving for energy

Any form of exercise is to be encouraged, as it undoubtedly boosts immunity and helps to relieve symptoms of depression and stress, but it doesn't have to be a chore. There are many ways of incorporating more movement into your working day:

- Everyone needs fresh air. Take a lunchtime walk around the school field or around the block and do some deep breathing as you go.
- Jog up stairs whenever possible.
- Walk short journeys instead of relying on the car. This is not always easy for a teacher, with books, boxes and bags to carry, but certainly possible on occasion.
- Give yourself some time each day to move freely. You might like to do this in private! Allow your body to sway, dance, shake, etc. – whatever it wants to do.
- Work into your diary a regular slot each week for an organized sporting activity, such as a class, or a game of tennis or badminton with a friend. These exercise slots will soon become sacrosanct!

Stretching is a wonderful way to tone muscles, increase suppleness and allow oxygen to flow freely around the body. Get into the habit of doing some simple stretching exercises in the morning, and throughout the day as appropriate. (See Appendix 11 for further reading.)

ABOUT SNACKING AND HYPOGLYCAEMIA

When the brain is starved of glucose (which is carried in the blood), the body cannot function properly. Most people have experienced attacks of low blood sugar (or hypoglycaemia) and know how uncomfortable the associated feelings are, such as sweating, shaking, feeling irritable and confused and suddenly, ravenously hungry. Usually, these feelings can be relieved by eating, but if they aren't you must visit your healthcare practitioner. The best way to balance blood sugar levels is to eat little and often. Fortunately, the teaching day lends itself to snacking in this way, but it is important to snack on the right foods.

According to the Institute for Optimum Nutrition, the best snack is one that consists of a carbohydrate plus a first-class protein (e.g. white meat, fish, dairy produce or tofu). This means eating, for example, a crispbread with cottage cheese, or raw vegetables with tuna pâté. This combination of carbohydrate and protein produces the optimum rate of sugar release into the bloodstream, which sustains even energy levels overtime.

Disease prevention

People can have a very strange attitude towards illness and disease, or 'disease'. Preventing ill health takes a low priority, yet when illness does strike we think it has done so unexpectedly, and feel victims of bad luck. Illness is simply evidence that your body is fighting to rebalance itself. Your body is your last line of defence and, before manifesting symptoms, it will have been sending signals that all is not well. Physical or mental disease is the loudest signal it can send, so you owe it to yourself to listen.

A GP is usually the first port of call when illness strikes. Before you attend the surgery, you may have already taken time off work and tried various over-the-counter remedies. However, if you take a preventative approach, you may be able to stop your symptoms from taking hold. Fortunately, there are now many widely accepted complementary therapies, such as homoeopathy, acupuncture, massage and reflexology, which work by boosting immunity and vitality through taking a holistic approach. A complementary practitioner will look at all aspects of your life in the process of healing.

For ease of reference, the following section has been divided into physical health and mental health, although it is important to consider both, and not necessarily as separate entities.

Physical health

The best way to prevent physical disease is to boost your natural immunity to illness. When you consider the number of people a teacher interacts with every day and that each individual carries a different cocktail of germs, a healthy immune system is essential.

Frequent infections, colds, coughs, sore throats, allergies and even persistent tiredness are all signs of an immune system under pressure.

Become self-observant and listen to your body's needs. There are valid reasons for feeling tired; most cell repair takes place while we sleep. If we ignore tiredness, we are preventing this from taking place.

ABOUT TAKING TIME OFF SICK

It can sometimes be easier as a teacher to struggle through feelings of ill health rather than take time off and organize work for missed classes. Struggling on to avoid the guilt so often associated with taking time off will not be positive in the long run. Inconvenient as it may seem, take a day sooner rather than a month later. Not surprisingly, recent research has shown that teachers (along with nurses, childminders and carers) have the highest rates of turning up to work when sick.

If you do need to take time off, follow your school's procedures for this closely. You will need to keep your headteacher informed and, if possible, anticipate how much time off you will need so that cover arrangements can be made (this is not always possible, so don't worry if you cannot be specific). Ask your school or union for advice on self-certification and GP certification for illness.

Other ways to boost your immune system include:

- Increase your intake of antioxidants, which help to boost your immunity. Vitamin A strengthens cells that keep viruses at bay, and vitamin C will fight any that do get through. Zinc helps immune cells to mature, and selenium helps them to identify invaders. Eat more apples, oranges, red, green and yellow vegetables, carrots, potatoes, grains, seeds, nuts and cereals.
- Take an immunity-boosting supplement such as echinacea, aloe vera, garlic or bee pollen. Your local health-food stockist will help you identify which one is most suited to you.
- Keep your lungs healthy by exercising, singing or playing a wind instrument.

ABOUT CHOOSING A COMPLEMENTARY PRACTITIONER

We should take as much care over choosing complementary therapists as we do over choosing a conventional doctor. Follow these guidelines to avoid the 'therapy merry-go-round':

- Read about different therapies and make a list of the ones that sound interesting.
- Look for local practitioners in the *Yellow Pages* or on notice boards in health shops and health centres, or by asking friends and family for personal recommendations. Make contact with your chosen practitioner before making an appointment to establish whether you think he/she can help you.
- Ensure that the practitioner you have chosen is fully qualified and a member of a recognized, professional body with specific codes of practice. Does he/she have insurance to cover his/her actions as a healthcare practitioner?
- Many complementary therapies are now available on the NHS. If money is restricted, ask your GP if you can be referred.

Remember that you are in control of any form of healthcare, be it allopathic or complementary.

ABOUT FIGHTING COLDS

> Take rest; a field that has rested gives a beautiful crop.
> (Ovid)

The staffroom that doesn't have at least one teacher crouched in a chair desperately trying to muster the energy to teach through a severe cold simply doesn't exist!

At the first sign of congestion:

- Take high doses of vitamin C (one gram three times a day). Vitamins A and B-complex will help too.
- Suck a zinc lozenge. Zinc is thought to reduce the time you are sick.
- Eat lightly and drink plenty of water, as this washes out toxins.
- Use eucalyptus essential oil to clear sinuses.

Mental health

A key word in the maintenance of good mental health is 'balance', more specifically balance between home commitments, including family, personal needs such as social activities and self-pampering, leisure and rest, and the demands of work. Ironically, many new teachers find themselves in the 'Catch-22' situation of not having time to create balance, yet suffering because of the resulting imbalance.

A big step towards regaining balance is to recognize what aspects of your life you can be in charge of, and retaining that control. For example, your timetable commitments are part of your contract, and you cannot arrive at school one day and say 'I really need some time to prepare for the science afternoon, so can someone else teach year 3 this morning?' However, you can arrange to set work requiring minimal assessment during weeks when you know your workload will be especially heavy. Remember that you have choices and control. Put your needs first.

When pressures are mounting and the control is slipping away, be assertive in asking for support and limiting the demands made on you. There is not a teacher in the profession who has not had to take stock at some stage, and this is much harder to do alone. Support can come from:

- other NQTs;
- your induction tutor/mentor;
- your head of year/school/department;
- friends and family.

Ignoring signs of overload can lead to anxiety, depression and stress.

ABOUT PANIC ATTACKS

These episodes, which may involve shortness of breath, palpitations, sweating and a feeling of impending doom, signify severe discontent and must be taken seriously. However, they are perfectly treatable and there are many techniques that can be employed to restore balance. Do visit your healthcare practitioner if you suffer a panic attack.

There are four particularly effective ways to improve mental health that even the most serene could usefully employ:

- Deal with your emotions. It might not be appropriate or constructive to shout at a class, however angry you feel, but that emotion must be discharged later on. Frustration and anger at pupils or colleagues can be vented on a pillow, or in a car parked in a secluded place (open the windows and yell it out). Do be sure to address the problem calmly when the initial anger has subsided. Seek counselling (Contact the Teacher Support Line: 08000 562 561) if it would help.

- Utilize your inbuilt remedies. Crying is an excellent way to release emotion, and research has shown that laughter can help to cure even the most serious of illnesses. Some staffrooms have a joke board, which encourages laughter and lifts tension, helping staff to regain a positive perspective. Try watching comedy shows and films, or reading a few pages of a funny book each evening.

- Develop relaxation skills. Not only will all aspects of your life seem more manageable, but there will be noticeable improvements in your physical health too. When we are deeply relaxed, our pulse and breathing rates slow down and blood pressure drops. However, few people are able to relax deeply without learning techniques from a book or a class. Information on local classes can be found in health centres, libraries and adult education programmes. You may prefer to learn yoga or t'ai chi, both of which incorporate movement with relaxation and meditation.

- Utilize the power of the mind to cultivate a positive attitude. There are always two ways to view any situation, positively and negatively; remember those choices. Affirmations can be very useful in helping to assert the positive and minimize the negative.

ACTION

When a problem or anxiety is getting out of hand, write it down as a heading. Underneath, write answers to these questions:

- What is the core of this problem?
- What can I do about it?
- Can anyone help me out?
- What can he/she do about it?
- What are the best and worst scenarios?

This should help you to see that the problem is not insurmountable.

Looking after yourself

Fear less, hope more; eat less, chew more; whine less, breathe more; talk less, say more; love more, and all good things will be yours.

(Swedish proverb)

Most teachers are extremely conscientious when it comes to nurturing those in their care, but don't extend that generosity to themselves. It cannot be expressed strongly enough how important self-nurturing is for NQTs. Do not take yourself for granted. Rather, engage in meaningful self-care.

Day-to-day maintenance

> Happiness is neither virtue nor pleasure nor this thing nor that but simply growth. We are happy when we are growing.
>
> (William Butler Yeats)

Making improvements to your health and lifestyle is best done gradually. Dramatic changes will probably lead to a reversion to the old way. Try adopting one item at a time from the list of day-to-day maintenance and then reap the rewards.

- Take care over breathing. Rapid, shallow breathing can lead to varying degrees of hyperventilation, the symptoms of which can be dizziness, irritability, tension in the abdomen and excessive sighing. Spend a few moments several times a day doing simple breathing exercises, for example: breathe in to a count of four, hold for two, breathe out to a count of four and pause for two. Repeat five times. This is not only calming, but energizing too.
- Develop awareness of your slack times and learn to anticipate them. Treat energy slumps with breathing exercises and appropriate snacks, and pace yourself.
- Pay attention to your posture. You should aim for a balance between tension and relaxation, with your back straight and shoulders down.
- Create good sleeping patterns rather than 'crashing-out' patterns. If you don't wake feeling rested, aim to get more hours of sleep before midnight.
- Talk about work frustrations with colleagues. Start a support circle for this purpose if there is no forum for this sort of discussion at your school.
- Pursue a hobby – something you really enjoy. Be it painting, ceramics, woodwork, sport, gardening or cookery; just let your creativity flow.
- Get used to saying 'I can't afford it!' – not the cruises and convertibles, but the multi-tasking and working without adequate breaks!

ABOUT VOICE PROTECTION

It will come as no surprise that teachers are among the most likely to be referred to a speech therapist for help to minimize permanent voice damage.

Of course, that does not mean that you will necessarily suffer – susceptibility plays an important role – but being aware of how you can protect your voice is invaluable. Common throat disorders that teachers seem to suffer from are pharyngitis, laryngitis, vocal cord polyps, vocal cord nodules and contact ulcers (sores on the mucus membrane covering the cartilages to which the vocal cords are attached).

To preserve the good health of your voice and throat, try these ideas:

- Develop non-verbal cues for your class(es) to follow, such as standing in a particular place when you want to issue instructions or tapping a desk with a pen to get the attention of those around you.
- Avoid shouting in the classroom at all costs. It is terrible for your voice as well as disturbing to other classes around you.
- Consciously relax you neck and jaw as often as possible. Yawning is an excellent way of doing this. Aim to lower your shoulders as soon as they rise in tension.
- Drink plenty of water throughout the day. This helps to keep your throat lubricated and avoids the potentially scalding effects of hot tea and coffee.
- Avoid drinking spirits neat.
- Cut down on your dairy intake to reduce the formation of mucus.

For more information on voice care, visit: www.voicecare.org.uk

ABOUT HEAD LICE AND NITS

Head lice are small insects that live on the human scalp. Just a few millimetres long, they are a light greyish brown in colour. They feed on human blood and lay their eggs (nits) on the hair shaft, securely glued on. Nits have a 7- to 10-day gestation period in the warmth from the head. When the new lice hatch, the cycle begins again.

Lice cannot jump or fly so they require head-to-head contact in order to walk from person to person. They also need warmth to survive, so they cannot live on coats and scarves and other clothing or bedding.

Head lice are a community problem, but it seems that 80 per cent of those affected are aged between four and 14. Estimates suggest that in primary schools one child in 10 gets infected each year.

Routine head inspections are no longer carried out in schools. Responsibility for checking for lice lies firmly with a child's parents. If you see live lice on a child, you should notify the parents as soon as possible, and be particularly vigilant of children who appear to get frequent infestations. Your school may be adopting a whole-school approach with 'Bug Busting' days (for more information on the 'Bug Buster' kit, visit www.chc.org/bugbusting).

What to look out for

Children who scratch vigorously, especially behind the ears and the nape of the neck where the hair tends to be thicker and warmer.

Treatments

An occupational hazard, especially for teachers of the very young, is catching head lice:

- Using a nit comb, comb your hair, when wet over a sheet of white paper. This may give you a clear indication of whether you have been infected, but it is not wholly fail-safe, so don't assume you are free from them if you find none in this way.
- There are specific insecticide treatments for head lice but these are thought to be pretty ineffective, as not only do the lice become resistant to the chemicals but the chemicals are thought to be potentially harmful to human health.
- One method of treatment that many swear by is to apply an excessive amount of conditioner to the hair after washing. Then, using a fine nit comb, comb through the hair from the roots to the very tips in an organized way, checking the comb after each sweep. The conditioner makes it impossible for the lice and nits to cling to the hair. This treatment can be performed every other day for about two weeks for the best results.
- Another method of encouraging lice to leave is to wash hair in a basin of water to which lavender oil, lemon juice or vinegar has been added, and then to comb through as described above. Repeat often. Using olive oil rather than water makes it easier for people with very curly hair to get a fine nit comb through.
- If you find any live lice in your hair, then every member of your household should be treated.
- There are some homoeopathic treatments available. A qualified practitioner will be able to advise. Likewise, a trip to your local health store may offer treatments that are alternatives to the insecticides available.

Finding that you are host to head lice is no indication of the cleanliness or condition of your hair. They are not at all fussy and simply need blood and warmth in order to survive.

Find out more . . .

- You can find out all you need to know about work/life balance and teacher well-being in all aspects of your work in *Teacher Well-being: Looking After Yourself and Your Career in the Classroom*, also published by Routledge.
- In June 2008 the DCSF published guidance for schools on staff well-being. Titled *Common Mental Health Problems: Supporting School Staff by Taking Positive Action* (reference: DCSF-00380–2008) it has been designed to help schools to support teachers who may be struggling with well-being issues. It would be worth reading this document, which is available to download from www.teachernet.gov.uk, so that you are familiar with your school's obligations regarding the duty of care which your employers have, the Health and Safety at Work Act and the Disability Discrimination Act.

Chapter 8

Working with colleagues and parents

> If we would just support each other – that's ninety percent of the problem.
> (Edward Gardner)

You're a teacher, highly trained, skilled at what you do, with a passion for nurturing children and young people. Demanding as the job is, though, you'll already be well aware that's not all it entails. In order to support your relationships with colleagues and parents, this chapter focuses on:

- Getting on with colleagues
- Dealing with staff 'bullying'
- Consultations with parents
- Other adults in your classroom – TAs and adult helpers.

Getting on with colleagues

> The best teachers are positive teachers.
> (Robert Grice)

While there is an obvious need for members of staff to be cooperative and mutually supportive regarding the work they do as teachers, there is also a need for the 'softer' side of working in a school to be acknowledged. In other words, it's not all about work, it's also about relationships; the kind of relationships that facilitate effective teaching. And a good proportion of relationship building will take place in the staffroom. This has often been described as the 'backstage' area of a school and this is quite a useful analogy. Just as the audience in a theatre rarely glimpses what happens behind the scenes, so too are pupils banished from this most sacred of safe havens while teachers 'rest' after their 'performance'.

Find your place in the staffroom by following these tips:

- Don't be daunted by other teachers' approaches to their jobs. Some will be bursting with enthusiasm while others will be counting the days to the next holiday. Try to retain your own perspective.
- Don't judge your fellow teachers too harshly. Everyone has reasons for the way they are, and a little understanding can go a long way.
- Remove yourself from any situation or conversation that makes you feel uncomfortable. Teachers always have a plethora of excuses that they can employ to excuse themselves, e.g. an arrangement to see a pupil, preparation to do or books that urgently need marking. If you don't like the atmosphere, take a walk outside in the fresh air for a few minutes.
- Be yourself. The staffroom is your place to rest and recuperate in time for the next lesson as well as being a busy space for communication between teachers.
- Be discreet when others confide in you. Also, take care over discussing confidential matters within earshot of colleagues, who may not be aware of the sensitive nature of the discussion.
- Try not to use the staffroom as an extension of your working space. Not only is it hard to concentrate in a room full of chattering people, but your mess could annoy your colleagues. Clear your lunch things away too – you won't be popular with the cleaners if you leave it all to them!

ABOUT GETTING ON WITH YOUR COLLEAGUES

It can be easy to forget what impact other people are making in order to ease your day when you are busy and rushed off your feet. However, it is important to recognize the efforts of others. It is also vital that you get to know the pressures that other people are under. Positive comments about what other people have done for you will never go amiss. Do what you can to develop and maintain positive working relationships with as many people as possible and you will certainly reap the benefits.

Dealing with staff 'bullying'

It is worth mentioning here that, in spite of the good intentions of the vast majority of teachers to build and maintain healthy relationships with colleagues, sadly, what is described as 'bullying' can occur between employees in a school.

Research suggests that teachers form the largest occupational group to suffer from workplace bullying – it appears that schools can be hostile places for some teachers. For NQTs, being forewarned is being forearmed. Bullying and stress are closely linked and negative stress invariably seems to lead to illness. Bullying amongst staff presents great complications, not least because there is no consensus of opinion over how it should be dealt with. However, your school should have devised a specific policy, rather than squeezing it under the heading of 'harassment'.

Identifying what bullying is

It is important to establish a definition of bullying as opposed to a personality clash or difference of opinion. True bullying can involve:

- insidious, relentless criticism;
- fault finding;
- humiliation;
- excessive work expectations;
- abuse of discipline and competence procedures;
- inappropriate forms of communication (e.g. shouting, ordering or 'death by a thousand memos');
- inexcusable blocks to promotion and training;
- withholding of recognition for performance;
- manipulation;
- lack of compassion in difficult circumstances.

ABOUT PERSONALITY CLASHES

Personality clashes are almost inevitable, especially in large schools with huge numbers of staff. It could be that the person you are having difficulties with is someone that other teachers find hard to relate to as well. Some surreptitious observation may help you here.

Never write off a relationship as being beyond hope. It may be stretching your skills of compassion, but there is always a thread of empathy that can be built on. You don't always have to agree with the opinions of others, but you can try to understand why they hold their opinions and why they behave as they do. You may find that those with whom you initially clashed become your closest allies.

ABOUT ADULT BULLIES

An adult bully aims to exert power negatively and consistently over another person with the purpose of inciting fear and causing professional and emotional damage. The bully is inherently destructive, but his/her actions could result from feelings of inadequacy, which have been deflected on to another person, who may be accused of the very flaws that the bully detects in him or herself.

How bullying can affect you

Victims of bullying often have to cope with a multitude of symptoms. Most victims of staffroom bullying find themselves dealing with some of these:

- reactive depression;
- hyper-vigilance;
- shattered confidence;
- anxiety;
- fatigue;
- negative stress;
- digestive disorders;
- menstrual disorders.

This is perfectly normal under the circumstances, and can be short-lived as long as the cause of the bullying is dealt with. Victims of bullying can also anguish over the question, 'Why me?' The answer is often the same as for a child who is bullied – peers may perceive the person as being too popular, too accomplished, incorruptible or highlighting incompetence through competence.

EXAMPLE

As soon as she realized that one member of staff was responding to her negatively, NQT Nessa started to develop a selection of symptoms, most worrying of which was uncharacteristic introversion. She started to question every action she took, which had a negative effect on her work. It became a downward spiral, with every criticism leading to a worsening of her performance and so attracting further criticism.

Strong management or bullying?

> Never pay attention to what critics say . . . A statue has never been set up in honour of a critic!
>
> (Jean Sibelius)

There is a clear difference between strong management and bullying. All managers have the facilities to correct the behaviour or work performance of an employee, but this must be done in accordance with proper procedure. A sign of good management is how nurtured and encouraged you feel after a 'pep talk'. If you are left feeling despondent or humiliated, it is likely that bullying tactics have been employed. Good managers will observe aspects of your work performance that might need correcting and advise you in good time. In fact, they are obliged to do so. Your side of the bargain is to take on board what has been said and act on improving the areas that need attention.

However, there are tell-tale signs of bully-tolerant institutions. High absenteeism and turnover of staff seem to indicate staffroom distress. This in turn reduces the morale of the staff and a subculture of disrespect towards the management quickly develops.

Workplace bullying is illegal on several grounds. The responsibility for its prevention lies firmly with your employers.

EXAMPLE

I found my induction tutor and headteacher to be really unpleasant. I couldn't pick out anything positive about the way they treated me. My experiences at the school went from bad to worse and by the end of my first term I was really ill. I ended up leaving the school and the area and doing day-to-day supply to rebuild my confidence. It has interrupted my induction period, but I knew that I had to get out of that environment. I still feel confused about why I had to suffer such a high level of personal criticism.

(NQT)

Dealing with bullies

If you feel that you are experiencing bullying at work, there are many things you can do to minimize its ill effects. Try following this action plan:

- Talk to a trusted friend about your experiences. A second opinion can really help to give you a sense of perspective about the situation and will help you to decide whether to take action.
- Reread your job description, the Standards for Qualified Teacher Status, the Core Professional Standards for Teachers and any information on the responsibilities of teachers available from your school and union. This will reaffirm what tasks you should and should not be performing in your job. It is also worth reading the latest version of the *Governors' Guide to the Law*, which will inform you of procedures relevant to your situation. Be sure to read the correct version, as they vary depending on the type of school. These guides can be downloaded (see www.governornet.co.uk).
- Attend an assertiveness course, or read about it. Your professionalism may be under question and you will need to be able to deal with it calmly and rationally. Confidential professional counselling would also be a good idea at this stage and may be on offer from your local authority. Again, retaining perspective is crucial to the way in which you approach your

bully. Try to avoid allowing the situation to permeate every aspect of your life.

- Seek advice from your union. Bullying destroys good teaching and you don't want to be facing accusations of incompetence in addition to the bullying. Most unions have their own documents on dealing with bullying, which are available to members and non-members. Read the literature from all of them.
- Ask for a copy of your school's policy on workplace bullying.
- Read about workplace bullying. There are some excellent books available and these will serve to reassure you that this problem is widespread – you are not alone (try *Fighting Back: How to Fight Bulling in the Workplace* by David Graves).
- Gather support for your cause by speaking to carefully selected colleagues. Divulge a little of what is happening to you and you may find that other members of staff come forward as sufferers too.
- Document all communication you have with your bully – even relatively informal contacts. This is not being unnecessarily paranoid, but will serve you well at a later stage if you need to refer to previous conversations. Aim to ease any possible stress and anxiety.
- Refute all unfair claims that have been made against you – in writing if necessary – and keep records of anything you say or write.
- Monitor changes in your work performance due to bullying. This might include getting behind on marking and preparation, or feeling inhibited in your teaching. Keep copies of any induction assessments, appraisals and OFSTED reports you may have and read all the positive comments when your confidence is low.
- Visit your GP, even if your health doesn't appear to be suffering. It is sensible to have formally recorded what is happening to you and whom you consider to be responsible. Your GP will be able to offer constructive stress-busting advice and will be a source of support should you need to take time off school. If your GP recommends sick leave, follow his/her advice. Time taken now could prevent a health crisis. You should record any ill health resulting from bullying in your school's accident/incident book.
- Never be encouraged to 'slide out gracefully' or leave the profession if that is not what you want to do.

Seeking help

It is an unfortunate character trait of many competent professionals, such as teachers, not to ask for help when they could benefit from it. In the case of workplace bullying and other abuses of power, the more advice you can get from different agencies and individuals the better.

Possible sources of help from within your school

Anyone who is not your bully could be the source of valuable support, so be open to the advice you are given. More specifically, try these sources:

- your induction tutor/mentor;
- other NQTs;
- your union rep;
- the person with responsibilities for staff welfare (usually a deputy headteacher);
- a governor who is attached to your class or department.

Possible sources of help from outside your school

These sources include:

- your union;
- your local authority;
- books on dealing with bullying;
- your GP or other healthcare practitioner;
- family and friends;
- the Internet.

ABOUT ACTING PROMPTLY

As soon as you think you may be victim to bully tactics, seek help. Acting promptly can help to circumvent more serious situations such as a disciplinary or incompetence claim being made against you. Gloomy as it may sound, the longer you leave it to act, the harder the situation will be to resolve. There is a wealth of support for victims of bullying – you don't have to suffer alone. Just don't sit on any experiences of bullying you may have had without talking to someone.

Consultations with parents

Sometimes referred to as 'open evenings', 'appointment evenings' or 'parents' evenings', you will probably have to face several throughout the school year. They can be daunting, especially if you did not get a chance to attend one during your training but, with a little preparation, they needn't be a big deal.

Before the big day

- Don't save important concerns about a child until consultation time, as you may be met with anger and defensiveness. Aim to communicate with parents sooner rather than later about behaviour or work problems.
- Prepare for the night by having pupils' books marked up-to-date, and records of attendance, homework, general participation in class etc. to hand.
- Make sure you know who is coming to see you and what their relationship is to the child. Be prepared to see older siblings in some cases, and occasionally divorced or separated parents may want two appointments.
- Talk to colleagues about who is coming to see you to make sure you will not be meeting any parents known to be difficult or aggressive, either towards staff members (relatively rare) or their children. You may want to ask a member of the senior management team to hover near you when you are talking to such a parent.
- Be prepared for a long evening. Make sure you have plenty of sustenance with you, especially if you won't have time to get home before the evening begins.
- Aim to have a free evening as far as marking and preparation are concerned. You won't feel like doing much by the time you get home.

On the night

- It is worth making the effort to look smarter than usual when meeting parents, especially for the first time.
- Have a name card on your table (these are usually provided by the school).
- Stand up when greeting parents. It may feel as though you are bobbing up and down all night, but staying seated can appear rude.
- Don't use educational jargon. Explain everything, as a parent may not want to ask for clarification. These evenings can be just as daunting for parents as well.
- Let parents know exactly what you expect of their child.
- Focus on the progress the child has made. He/she may be top of the class, but has he/she improved?
- Show parents evidence of the child's achievements. Let them look through books etc. Talk about your assessments in order to help parents make meaning from them.
- Record what happens at each interview. You don't need to include much detail, but it will be useful for future reference, especially when writing the next round of reports. You could have a form ready (see Table 8.1 below) to minimize work on the night.
- Don't slot extra consultations in that haven't been booked unless you have clear gaps.

Table 8.1 Parent evening specimen form

Parent	Pupil	Key points	Action	Target date
Mrs Barker (mother)	Kevin Barker 8DS	Civil War extension work	Give Kevin additional reading references and exercises if wanted	Start asap and review after a few weeks

- Be professional when other staff members or pupils are being discussed.
- Aim to give advice on how achievement can be improved. Make this advice easy to adopt and encourage the parent to pass the information on to the pupil.
- Do not get drawn into making predictions about a child's future performance. Parents may hold you to what you say.
- Try to focus immediately on the task in hand. Don't get sidetracked by general conversation; otherwise you'll get irretrievably behind.
- Take drink breaks whenever you need them. Most schools arrange for drinks to be brought to teachers.
- If you find yourself with some spare time during a parents' evening, ask a colleague if you can observe him/her in action.
- Don't worry if things don't go according to plan. It will be a learning process, and you, your induction tutor/mentor or a member of the senior management team can deal with every situation.

Being heard

- The best way to ensure that you are heard is to show that you know how to listen. Demonstrate your attentiveness and empathy and the parent will be more likely to listen to what you have to say.
- Encourage parents to say what they want to say in order to keep the dialogue going. This is, after all, an opportunity for parents to speak as well as you.
- Think about your tone of voice. Always meet rising tension with calm. If a parent's voice rises, lower yours.
- Don't dilute what you want to say about a child to try to pacify a dominant parent. The key is to be truthful rather than blunt.
- Reiterate the fact that your main concern is the child and how he/she can develop his/her potential.

Facing a refusal to listen

Occasionally, adopting the above tips on being heard by a parent won't work and you may face a point-blank refusal to listen to your reasoning. Read the following section in advance to help should such a situation arise.

Dealing with 'difficult' parents

It seems inappropriate to apply the word 'difficult' to a parent. After all, they invariably want the best for their children and are very much part of the team that helps to nurture them to their best potential. However, things don't always run smoothly.

Do:

- Be aware of prejudices that parents may be airing. It may be necessary to discuss what the parent has said to you with your headteacher.
- Be concise and consistent and have justifications for your views.
- Maintain eye contact as much as possible.
- Focus on achievement and behaviour, both good and bad.
- Explain that everyone has many facets to their character and that the child's behaviour and attitudes at school may not necessarily reflect the way he/she is at home.
- Try to motivate the parents into joining you in working for the child. Encouraging a partnership can often work.

Don't:

- Retract any statements that you have made about a child simply because the parent won't accept them.
- Try to force the parent to see your point of view, but present your opinions and trust that they will be digested eventually.
- Focus on problems. Rather move towards solutions.
- Focus on personality.
- Forget that the parent may be feeling embarrassed by and disappointed with the child.
- Struggle on with a conversation that is not moving forward positively without offering the parent the opportunity to talk to a member of the senior management team.

Seeing parents at other times

It is wise to have an 'open-door' policy when it comes to seeing parents and your school may well have a policy on this. If you encourage an ongoing dialogue with them, you are less likely to get into difficult situations on parents' consultation evenings.

- Let parents know the best way for them to get in touch with you if they want to discuss anything. Do you have a good time when they can ring you or a good day when they can call in after school? Make sure you keep such arrangements contained, and on your terms.

- If you have a need to talk to a parent on the telephone about his/her child, prepare a script, or some notes at least, and have to hand all the information you need.
- Parents are entitled to see their child's records, but this is definitely a senior management matter. Pass the request on.

EXAMPLE

The most difficult aspect of this year has been that, more times than not, my parents have perceived me as the 'enemy' and think that I really don't have their child's best interest in mind. Thankfully, I have an administration that is on top of their faculty and they know exactly what's going on in my room and support me 100 per cent. Otherwise, if I had not had the support, I think that I would've crumbled under the pressure. It's tough being young and without children of my own when I try to give guidance on particular situations. Not only do I have to be policeman, nurse, mother, entertainer, counsellor and teacher all in one, I am also forced to be a Dr Spock or James Dobson-type family counsellor who gives advice on child rearing!

(Katherine L Cole, USA)

ABOUT DOCUMENTING YOUR VIEWS

If a difference of opinion arises between you and a parent, it may be pertinent to document your views and why you hold them. This is so that you can refer to the conversation later, should you need to. You may also want to discuss what you have written with your mentor or a member of the senior management team. Place a copy in the child's records and keep a copy for yourself.

Other adults in your classroom: TAs and adult helpers

The involvement of support teachers in classrooms of mainstream and special schools across the country has increased quite dramatically over recent years. In primary schools in particular, many teachers would not be able to function efficiently without the input of teaching assistants (TAs) and adult helpers.

The role of TAs and higher level teaching assistants (HLTAS) has developed significantly in recent years, so it is worth being fully aware of how they are being deployed in your school. Talk to as many TAs as you can about how they view their role, what they do and what helps them to be most effective in the classroom.

The head of a school appoints most TAs and helpers, both paid and voluntary. It would be unusual for you to arrange your own helpers, as schools carry out CRB checks on all adults with access to pupils.

If your school has a policy on dealing with adults in the classroom, use it. If not, these ideas will help:

- Make sure you know why the adult is helping you. Is the adult there for learning support for one pupil or as an extra pair of hands and eyes for you? Is he/she paid or voluntary?
- Inform your helpers of your classroom rules and routines and the reasons for them.
- Inform helpers of first aid procedures in your school and routines for fire practice. They'll also need to know about tea and coffee arrangements and where to put bags and coats etc., although your school's management team should arrange for them to receive some induction.
- Make sure that your helpers understand the need for confidentiality. You don't want your pupils and lessons being discussed outside school.
- Back your helpers so that pupils see you presenting a united front.

Making your intentions clear

The only way to be clear in what you need your helpers to do is to know for yourself. What, exactly, are your learning intentions for your pupils? How can your helpers enable pupils to achieve them?

If you are fortunate enough to have regular helpers with whom you can build a good relationship, they will be able to follow your lessons as you go along, without too much need for planning discussions. If not, you will need to brief your helpers so that they don't have to bluff in front of pupils. Don't expect them to be familiar automatically with the intricacies of the curriculum you teach.

An interesting exercise is to place yourself in the position of a support teacher in one of your lessons. Do you know what you are doing and why? Do you know where this work is coming from and where it is going? The need for communication between you and your support teachers is great and you may have to be 'creative' in looking for opportunities to meet.

Maximizing the use of classroom support

The most effective way of maximizing the use of other adults in your classroom is to raise the status of in-class support amongst the children you teach. This will ensure that pupils view your helpers as a valuable resource that they should make use of rather than an embarrassing reminder of their self-perceived 'inadequacies'.

You may also want to think about preparing an information sheet for helpers in your classes, or perhaps giving some brief training sessions on certain aspects of your work, such as hearing children read etc. Mutual feedback is always valuable. If you don't have time to talk immediately after a lesson, ask your helpers to jot down any points that they would like to raise and arrange a mutually convenient time to meet.

TAs can help you to mark your progress through your induction period in a way that your induction tutor cannot, simply because they will be witnessing your work on a daily or weekly basis for the full length of a lesson. They will see how your relationships with the pupils develop over time and how effectively you relax into your job in ordinary, unobserved circumstances. TAs can also give you valuable insight into how key pupils behave in the presence of other teachers, a perspective you couldn't possibly achieve alone.

Delegating tasks

Paid support staff will have guidelines to follow regarding their work in your lessons. However, volunteers who help in your classroom are often giving up valuable time and it is worth organizing some structured tasks so that they do not feel they are surplus to requirements or wasting time. Perhaps ask helpers if there is anything they want to get involved in, or if they have any particular skills that can be utilized.

Think about how they can save you time by doing work displays or mounting, general tidying, collating worksheets, preparing materials etc. However, avoid the trap of relying on volunteers too heavily. You don't want your lessons to collapse if you find they can't be there for any reason.

> ### *ABOUT* DELEGATING TO HELPERS
>
> Do not ask helpers to perform duties that should only be done by a qualified teacher, tempting as it may be, e.g. marking, curriculum planning, report writing etc. You are ultimately responsible for what goes on in your classroom. You could, however, keep a notebook of ongoing tasks in your classroom to which helpers could refer.

Find out more . . .

- Your union will be able to advise on all issues to do with staff on staff bullying.
- The Teaching Expertise website carries articles on how schools can make the most of their teaching assistants (see www.teachingexpertise.com).
- *FAQs for TAs: Practical Advice and Working Solutions for Teaching Assistants*, published by Routledge, also covers the teacher/TA relationship in detail.

Chapter 9

Tutoring and beyond

The highest education is that which does not merely give us information but makes our life in harmony with all existence.

(Rabindranath Tagore)

Having your own class or group can be one of the most rewarding aspects of being in the teaching profession. It offers the opportunity to get to know a group of young people well and to follow their development over time. It's also a great way of becoming immersed in school life. This chapter takes a good look at all you need to know about tutoring, including:

- Dealing with personal issues
- Effective tutoring
- Setting the tone of your group
- Tutoring folklore
- First aid in the classroom.

Dealing with personal issues

There are bound to be occasions when discussions with pupils move away from the curriculum. Being prepared for such situations will save unnecessary embarrassment and protect you from possible future criticism.

Your own issues

Regardless of the age of your pupils, you will almost certainly face from them some degree of interest in your personal life. While keeping yourself a complete mystery is neither necessary nor desirable – it is good for pupils to have some insight into the lives of their teachers – the skill is in achieving professional balance.

How much should you tell?

This is entirely for you to decide. The main thing is to be aware of your motives for revealing aspects of your life to pupils. Is it:

- because they frequently ask you?
- because you really do see some of them as friends?
- because you feel it may excuse your mood/behaviour?
- because it is relevant to a particular lesson?

You will know when you have established a good relationship with your pupils and when you have crossed the invisible boundaries of professional discretion.

Some points to remember:

- It can sometimes be appropriate to talk to a pupil about an aspect of your personal life to reassure him/her. For example, if a pupil is suffering from a broken heart, there can be no harm in empathizing and telling a brief anecdote about your experiences. This illustrates your understanding of issues facing your pupils.
- Never reveal something to a pupil that should then be considered a secret. This places unfair expectations on the child and crosses professional boundaries.
- Be prepared for distorted repetitions of your revelations.
- Keep certain aspects of yourself back from the full knowledge of your class. It's not desirable for them to know all about your partner, children, hobbies, home, family, aspirations or dreams and, in any case, they probably won't be interested.
- Divert attention away from yourself by focusing on pupils. If you feel uncomfortable under questioning from pupils, establish early on that you would prefer it if they did not ask personal questions.
- In many ways, it is a compliment to your abilities to relate if pupils want to know more about you. However, flattering as this intrigue may be, inappropriate 'chumminess' can be damaging to your career, and your more astute pupils will interpret it as insecurity and sense weakness.

Pupils' personal issues

This is something that you will face time and again throughout your teaching career, from dealing with a child who has wet him/herself (depending on the age range you teach) to helping a child through the grieving process.

How much should you ask?

It can be easy to work out which pupils are carrying burdens above those of childhood and adolescence. There may be changes in behaviour and character that need addressing or dramatic changes in work performance. Even improvements can be cause for concern as they can be indicative of a child who is escaping from a situation by throwing him/herself into work.

- It is important to tread extremely carefully when talking to a child you feel may be suffering a personal difficulty. Your school may have guidelines to follow but, if not, talk to the child's pastoral head before doing anything. He/she may know the family, or know how to approach the problem.
- Discuss the child with colleagues to establish whether others have noticed a change.
- Always get guidance from pastoral heads and tutors before asking to speak to the child's parents or carers.
- If you decide to approach the child directly, having spoken to colleagues, do so in a relatively light-hearted (but not flippant) way. Ask, in passing, if there is anything wrong. Avoid saying 'I've noticed you haven't been yourself recently', as this may place the child under undue pressure to discuss private matters. Pave the way for the child to come and talk to you if he/she wants to. You could say 'You know where I am if you want anything, don't you?' Then keep a close, surreptitious eye on the child for a week or so before trying again if things have clearly not improved.

Helping versus interfering

Your memory will tell you that many childhood and teenage issues often resolve themselves with time. Once you have established with pupils that they can talk to you, or a colleague of the opposite sex, whenever they need to, further questioning could well be construed as interfering. Unless you suspect some form of abuse or neglect, in which case you must speak to the named person dealing with all child protection issues, take a back seat and observe for a while, so as to preserve the relationship that you have already created with the child.

> **ABOUT** PUPILS GETTING PERSONAL
>
> Intimate relationships (or even discussions) between teachers and their pupils should always be avoided. They represent a gross misuse of a teacher's professional status.

However, there may be situations when a pupil involves you in an issue of a personal nature – perhaps the pupil declares undying love for you. It goes without saying that you must respect and accept what the pupil says, but don't attempt to deal with the situation alone. Protect yourself by referring the issue to the child's pastoral head or tutor and make sure that, whenever you speak to the pupil, you do so either when there are others present in the room (preferably a colleague) or in a public place where others may be passing through.

Effective tutoring

The system of tutoring delivered through tutor groups or houses is one way in which a school cares for its pupils.

Pastoral care should never be confused with discipline – in fact, the two are quite separate. When you discipline a child, you are reacting to his/her behaviour, not to the person. Effective pastoral care is proactive and responsive and cannot really be confined to the tutor group. Especially in the primary sector, the roles of individuals as teachers and tutors are inseparable.

Tutoring can be defined as the dimension of teaching that encourages young people to discover the kinds of personal, social and academic strategies that can help to enhance their experience of school and life.

Most people can think of times when they have not felt nurtured. Maybe this was at school or college, perhaps being ignored in a shop or failing to have needs met in a relationship. Those times usually result in demotivation, despondency, demoralization, frustration and even anger. Using those memories to empathize with the tutees in your care makes it easier to understand the importance of meeting all the needs of pupils to ensure that they believe in their personal value to the school community.

Ideally, you will not be given a new group in your first year of teaching, as problems can arise when both teacher and class are new. You may be a co-tutor in your NQT year but will almost certainly be a tutor in your own right in your second year. However, you are not expected to sink or swim. There will be a pastoral team for you to call on and even pastoral heads may bring in experts to deal with certain situations, e.g. bereavement counsellors or drugs-awareness experts.

This section is based on the assumption that personal, social and health education (PSHE) is provided for elsewhere in your school's curriculum.

Your role as a tutor

As a tutor, you are in an extremely powerful position. You can make (or break) a child's experience of school life through your care for, and interpretation of, the issues important to your tutees. Make sure that you have been given all the relevant documentation regarding your job as a tutor. You could also get ideas from colleagues and select what you feel would suit your group. Seek help if there is any issue that you do not feel happy dealing with alone. There will be other members of staff to refer to for advice, for example the pastoral head, your induction tutor or the SENCO.

It is wise to take all opportunities to get to know the families of your tutees. In particular, be aware of those who do not live in nuclear families, and who the home caregivers are.

EXAMPLE

One NQT taught a boy who only had one leg, but it took the NQT a year to realize this! Since then, he has read all the information on his tutees carefully.

Aspects of your role as a tutor

A tutor is at the very least all of these:

- inspirer/morale booster;
- listener;
- counsellor;
- communicator;
- problem solver;
- nurturer;
- enabler;
- monitor of academic progress;
- monitor of social development;
- manager of behaviour;
- praise giver;
- motivator;
- team builder;
- confidant.

Inspirer and morale booster

There will be times when you will have to try to inject some enthusiasm into a demoralized group. Perhaps they are suffering under the pressure of exams, or have been reprimanded all morning for the poor behaviour of certain members of the group. Your role is to draw the group together and boost morale sufficiently for them to continue the day. Try to create in them a sense of enthusiasm for each other, and for learning.

ABOUT THE ROLES OF THE TUTOR

Be an actor, not a reactor.
(Dr Maxwell Maltz)

Whatever you read about the roles of a tutor; it is important to develop your own ideas. Use personal experiences to devise thoughts on what you want your role to be. As long as you fulfil your school's requirements of its tutors, you can expand your role as you see fit. For example, you may want to organize a trip for your group – perhaps to the cinema – as a way of creating the sense of being part of a team. However, keep the growth of pupils central to your thoughts, abide by local practice (which will be set down by your headteacher and governors) and strive to make school life a more humane experience for your tutees. Good pastoral care can enable pupils to become better learners, so keep in mind the power that your role as a tutor holds.

Listener

Listening is an important aspect of tutoring, and knowing how to listen is an essential skill. Pupils may simply want to express what they are feeling without the intervention of a problem solver, or may want you to act in their defence. Your job is to know the difference, and that will only become evident through listening. Allow pupils to describe their emotions.

Counsellor

There will be many occasions when pupils need the skill and understanding of a counsellor. As an NQT, you may not be qualified in counselling, but will certainly use some counselling skills. You can always refer to a professional for anything that you are not happy dealing with, such as a child's bereavement.

Communicator

Not only will you have to relay messages from other members of staff, but you will also have to communicate your own requirements to your group. The way in which this is achieved will have an impact upon the tone of your group.

Problem solver

Tutors often have to inject a sense of reality into fraught and emotional circumstances. Your job here is to find solutions, or help those involved to find solutions, to the problems that your tutees present that are acceptable to all involved. However, there may be times when you will have to be honest and say 'I'm sorry, but I don't know the answer to that.' There is never any shame in this, as long as you find out the necessary answers – this could even be done as a group.

Nurturer

Being a nurturer involves boosting the self-esteem of all the pupils in your care – even the ones you simply cannot get on with. A tutor can help to minimize what can be the cruelty of school life for children by boosting their self-esteem. Those with high self-esteem can retain perspective under pressure, and self-esteem is most likely to be nurtured when children are dealt with consistently. You will need to give tutees proof that they are gaining in competence and that you are genuinely interested in them.

Enabler

The role of enabler is closely linked to your nurturing roles and involves creating the circumstances in which your tutees can gain maximum benefit from their school life. You will enable them to succeed. You can also ensure that your tutees have the maximum opportunity to make informed decisions. However, be sure to educate rather than advise. Don't inflict your opinions – allow them to create their own against a backdrop of sound information. This links in with the current trend for schools to be proactive as opposed to reactive when it comes to pastoral care.

Monitor of academic progress

As a tutor, you are in the optimum position to track the academic progress of your pupils, including monitoring the time they spend on homework etc. When it comes to reports and assessments, your input is essential. In some schools, parents are invited to speak to form tutors as well as subject teachers at parents' evenings.

Above all, you want to encourage your tutees to become reflective practitioners and observe for themselves what is at the heart of all their schoolwork. What common threads are there? Why are they doing what they are doing? You could ask them to talk about what they have learnt and the processes they used to achieve a learning outcome. Create the environment in which it is safe for pupils to praise each other.

Monitor of social development

The time spent with your tutor group is likely to be when social development (or lack of it) is most apparent. The tutor's job is to monitor this to ensure that all pupils are given the opportunity to grow socially. Most children at some stage face difficult questions of identity such as 'Who am I?' or 'What am I?' They will have to develop self-knowledge, self-growth and the capacity to adapt to situations and go with the flow, not to mention rational autonomy and the understanding of the impact of the self upon others.

Pupils also have to develop the ability to be flexible and responsive to their environment, especially as they move through the school system and have to interact with increasing numbers of teachers and styles.

Manager of behaviour

There may be occasions when colleagues complain to you about the behaviour of a member of your group. While the colleague may have dealt with the misbehaviour, he/she may also look to you as a tutor to reinforce the standards that are expected. You will also have to keep an eye on the general level of behaviour in your group and praise or reprimand as appropriate.

ABOUT REPRIMANDING INDIVIDUALS

If you do have to reprimand a member of your group, it is imperative that the pupil understands why. What was his/her role? How did he/she personally contribute to the situation? Ask the child to explain exactly what happened and be open to the possibility of a misinterpretation of events, without expressing doubt at a colleague's understanding of what happened. Throughout your dealings with the child, think of ways of enabling the child rather than pushing him/her into a corner. How can the child be guided to a solution? Encourage tutees to be honest about their feelings, even if it does mean listening to 'I hate Mr Boyd', so that you can seek to find ways of turning these negative emotions into positive ones. Whatever the outcome, it must allow for good working relationships to be re-established.

The best way around this sort of situation is to prepare for it in advance. Many teachers run 'What would you do if ...?' sessions, which give pupils many ideas to draw on as and when the situation arises. This will help to enable tutees to express grievances constructively and deal with the outcome sensibly.

Praise giver

An unfortunate fact of school life is that you are more likely to hear about the misdemeanours of your group than their successes. You should aim to praise the group as a whole and individuals as frequently as possible. Remember how good it feels to be on the receiving end of positive feedback. Help colleagues in this role by reporting to them the good behaviour of their groups.

Motivator

Whether it is coping with the mid-term blues or dealing with a defeat in an inter-class football contest, there are bound to be occasions when you will have to lighten the tone of your group and motivate your tutees.

Team builder

The only way to create a class that is happy to work together cooperatively is to spend time team building. As a tutor, you are at the centre of your team. Talk together, encourage unity and emphasize group successes, for example 'Mrs Evans said you worked very cooperatively in Art today – that's great to hear. Tell me about what you did.'

Confidant

There are likely to be situations when tutees confide in you. However, you do have legal obligations to look after the welfare of the children in your care. This may entail passing information on to other agencies if necessary; therefore you must never promise to keep secrets. A teacher cannot be bound by a pupil's request for total confidentiality.

ABOUT DETECTING SIGNS OF ABUSE

Tutors are obliged, as part of their role as teachers in safeguarding children's welfare, to observe tutees for signs of neglect and abuse. Be aware of changes in behaviour such as increased aggression, withdrawal or overdependence, as well as physical signs such as bruising etc.

Always follow your school's guidelines on dealing with suspected abuse. Never try to tackle this complex area alone.

Setting the tone of your group

Your personality will be the main factor controlling the tone of your tutor group. You can set your own rules and limits for your tutees, although involving older pupils in this can work extremely well.

Consider some of these points:

- If you are punctual, your pupils are more likely to be.
- Make the administration side of your tutoring duties slick and efficient. A stock of class lists will be extremely useful for keeping track of reply slips returned etc.
- Place importance on preparation for the school day. Urge pupils to be fully equipped.
- Create routines and stick with them, for example silence when the register is being taken, any notices to be read out immediately after the register has been taken etc.
- Encourage tidiness and pride in your room.
- Constantly reiterate the purpose of your role – you are there for your tutees.
- Encourage togetherness and celebrate differences.
- Strive for balance and fairness.

Maximizing the opportunities of tutoring

Whatever the extent of your role as a tutor and the lessons you have to deliver, there are always methods of maximizing the opportunities that tutoring presents:

- Use any spare time in tutor periods to chat to your class, whatever their age group. Perhaps treat it as 'circle time'. You can glean so much about your tutees, the way they work and what motivates them in this way. Just make sure that those who want to speak have the opportunity and that such chats are not dominated by the few.
- Create the opportunities for tutees to talk to you when they want to. Approachability is an important characteristic for a good tutor to have.
- Remember the finer details of your tutees' lives. Draw attention to birthdays (you could even give a card or small present) and celebrate the achievements of pupils in your group, as a group.
- Pay attention to your obligations to provide equality of opportunity for your pupils.
- Discuss the strengths and weaknesses of the group and devise strategies for improvement.
- Encourage a climate of openness.

- Never forget the role of the tutor in boosting self-esteem. You will probably find that this becomes a two-way process!
- Keep track of pupils who may need follow-up care after a personal trauma.
- Be prepared for tutorial periods, as you would be for a lesson. Leave your subject behind and get to know your tutees as individuals. You should aim to have learning intentions for tutor periods as well as lessons.
- Liaise well with the coordinator of tutor groups in your year and also with the person in charge of personal and social education. If someone else is planning activities for you to do with your group, let him/her know if there was anything that worked particularly well or anything that was a complete disaster.
- Know the line of pastoral authority in your school. You may need to seek help urgently to deal with a situation and should know exactly whom to turn to.
- Ask your tutees what they would like to do or discuss. You could set some time aside each week or month to focus on their choices.

ABOUT GIVING PUPILS BAD NEWS

There may be occasions in your career when you have to break bad news to pupils. This can stretch the skills of the most experienced teachers. If you do need to break some bad news to a pupil, bear these points in mind:

- Arrange it that a colleague is with you when you break the bad news. This is particularly important, as the pupil will need some form of comfort.
- Try to detach yourself from what has happened and focus on the immediate needs of the pupil. You may need to arrange for the pupil to be taken somewhere.
- Make sure you know all the facts and try to answer the pupil's questions as honestly and tenderly as possible. Have tissues and a drink ready (but not in view).
- Allow the child to express his/her emotional reaction as freely as possible.
- Think about how much you need to tell other pupils. Seek advice from your headteacher on what should be said and when.

ABOUT THE MENTAL HEALTH OF YOUR PUPILS

Mental illness is a feature not only of adult life. Increasing numbers of young children are being diagnosed with mental health problems and there is no doubt that teachers can play an important role in the healing process for such children.

Recognizing mental illness in the young can be very difficult; after all, when does the angst of growing up actually become a health issue? However, there are some tell-tale signs that should be looked for:

- excessive introspection;
- loss of appetite;
- tearfulness;
- dramatic changes in behaviour/character;
- obsessiveness;
- mood swings;
- declines in standards and quality of work;
- obvious anxiety/panic attacks.

If you are concerned about the mental health of a pupil, you should seek the advice of your induction tutor/mentor and/or the child's pastoral head. It may be necessary to contact the child's parents, but do not do this without the full backing of your managers. Once mental illness has been diagnosed, the child will begin what is likely to be a difficult haul back to health. During this time, he/she will need all the support you can give. Mental health services for young people vary tremendously around the country and, unfortunately, mental illness still carries a stigma that many cannot handle.

Your SENCO may be able to point you in the direction of literature on helping a pupil through mental illness, as may the Mental Health Foundation (see www.mentalhealth.org.uk) or Mind (see www.mind.org.uk).

Tutoring folklore

> Remember that a man's name is to him the sweetest and most important sound in the English language.
>
> (Dale Carnegie)

There is no doubt that sound tutoring is a skill that may come naturally to some teachers and not others. A great deal of your success in tutoring will come as a result of trial and error and it isn't possible to present a winning formula for this complicated task. However, you will pick up hints and tips from colleagues and books, which can inspire you into loving this aspect of teaching.

Ideas that have worked for others

Use these as inspiration, but don't feel under pressure to try them all!

- Take photographs of your tutees to put up on the wall. Pupils could add to the gallery photographs of sporting achievements or school trips etc.
- At the start of the school year, ask your group to write down their hopes and fears for the year/term. Store their ideas away and review them at the end of this period. This is a particularly good exercise to use to illustrate the personal development of your pupils over time.
- Keep a folder for each member of the group in which they can record the work done in tutorial periods.
- Some tutors keep their own records of their tutees in addition to the school records. These can be useful in monitoring progress over the year and for report writing. They also help for reference writing. These records should be considered confidential. You could also include references made to your group by other teachers.
- Encourage your pupils to help you to settle in to your new school (providing they aren't new as well). Ask them about the school and its history etc. Try not to get drawn into discussions about other members of staff – this is inevitable, but remain professional.
- Create a list of discussion topics that pupils can choose from for specific purposes. These could include just about anything from smoking, citizenship or rites of passage to animals, music or body language. Involve pupils in this process.
- Organize cards and/or presents from the group for your cleaner, certainly at Christmas time but at the end of each term too. This encourages pupils to be more responsible for their actions as they become aware of the thanking process and why this needs to be done.
- Some tutors like to split their tutor groups into smaller 'care' groups. These groups can be responsible for making the room tidy at the end of each day, or doing any 'housework' tasks that need to be done. This encourages pride in the group's immediate surroundings, while ensuring the work is done on a rotation basis. End-of-term parties are relatively easy to organize yet will mark important transitions for you and your group. You would have to check this out with the powers that be in your school, but it may be possible to organize some food and drinks as well, perhaps with small contributions from your pupils. Be sensitive towards anyone who does not celebrate Christmas and Easter – it can be better simply to celebrate the end of the term or year, or the season.
- Ask pupils to write a 'this is me' letter to include details like where they live, who lives with them, likes and dislikes, hopes, fears and aspirations etc.

- Gain as much experience as possible. Observe other tutors in action and talk about ways of adding to your tutoring skills.
- Give pupils an inspirational quote as thought for the day/week.
- Encourage ongoing tournaments, perhaps with cards, a computer game or Scrabble etc.
- Work as a group to solve problems. For example, if the group is not responding to a particular teacher, work together to devise ways of remedying the situation.
- You could give pupils something to think about while/if you call the register, for example something they learnt that day, something that would improve their achievement, someone they would like to thank, the best thing they did that morning, someone they need to apologize to, how they are feeling that day on a scale of 1–4 etc. Do, however, make sure you allow time for a quick feedback.
- Always explain to your tutees why you are doing something. If you can't do that, the process or procedure doesn't need doing.
- Reassure colleagues that you will deal with their complaints about any member of your group. Both teachers and pupils have to believe that teachers are united.
- Some tutors write to their tutees' parents at the start of the year to introduce themselves. This is also a good opportunity to express your hopes for the group and explain the best way for parents and carers to contact you. Not only does this put you in control of the demands made of you, but also it establishes, from the start, lines of communication. Do get clearance from the pastoral heads first, before going ahead and sending letters home.
- Observe your group while they are being taught by another teacher.
- Consider how you might use peer tutoring. This is becoming increasingly popular both overseas and in the UK.

ABOUT CHILD BULLYING

This is a hugely important aspect of school life – too great to deal with here in detail. Research indicates that way over 50 per cent of pupils experience bullying at school at some stage, and all teachers have a clear role in helping to prevent it, recognizing it when it happens and responding to it effectively.

Make sure that you read your school's policy on dealing with child bullying and any advice that is issued by your local authority. Talk to teachers who have tackled bullying in the past about techniques that have proved successful. It is also worth reading some of the excellent books on bullying that are available and discussing the issue regularly with your tutor group. You could devise a role-play or encourage your class to talk openly about bullying they have witnessed.

Taking time to look at language, how it is used and how it can be misinterpreted also leads to a greater understanding of bullying situations. Try to encourage pupils to view the bullying from both sides, thereby developing skills of empathy with all involved.

The website www.bullying.co.uk is a useful resource for teachers dealing with child-on-child bullying.

First aid in the classroom

> Accidents will occur in the best-regulated families.
> (Charles Dickens)

Without being too dramatic, your ability to administer first aid can mean the difference between life and death. Quick action to help a child suffering a health crisis will greatly ease his/her distress and the physical trauma suffered.

Individual schools and local authorities will have developed their own procedures regarding first aid and the administering of medicines, so make sure you have been appropriately informed (you should never be directed to give a child medicine). While responsibility for first aid will rest with the qualified first-aiders and 'appointed persons' in your school (know who they are and where they can be found at any time), knowing what to do in certain circumstances will add to your confidence in the classroom.

Your induction programme should cover first aid information, which should also be included in the staff handbook. As a teacher, you are not obliged to give first aid, but you are expected to do your best for the welfare of a child.

- Do find out as soon as possible if you are indemnified in the event of any claim of negligence made against you. Your union can help you here and your employer. Also find out if assisting with any form of medical procedure comes under the scope of your employment.
- You may consider obtaining a first aid qualification yourself. Courses are run by the British Red Cross, St John Ambulance and sometimes local authorities. Becoming a first-aider should be undertaken on a strictly voluntary basis. Under no circumstances should you ever be persuaded or 'encouraged' to take this on.
- If you do decide to volunteer to undertake first-aid training, your employer should provide it or, at least, pay for an outside agency to provide it.

- According to the *Dorling Kindersley First Aid Manual* (which is regularly updated and available through all good high street and online book-shops), an important rule of first aid is 'First do no harm.' Bear this is mind when looking after a child, and be aware of your limitations. If for example the sight of blood really does cause you to pass out, you need to get someone else to deal with the situation immediately so that there aren't two casualties in the classroom. A copy of the *Dorling Kindersley First Aid Manual* will probably be available in every school – if not, buy yourself a copy to keep in your classroom.

- It goes without saying that you must protect yourself at all times. If you have to deal with a child's body fluids in any way, always wear protective gloves. It's a good idea to keep a pair handy, but remember to throw them away and replace them after use.

- If there is a medical emergency while you are teaching, consider the rest of the class. There may be pupils who are shocked or affected in some way and it could be necessary to clear the room of everyone except the casualty. A teacher in a neighbouring classroom should be able to help you out here. This will also help to protect the dignity of the casualty.

- Remember to follow your school's regulations on reporting accidents and incidents. In brief, you will need to know the date, time and place of the incident, the name and class of the injured/ill person, details of the injury/illness, details of the first aid given, what happened as a result, and the name of the first-aider dealing with the incident.

- You may feel perfectly calm and able to cope while you are dealing with a situation, but be prepared for a possible reaction afterwards. You may need to nurture yourself a little after the event.

Typical childhood ailments

There are a number of medical situations that you could encounter in your classroom. The following advice is designed to give basic information and is not a replacement for qualified medical advice, which you should seek at the earliest opportunity. Send a child to the school office with a request for immediate first-aid assistance, so that you don't have to leave the casualty.

Accident injuries

Depending on what subject and age range you teach you could encounter varying degrees of injuries from accidents that have happened in your class-room. The first thing to remember is that accidents do happen. There is usually little reason to blame yourself for an accident that has happened to a child in your care, as long as you are aware of basic accident prevention.

ABOUT ACCIDENT PREVENTION

Some areas of a school are potentially more hazardous than others, such as science rooms, technology rooms and workshops. However, all classrooms present potential risks, so taking these steps could reduce the possibility of an accident taking place in your room:

- Take a look round your classroom regularly throughout the day to make sure there are no obvious hazards such as chairs out of place or broken furniture.
- Make sure the windows in your room are all safe, that the catches work and there is no cracked or broken glass. If necessary, make the window area a pupil-free zone. Be sure to report any necessary repairs to your headteacher or site manager.
- Check your room for leaks. One teacher had to spend a lesson that was being observed by an OFSTED inspector finding suitable receptacles for rainwater that was dripping through the ceiling on to her guest!
- Check the furniture in your room regularly for damage, cracks and splinters. Ask your classes to inform you of broken items.
- Make sure any necessary repairs are carried out promptly. You may have to remind the powers that be about what needs doing.
- Be strict about the way that pupils enter and leave your room. Also be firm about the way pupils move around the classroom.
- Make sure pupils' bags are safely stowed away during lessons. Many a teacher has tripped on stray bag straps as he/she moved around the room to work with children.
- Be strict about food consumption in your room. Children who are trying to surreptitiously chew gum or suck sweets are more likely to choke.
- Check that any leads and wiring in your room are safe. If you are not sure, ask a colleague to check for you.

Bleeding

With gloved hands, apply pressure to the wound. Take great care if an object is embedded in it – you may only be able to raise the wound so that it is above the child's heart. Wait for help to arrive – a first-aider should do any bandaging or call for an ambulance if necessary.

Broken bones

While you are waiting for help, simply protect the injury site from further damage. Don't forget to reassure the child, who may be in great pain. You could talk the child through a visualization of a peaceful scene to prevent panic setting in. Only move the child with the help of a qualified first-aider.

Eye injuries

Personal experience will probably tell you how excruciatingly painful an eye injury can be. Immediate medical assistance is required for anything more serious than simply dust or grit in the eye – use your discretion. You may need to comfort the child who should be sitting still. The child will probably be protecting the site of the injury with his/her hand – this is fine as long as he/she does not apply pressure.

Head injuries

If the child is bleeding, apply the same advice as given above. It is possible that the child may be suffering concussion, the symptoms of which may not become evident immediately. For this reason, a doctor must see a child who has suffered a head injury as soon as possible. Confusion, vomiting, sleepiness and uncharacteristic aggression are all signs of concussion.

Anaphylactic shock

Anaphylactic shock is a severe allergic reaction to a particular substance. This could typically be a bee sting, nuts or drugs, or anything that the particular individual happens to be allergic to. The onset of symptoms, such as increasing difficulty breathing, tends to be rapid and requires immediate medical attention. Sit the child somewhere quiet and try to stop him/her from panicking while you wait for help. The child may carry adrenalin (if known to have an allergy), which can be administered by either the child or a suitably qualified adult. Don't be fazed by the speed with which the child's condition may deteriorate. This is usual under the circumstances and can be corrected if the right medical assistance is given in good time.

Asthma

Children known to be asthmatics should know what to do in the event of an attack. Many will have their own inhalers, which they can administer themselves. It is essential to call for immediate assistance and while you wait encourage the child to sit upright as this eases breathing. Do not put your arm around his/her shoulders but offer verbal reassurance instead. The child may naturally place his or her arms up on a table; this is a natural reflex that also aids breathing. Try to encourage the child to breathe in through the nose and out slowly through the mouth. This helps to prevent hyperventilation.

Choking

This is a difficult situation to deal with unless you are a fully qualified first-aider. The only safe thing for you to do is to look for any obvious obstruction in the child's mouth that could easily be hooked out with a finger. Medical assistance is urgently required.

Diabetes

Many people suffer sudden drops in blood sugar and will recognize the urgency for food that this causes. In normal circumstances, blood sugar can be regulated by eating something sweet, but in diabetics treatment can be more complicated and the fluctuations in blood sugar more dramatic. The child may also suffer from sweating, shaking and loss of concentration. Your role, having called for assistance, should be to support the child's needs. Allow him/her to eat immediately, if you are certain that it is in the child's best interests, regardless of any rules about food in the classroom.

Epilepsy

You should have been informed of any children in your classes known to suffer from epilepsy, but remember a child's first fit may occur in your classroom. There are different classifications of fits, some more severe than others. Minor fits may simply involve temporary losses of concentration, in which case you may need to repeat instructions to a sufferer or offer some reassurance. However, in the case of a serious fit, after calling for assistance you need to ensure that the area around the child is cleared of any potentially dangerous objects. Lay the child on his/her side and watch for any changes in his/her colour or choking. Try to protect the child's head but do not restrict his/her movement in any way. Talk reassuringly to the child throughout the whole fit, as this is thought to ease anxiety. It may be essential to clear the other children from the room, as a fit can be frightening to witness and embarrassing for the sufferer on recovery, as it is common to be incontinent during a fit.

Fainting

Children can faint for a variety of reasons. For some, simply standing for an extended period of time will be enough to bring on a faint. There is usually little warning of an impending faint and the first you may know is when a child hits the deck! If this is the case, place something soft under the head, raise the feet above the level of the heart and talk reassuringly as he/she comes round. The child may be confused or disorientated. After a faint, a child should be encouraged to drink water, eat something and rest until he/she feels fully recovered. Medical assistance should be sought, as fainting can be a symptom requiring further investigation. If a child reports feeling faint, place his/her head between his/her knees and talk reassuringly until the feeling has passed.

Headaches

Children can get headaches for a variety of reasons such as stress and tension, food intolerance, dehydration or the onset of a deeper ailment such as a virus or infection. Very occasionally, a headache can indicate a far more serious condition such as a tumour. If a child complains of a headache during class time, watch for accompanying symptoms he/she may have such as feeling nauseous or dizzy, or having a raised temperature or disturbed vision. Be guided by the child; he/she may prefer to remain in your classroom doing a quiet activity, or may want to be excused from the room. Headaches can often be cured by rehydrating the body so always offer the opportunity for the child to get a drink of water. Check the temperature in your room too. If it has become hot and stuffy, those sensitive to temperature will begin to suffer. If the same child appears to be experiencing a cluster of headaches over a period of time, discuss the matter with your induction tutor or with the child's pastoral head.

Nosebleeds

These are relatively common in children as receiving a hit on the nose or blowing and picking the nose can bring them on. Often, nosebleeds are slight and do not require any intervention. However, if the bleeding shows no sign of abating, place the child's head in a forward position and pinch the fleshy part of the nose (not the bridge). Take every precaution to protect yourself.

Period pains

Period pain can be severe in some adolescent girls and it can be mistaken for other ailments such as appendicitis. A girl suffering from excessive period pain should be encouraged to seek medical assistance, as it could be indicative of an underlying condition such as endometriosis. This situation needs to be treated with sensitivity, particularly because the girl may not want to reveal why she feels unwell. For this reason, it would be sensible to enable the girl to spend some time away from the class, perhaps doing some work in an office or medical room. A qualified first-aider may decide to send the child home where painkillers can be administered.

Vomiting

Hopefully, the child will have given you plenty of warning of feeling sick, but this is not always the case. If a child vomits in your classroom, you need to arrange for it to be cleaned up as soon as possible. Usually, the caretaker has this unenviable task! If possible, cordon off the area. In the meantime, do your best to clean the child's face (or offer tissues for the child to do this him/herself) and reassure them that all is well. A first-aider will probably suggest that the child goes home. In any case, arrange for the child to have a glass of water if the child feels he/she could manage this and to change his/her clothes if they are soiled.

Find out more . . .

You can find out more about the pastoral side of your job from www.schoolsweb.gov.uk and from websites such as Teaching Expertise (see www.teachingexpertise.com).

Chapter 10

Non-teaching commitments

> Never promise more than you can perform.
> (Pubilius Syrus)

As your training will have shown you, being is teacher is about far more than just teaching! There are numerous other activities that you may be involved in. This chapter explores some of them, taking in:

- Taking on extra commitments
- Being assertive – can you say no?
- Organizing school visits
- Writing reports.

Taking on extra commitments

From school plays, outings, clubs and gardens to PTAs, staff committees and looking after class pets, there is no end to the extra commitments you may be cajoled into making. It is also no coincidence that NQTs often get asked to do extra jobs; existing staff have been there and done that and now say 'Sorry, I don't have time to take anything else on'.

Knowing your natural limits

The best line to take with extra commitments is to avoid them, if possible, in your first year unless you really want the experience that the commitment will provide, or unless it will add to your relaxation, e.g. acting in the school play if drama is a recreation for you. You will have enough on your plate working through your induction year without adding to the demands on your time. Taking extras on can result in you working at a pace above your optimum, which would reduce your effectiveness.

If you are not sure whether you can manage an extra commitment, agree to do it on the condition that you can review it after a few weeks. Provide yourself with a get-out, and the extra work will not seem like such an added stress.

If you are asked to take on duties in your department or curriculum area, such as being an ICT coordinator or being responsible for SEN, talk to your induction tutor/mentor. There will probably be a clause in your contract giving your headteacher the ability to ask you to do what he/she deems reasonable, but it is not practical for you to take on such duties as an NQT.

Being assertive: can you say 'no'?

Most teachers, when asked if they are assertive, will reply positively, simply because of the nature of their job. Yet, if they are asked the question 'Do you ever feel put upon?', they will still give a positive answer. So how does this add up? Perhaps some teachers are not as assertive as they think they are. In order to express yourself assertively, you have to be able to view yourself and your work positively. If you don't, you can hardly justify why others should listen to your assertions.

There are three main reasons why some teachers find it difficult to say 'no' to additional tasks that they don't want to take on:

- Managers lead them to believe that they are obliged to complete the extra tasks.
- They are insecure in their performance and think that performing the extra tasks will improve their feelings of self-worth.
- They want to create the impression that they are ready for anything.

These reasons are more destructive than positive. There is no doubt that it is the assertive (as opposed to aggressive, dominating or weak) individual who gains the most respect in the workplace.

ABOUT BEING ASSERTIVE

An easy route to stress and anxiety is by committing to too many projects. This usually results in feelings of being overwhelmed and unable to cope.

- An important step in the development of assertiveness skills is to practise some positive self-recognition. If you allow yourself to acknowledge what you are good at, you will boost your feelings of self-worth.
- Use affirmations daily, based on your skills. This will help to remove the need for positive strokes through taking on additional work.
- Accept any positive recognition that others give you.

- When you are in the position of needing to express yourself assertively, use these ideas:

  - Use 'I' statements to express yourself positively, for example 'I would be interested in playing the part of the beast in *Beauty and the Beast* but I feel it would adversely affect the way I manage my workload at the moment'.
  - Don't put yourself down. Say 'I don't feel that is appropriate for me at the moment' rather than 'I can't do that'.
  - Think about how you are using your body when you are being assertive. Tone of voice, body language, eye contact, etc. all make a difference to the way your words are received.
  - If you are anticipating a situation when you fear you will be 'put upon', use creative visualization to enable you to 'see' yourself behaving assertively. Focus on the best possible outcome for you.

Being assertive is not just about saying 'no'. It is also about making requests yourself. 'I need', 'I would like', 'Do you think I could have . . .?' are all phrases that NQTs will need to use throughout their first year of teaching, and probably beyond.

Organizing school visits

Taking on the organization of a school visit is something that even the most experienced teachers find time-consuming and potentially troublesome. Your school should have clear guidelines for teachers to follow when organizing visits, and if you do find yourself at the helm take as much advice from colleagues as you can.

The DfES document *Health and Safety of Pupils on Educational Visits* (1998) states that: 'Pupils can derive a good deal of educational benefit from taking part in visits with their school. In particular, they have the opportunity to undergo experiences not available in the classroom. Visits help to develop a pupil's investigative skills and longer visits in particular encourage greater independence.'

Although, as a new teacher, you probably won't be landed with the task of organizing a school visit from scratch, and certainly should not be asked to lead a residential visit, you will almost certainly be involved in them at some level. Before organizing a school visit, make sure you read a copy of the above document, which is available on request from the DCSF Publication Centre: 0845 60 222 60. Your school may also have a copy. It contains all the information you need regarding the legality of different kinds of school visits as well as health and safety considerations for all on the visit. It also has an extensive list of useful contacts. Do also visit www.hse.gov.uk/education/visits.htm, which lists more of the guidance which exists for those organizing educational visits for children.

> ### ABOUT 'STAYING SAFE'
>
> The Staying Safe Action Plan was launched by the DCSF in 2008 to help make it easier for teachers to take pupils on school trips. Keen to promote learning outside the classroom to enhance knowledge, boost confidence and achievement and encourage pupils to understand more about managing risk, this Action Plan and associated *Out and About* guidance builds on *Health and Safety of Pupils on Educational Visits* (see above) and is essential reading for all teachers involved in organizing trips and visits. You can find out more here: www.everychildmatters.gov.uk/stayingsafe/

Checklist for planning a visit

The first stage of planning a visit is convincing your headteacher that the trip is worth doing, that it fits into the curriculum you are teaching and that it carries minimum and managed risks. This is because your employer is still responsible for the health and safety of their employees (who carry a duty of care for pupils) when out on visits, as well as having to account for the way time is spent in their schools. Go no further than this at first because, if you don't get approval of the idea in principle as well as permission from your headteacher, the trip cannot go ahead.

When you present the idea to your headteacher (or head of department) have your justifications for the trip well rehearsed. It's a good idea to have a printed sheet ready to leave with the headteacher. On the sheet you should include:

- where you propose to take the children;
- whom you propose to take (including staff, supervisors and children);
- why the trip is necessary;
- what aspect of the curriculum you would be covering;
- how you would link it into work before and after the trip;
- how much you estimate the trip will cost.

Once you get the go-ahead to start the planning, use this checklist:

1   Find out if your school has guidelines for planning a visit (your head of department, induction tutor/mentor or headteacher should be able to confirm this). If it has, use them; otherwise, use this checklist.

2 Carry out a risk assessment. The DfES document mentioned above suggests basing a risk assessment on the following considerations:

- What are the hazards?
- Who might be affected by them?
- What safety measures need to be in place to reduce risks to an acceptable level?
- Can the group leader put the safety measures in place?
- What steps will be taken in an emergency?

The document also states that: 'A risk assessment for a visit need not be complex but it should be comprehensive . . . Pupils must not be placed in situations which expose them to an unacceptable level of risk. Safety must always be the prime consideration. If the risks cannot be contained then the visit must not take place.'

The document suggests that teachers consider these factors when assessing the risks:

- the type of visit/activity and the level at which it is being undertaken;
- the location, routes and modes of transport;
- the competence, experience and qualifications of supervisory staff;
- the ratios of teachers and supervisory staff;
- the group members' age, competence, fitness and temperament; and the suitability of the activity;
- the special educational or medical needs of pupils;
- the quality and suitability of available equipment;
- seasonal conditions, weather and timing;
- emergency procedures;
- how to cope when a pupil becomes unable or unwilling to continue;
- the need to monitor the risks throughout the visit.

Once you have completed your risk assessment, make sure all those involved in the trip (but not pupils) have a copy.

3 If possible, go on an exploratory visit to:

- ensure at first hand that the venue is suitable to meet the aims and objectives of the school visit;
- obtain names and addresses of other schools that have used the venue;
- obtain advice from the manager;
- assess potential areas and levels of risk;
- ensure that the venue can cater for the needs of the staff and pupils in the group;
- become familiar with the area before taking a group of young people there.

If you can't go on an exploratory visit, get the necessary information from telephone calls. You also need to make sure you have identified good places to designate as meeting points, especially for lost pupils.

4 Think about joining up with another teacher for the trip. Perhaps another year group would benefit from the visit, or you could link with pupils from another subject area.

5 Talk through the financial arrangements with your head of department or headteacher.

6 Make sure that you know who will be responsible for first aid on the trip. You will have to have a first-aid box with you (your school will provide this) and it is a good idea to find out where the nearest hospital will be.

7 Work out the best form of transport (which may not necessarily be the cheapest). If the group is small enough, a mini-bus may do, but usually a coach is the best option. Also consider walking (if appropriate) and going by train. Work out what would be the best pick-up and drop-off points.

8 Decide on the exact timing of the day, including toilet and lunch breaks. Prepare one itinerary for pupils and one for adults.

9 Who would be the group's leader? It is important to appoint one person (usually the organizer) to whom all other staff and supervisors may refer.

10 Work out how many adults need to go on the trip. Your headteacher will tell you what adult to child ratios you need.

11 Prepare a letter informing parents of the trip. Many schools have a stand-ard format for this. Aim to give sufficient information for parents to make an informed decision on whether their child should attend, but not be swamped with detail. Make yourself available for parents to ask you questions if necessary. You will also need to mention what clothing (if different) children will need, what food should be provided by parents and whether any extra money should be taken (perhaps for spending in a gift or souvenir shop etc.). It can be worth mentioning the standard of behaviour that is expected of pupils on the trip.

12 Think about whether you want to ban carbonated drinks, glass bottles, mobiles, iPods, etc. Follow your school's policy on this.

13 Keep equal opportunities issues in mind, especially when you arrange subgroups.

14 If possible, involve pupils in the planning of work to be completed on the trip. This helps to ensure that they understand the relevance of the trip and can place it clearly in the context of the curriculum they are following. It also encourages them to complete the work.

15 Get a list of any children with medical needs. Some teachers like to take a list of each child, the names of their GPs and next of kin and emergency contact numbers. This is usually unnecessary, as most trips are in school hours and, in the event of any emergency, you would contact the school, where all this information is held, as soon as possible.

16 Sort out insurance in good time. Your headteacher will be able to do this for you.

17 Discuss the standards of behaviour that you expect. It is particularly important that pupils realize how identifiable they are in school uniform.

18 Think about how travelling time might be used constructively. Perhaps give pupils a quiz to do based on what they might see on the journey.

19 Write a list of everything you will personally need on the day, from lunch to worksheets, waterproofs to registers.

20 Think about how pupils will complete their work on the day. Will they have time to do tasks? Will clipboards be necessary? Will they use exercise books, paper or worksheets with gaps to fill in?

21 Inform any colleagues who would have taught the pupils you are taking off site of the exact details of the trip. It can be extremely annoying if they have planned an exam or assessment for your group and half of them are not there.

22 Arrange work for a cover teacher to set for any classes you are unable to teach.

23 Inform catering staff of the numbers you will be taking off site. They will need to adjust the amount they cook for the day and plan any free lunches in advance.

24 Create a contingency plan for arriving back late. Who will you phone? Will he/she be able to contact parents?

25 Make sure that there is someone who is able to deputize for you in the event of an emergency. If you are incapacitated for whatever reason, the trip should not necessarily be called off. You will have to keep the person informed of all the arrangements.

ABOUT THE JOURNEY

The travelling time on a trip can be potentially problematic. Children may get travel-sick, become excitable or, worse, start misbehaving. Having a focus for the journey often helps to pre-empt any troubles and, if you can make this light-hearted, even better. A quiz with a prize for the winner is usually great for occupying the time and creating unity in the group through a common task. Try to invoke a sense of anticipation of the day.

Pitfalls to avoid

• Don't plan too much initially before getting firm approval from the powers that be.

• Once you have approval, pace your planning so that you don't have a last-minute rush. Remember that you will have to keep up with everything else on top of organizing the trip. Try to avoid being the sole organizer. This would be a pretty unfair expectation to make of an NQT.

- Don't get saddled with the cost of an exploratory visit. You should be able to claim your expenses back. Speak to the bursar.
- Don't make arrangements over the phone without asking for written confirmation.

Summary checklist for planning a visit

1   Get a copy of your school's guidelines.
2   Do a risk assessment.
3   Go on a preliminary visit.
4   Perhaps join up with another teacher/class.
5   Discuss finances with the headteacher.
6   Consider first aid arrangements.
7   Assess transport possibilities.
8   Create an itinerary.
9   Designate a leader.
10 Decide on supervision levels.
11 Inform parents of the details of the trip.
12 Think about banned items.
13 Remember equal opportunities.
14 Allow pupils to help you plan work.
15 Find out any medical needs.
16 Sort out insurance.
17 Discuss standards of behaviour.
18 Consider using travel time.
19 Create a list of personal things you will need.
20 Consider the practicalities of how pupils will work.
21 Inform colleagues of those you will be taking out if necessary.
22 Arrange cover work if necessary.
23 Inform catering staff about those you are taking out.
24 Create a plan for late arrival back.
25 Arrange a deputy for the trip in case of an emergency.

Checklist for the actual day

All your meticulous planning will pay off now as you enjoy a trouble-free trip. Use this list as guidance:

1   Start with a headcount. It's not sufficient simply to call a register.
2   Continue to count heads at regular intervals throughout the day.
3   Take a mobile phone (which should be provided by your school) and some spare cash (again, talk to the bursar) for emergencies.

4 Make sure that pupils are fully strapped in before the coach starts to move and that they stay strapped in throughout the journey.

5 Staff and helpers should be evenly spread throughout the group on the journey and through the day.

6 Ask helpers unknown to the children to wear name badges.

7 Make sure children know which adults are assigned to their group.

8 Designate a central point as a meeting place in the event of children getting lost.

9 If travelling by coach, make arrangements with the driver about where and when you will meet again. Make a note of the coach's registration number.

10 Note anything that works particularly well on the day.

11 Keep a record of behaviour, both good and bad. Pupils should receive feedback when they get back to school, and you will have to discuss this aspect of the trip with your headteacher when you get back.

12 Recap on the day on the journey back. You could also go over some of the work the pupils have done and explain what comes next.

13 Evaluate the day for the purposes of future trips. Is there anything you would change in the future, or anything you would never do again?

Pitfalls to avoid

- Don't forget a sick bucket/bag, a bottle of still mineral water for the vomiting child, plenty of tissues and some mints – he/she will want to be refreshed after throwing up!

- Don't think you can relax for a minute throughout the day. You will need to be more vigilant than usual.

- Don't be so concerned about how the day flows that you forget to enjoy it.

Summary checklist for the actual day

1 Count heads regularly.
2 Take a phone and some money.
3 Strap pupils in on the journey.
4 Spread helpers throughout the group.
5 Give helpers name badges.
6 Explain groups to children.
7 Decide on a meeting point.
8 Arrange when and where to meet the driver.
9 Note what works well on the day.
10 Record good and bad behaviour.
11 Recap on the day on the journey.
12 Evaluate the day.

Writing reports

Whatever schools call them, there's no getting away from the fact that you will have to write thousands of these throughout your teaching career! It's an onerous job; you will need to give accurate messages in an accessible form while under a great deal of time pressure.

Report writing

Do . . .

- take care over presentation, whether hand-written or printed. Would you mind if your reports were published?
- keep to internal deadlines. Your headteacher, head of department or year group leader will probably want to read them before they leave the building.
- set yourself mini-deadlines of 5–10 reports at a time.
- consider writing drafts, or at least jotting down key words for inclusion.
- start your comments positively and focus on progress.
- avoid educational jargon (of which there is a plethora). Remember that acronyms can be confusing.
- offer constructive suggestions for improvement.

Don't . . .

- allow a report out of your hands with errors and corrections. Start again if necessary.
- forget that it is the written comments that parents tend to take most notice of, as opposed to test results and attainment levels.
- attempt to do a whole class set in one go.
- forget your accountability. Can you substantiate all you write?
- express limits. It is better to focus on possibilities (as opposed to predictions).
- waffle. Select apt, crisp language.
- hide the negatives, but be aware that reports are not the place to spring nasty surprises on parents.

When considering the actual words you will use, take care over creating a stockpile of phrases to scatter throughout your reports, as it is essential that they should apply to a child's work and progress. 'Tries hard', 'Could try harder', 'Makes a good effort', 'Makes no effort', 'Talks too much' and 'Doesn't speak out' are all meaningless and reflect more on teaching style than any aspect of the child in question. (For example, why does the child make no effort? Because he/she is bored? Because the work is too easy? Be aware of how your comments could reveal shortcomings in teaching style.) As long as your comments are specific to the child and relate to the skills required of the subject, where appropriate, your reports will be valid and noted, and you will not lay yourself open to criticism from within or outside your school. Remember that your reports should be accessible in style to all parents, particularly bearing in mind those whose first language may not be English.

A quick search on the Internet will reveal the growing number of sites dedicated to report writing. Some schools, too, have created comment databases for teachers to use to ease the task. If you use such a database, remember the following:

- Each comment should be backed up with an example, either written in the report or spoken at the parents' evening.
- The language of such comment databases might not match the way in which you would naturally phrase things; therefore they are best used as inspiration to trigger your own thought processes.
- Each comment should add meaning and clarity to the report.

The following lists of positive and negative comments have been put together by staff at St Martin's School in Brentwood, Essex.

Positive comments

- Has proved to be an extremely committed pupil with genuine enthusiasm for the subject.
- Teaching ... has been a privilege. His/her constant enthusiasm and willingness to learn have been a pleasure to watch.
- He/she is extremely conscientious, has set him/herself high standards and is achieving them.
- His/her work reflects consistent effort.
- Possesses the ability to apply quickly what he/she has learned.
- Is a very conscientious pupil who takes pride in all he/she does.
- Has shown the ability to achieve a great deal in this subject.
- Has maintained the highest standards this year.
- Has demonstrated outstanding commitment.
- Seems determined to succeed.
- Has grown in confidence.
- Has improved greatly.
- Has shown a very sound/firm grasp of this subject.
- Is finding the subject difficult but always tries very hard to make progress.
- Can apply him/herself most effectively.
- I have been pleased with ...
- I have been encouraged by ...

- A perceptive/inquisitive/thorough approach.
- A lively intellect.
- A sensitive and mature student.
- A very encouraging start.
- Has worked conscientiously/effectively/diligently/enthusiastically.
- Has made enthusiastic/pleasing/outstanding contributions to class discussion.
- Has made pleasing/generally pleasing/very pleasing progress.
- Is developing into a mature and conscientious/committed student.
- Is a conscientious and committed student who has undoubtedly worked very hard this year.
- Has evidently worked at his/her best to produce such good results.

Negative comments

- . . . . .'s poor presentation skills have impeded his/her progress.
- Although keen to do well . . . allows his/her concentration to lapse far too often.
- . . . . . seems to have lost some of his/her willingness. He/she is an able pupil and usually conscientious but this must be a sustained feature of his/her work if he/she is to fulfil his/her potential.
- . . . . .'s expectation that others will give the answers in class often leads to a loss of concentration.
- . . . . . only works under pressure.
- . . . . . needs to organize his/her work more efficiently.
- . . . . . lacks commitment.
- His/her performance is erratic.
- Homework often appears rushed, has not been checked for avoidable errors and consists of a bare minimum.
- Should adopt a far more mature attitude.
- . . . . . has a considerable weakness in . . . . .
- Some weaknesses remain.
- Should not allow him/herself to be so easily distracted.
- Needs to become more effectively involved in group work/class discussion/etc.
- Needs to target/focus/marshal his/her energies/enthusiasm more appropriately/effectively/maturely.
- Lacks confidence but can make pleasing contributions.
- Can lack application at times.
- Has a tendency to be immature.
- Has shown a lack of regard for authority which has been profoundly disturbing in its intensity and scope.
- A lack of attention to detail has hampered his/her progress.
- Frequent absence has made genuine progress difficult.

- Has worked poorly.
- Needs to adopt a more rigorous approach.
- Can lack concentration.
- Can lack the application required at this level.
- Has struggled with some of the more difficult aspects of the course.
- Seems unable to cope with even the most basic concepts.
- Potential there, motivation sometimes lacking.
- A student whose boundless enthusiasm is channelled in any direction but mine.

Find out more . . .

- The Standards for QTS and the Core Standards (see Appendices 4 and 5) as well as your job description will give you information on what you can expect to undertake as a teacher.
- The Teaching Expertise website (www.teachingexpertise.com) is worth browsing for articles on these issues and more.

Chapter 11

Continuing professional development

> The aim of life is self-development. To realize one's nature perfectly – that is what each of us is here for.
>
> (Oscar Wilde)

As you reach the successful conclusion of your induction period, you can look ahead to a career in which you will face many challenges, changes and triumphs. There are so many directions that you could take and ways you can make a positive impact on the lives of your pupils in a society that now demands creativity and resourcefulness. To support your progress, this chapter looks at:

- Early and continuing professional development
- Planning for future directions
- Gathering evidence of skills and achievements
- Your individual professional development record
- Changing posts within your school
- Moving to another school
- Career satisfaction.

Early and continuing professional development

It is really important for all teachers to be motivated to take responsibility for their own professional development. This encompasses a pretty broad range of activities, but, in short, can be taken to mean that you will:

- identify the areas of practice you need to develop;
- set targets for your own improvement;
- work with others to set targets for your improvement;
- convey your learning needs;
- work independently at developing your specialist skills;
- make full use of the possible sources of professional development that exist;

- seek help when appropriate;
- give and receive help, advice and constructive criticism;
- contribute to the development of others.

The early professional development of NQTs is of great interest and importance to the General Teaching Council for England, the government and many other bodies with interests in education. For teachers to be successful educators, there is broad acceptance that their training should not end with the induction period and that teachers are most likely to remain in the profession if their early professional development needs are met.

Although the quality of the early professional development that you receive following on from your induction is in part dependent upon the attitude that your school and employers take towards it, you still retain tremendous scope to impact your own development in a positive way.

Each local authority will offer, through your school, opportunities for early professional development, which will typically include:

- school-based activities including action research;
- focus on classroom practice skills as well as management skills;
- peer mentoring/coaching partnerships;
- focused classroom observation;
- pupil tracking;
- subject self-review;
- using ICT;
- personalisation;
- focus on Every Child Matters and other national agendas;
- data analysis;
- action planning.

Recognizing development opportunities

Professional development does not have to mean attending a one-day in-service training course. There are many opportunities for professional learning facing most teachers on a daily basis. These include:

- focused observations of colleagues at work;
- studying your own teaching through video;
- action research;
- distance learning;
- reading professional journals and texts;
- engaging in online discussions and other technology-mediated learning;
- self-directed study perhaps linked to academic awards;
- giving and receiving tutoring and mentoring;
- working with a study or learning team;

- attending 'masterclasses';
- team teaching;
- planning and assessing with colleagues;
- developing resources with colleagues;
- peer coaching;
- collaborative school cluster projects;
- job shadowing;
- researching existing effective practice;
- personal reflection;
- observations and placements in other schools.

The chances are, you will have a clear idea about what it is that helps you learn best in your job, but it's likely that having the chance to learn from other teachers and going on good quality courses that offer learning that can be applied in your specific circumstances rate pretty highly.

If there is a culture of support for professional development at your school then there will be no problem in identifying the opportunities that may face you. If not, a degree of ingenuity might be needed. Remember that a main goal of professional development is to improve classroom practice, which leads to enhanced teacher effectiveness and a general raising of standards.

What we know about professional development indicates that the following features are most likely to lead to success in the classroom:

- coaching and feedback over a period of time in the classroom;
- the chance for teachers to understand the rationale behind new ideas and initiatives;
- being able to see theory in practice;
- being exposed to a variety of expertise;
- the chance to experiment;
- the chance to interpret new ideas at work, and to build on existing knowledge and skills.

ACTION

Using knowledge of the style of learning that suits you best, combined with the experience of your induction period, consider the kinds of professional development that you have found most effective. Is there anything that you have not had the opportunity to experience that would further your development? Is there anything that you have learnt but not been able to apply in the context of your classroom? Where would you like your professional development to take you?

ABOUT INDIVIDUAL AND INSTITUTIONAL DEVELOPMENT

Any continuing professional development that you undertake will necessarily need to balance your needs as a learning and reflecting practitioner and the needs of the institution to which you belong. Development priorities should be informed by both to avoid conflict and tension arising.

ABOUT THE CPD 'MINDSET'

The early stage of your career is a key time to harness a sound attitude towards professional development. There is the potential for development each and every day that you are in school, and the teacher who is adept at recognizing when these opportunities occur is the teacher who will ultimately be most effective and successful. Don't get hung up on a quest for perfection though; this is both unachievable and undesirable. Be aware, too, that your work/life balance should not be compromised. Giving thought to the motivations behind your professional development can help to conserve this. Finally, be honest with yourself about what it is that you do well. How can you assist colleagues in their development?

Planning for future directions

Although continuing professional development is largely your responsibility, your school should be ensuring that you have the opportunities to undertake appropriate, valuable development and that you are motivated in this. These questions may also help when planning for your future:

- Where do you instinctively want to go in your career?
- What existing skills do you want to develop? What new skills do you want to pursue?
- What funds are available to you?
- Can you identify distinct short-, medium- and long-term goals?
- Are you happy to be flexible in your goals (given that the experience and skills you gather may lead you in new directions)?
- Do you know where to get any information you may need?

Pacing your targets

As the induction period is so busy, it probably won't be until your second year at the earliest that you start to think about your own target setting for further development. When you do get round to this, pacing is crucial. Expect too much of yourself and your performance will suffer, not enough and you risk stagnation.

If possible, don't depend on future study for anything ('I must complete this MA in two years, as otherwise I won't be able to go for . . . by my deadline'). This will keep harmful stress at bay and allow you to work at a pace most suitable for you. Above all, make sure that any further professional development you do above the INSET that you are offered responds to issues raised by your induction and Career Entry and Development Profile and serves to fuel your enthusiasm for your career.

There is little value in targets that are not achievable. They will only serve as a source of unnecessary stress and anxiety. When setting targets, try to strike the balance between sensibly stretching yourself and going full out for every experience you have not yet encountered. Be realistic.

For every professional goal you set yourself, set a personal goal too, however small that may be. Don't neglect your non-working life, as the costs are far too high.

Gathering evidence of skills and achievements

> Looking back and evaluating is important. Your own achievement is one of your best inspirations. When you realize you have achieved something, it is one of your most reliable sources of strength.
>
> (Rimpoche Nawang Gehlek)

The phrase 'lifelong learning' is one that all teachers are being encouraged to embrace. Linked to this is the fact that all professional experiences form a valid part of your development; it is possible to learn something positive from every event in your career.

Many schools have devised their own individual professional development record that teachers can fill in and add to throughout the year. These are intended to supplement the Career Entry and Development Profile for NQTs. If your school does not have such a system of individual record keeping, use the framework in the following section to keep track of significant achievements and milestones. It will make any inspections and appraisals that you experience significantly easier to prepare for. Acknowledgements for the following ideas must go to Bishop Luffa CE School in Chichester and Davison CE School in Worthing.

ABOUT THE PROCESS OF GATHERING EVIDENCE

The whole exercise of gathering evidence of your skills and achievements should not become a chore. It is a necessary part of moving through any profession and should therefore be considered as an aspect of the maintenance of your work. Aim to update your records on a regular basis (perhaps once a month) so that the time you spend on the task is minimized. Don't wait until the end of a term when your energy and enthusiasm are likely to be at their lowest.

Your individual professional development record

There only needs to be a maximum of three parts to this record, the final part of which could be replaced by the Career Entry and Development Profile as appropriate. Create a file that you can add to easily and that can slip into your portfolio.

Start with a current CV, including your name, all contact details, all your qualifications, both academic and otherwise, the institutions that awarded them and when. Also include your full employment history (not just in teaching) and brief outlines of previous job descriptions, quantifiable achievements and transferable skills.

The second section should include your professional development experiences, and how they have impacted on your work and understanding. Such experiences need not simply be courses you have attended, but may include anything that has contributed to your professional skills and knowledge. Think about these suggestions:

- curriculum and departmental meetings;
- advice passed on from other staff members;
- training sessions attended both in school and outside;
- lesson observations;
- visits from local authority advisers;
- secondments and exchanges;
- visits to other schools;
- conversations with teachers from other schools;
- job shadowing;
- ICT training;
- cross-curricular meetings, e.g. SEN and ICT.

The impact of such experiences could initiate changes in the way you work, the way you respond to colleagues and the way you perceive your own professional development. You could put your findings under three headings: date, event and impact (see below).

EXAMPLE

How to record professional development

Date 3 March 2008

Event Observation of Bob Hill's ICT lesson with year 10

Impact By not attempting to have all 30 pupils on task 100 per cent of the time, Bob utilized the skills of the more able pupils to assist those who needed extra help. In this way, all pupils were able to maximize the learning potential from the lesson. The way the hour flowed showed me that children appreciate the opportunity to test what they have learnt.

If your school requires you to complete evaluation reports on training sessions, you could file them in this section too. Alternatively, evaluate courses using the above format. By recognizing how much you can learn from a variety of sources, you can realize how much you are able to help others.

The final section should cover your professional targets. For teachers with a Career Entry and Development Profile, this part is unnecessary but, for others, this is a good opportunity to draw together your personal goals and those that have been identified from assessments and performance management. You could use the format shown in Figure (11.1) for each goal.

Target	**Timescale**
Proposed activity	**Success criteria**
Evalution of outcome	

Figure 11.1 How to record your goals.

Changing posts within your school

> Well is it known that ambition can creep as well as soar.
> (Edmund Burke)

It can be possible (but not always advisable) for NQTs to move up the career ladder during the first year of teaching or in preparation for the second year.

While it is important to consolidate, there are many opportunities for taking on responsibilities of varying degrees. For the greatest chance of success, always think about why you want to progress.

Possible areas for promotion

For those keen to develop their work in a particular subject area, the obvious choice is to work up the departmental ladder. This could mean taking a second- or third-in-command post in your subject area or, if your school is small enough, it could mean taking a head of department or subject leader post.

If you don't want to take on a different post, but would like to take on more responsibility, talk to your line manager about working on a specific project such as writing exam papers or the development of a scheme of work. This can be a gentler route into middle management.

Outside your subject area, there are many opportunities to enhance your responsibilities. All schools have a pastoral team, and there are usually posts of varying degrees of importance to be had, such as head of house, head of year or head of school. Again, if this is your chosen route of promotion, don't feel you have to achieve it in one step. Shadow the person who is already in post to see if there is an aspect of his/her job you would like to take on or learn more about. Alternatively, there will be opportunities to coordinate many cross-curricular aspects of the school, such as special needs, ICT, literacy and numeracy, citizenship and personal and social education.

ABOUT WANTING TO CONSOLIDATE

With the current trend in the teaching profession to progress, diversify and push for professional development early in your career, it can be easy to be swept along, assuming that onwards and upwards is where you really want to be. There is nothing wrong with consolidating your position for a few years before even thinking about the next step, rather than leaping into a promotion simply because 'you would be foolish not to'.

However, you do have a professional 'duty' to remain up to date with your teaching skills and subject expertise, so even though you may be consolidating, you will still be progressing in terms of knowledge and skills.

ABOUT THE FAST TRACK

The Fast Track Teaching Programme is an accelerated development programme for teachers who want to be school leaders. In identifying the most talented teachers, it seeks to give intensive professional development to steer them to their full potential more quickly than might otherwise be possible.

For further information on Fast Track Teaching, take a look at the National College for School Leadership website (www.ncsl.org.uk).

Moving to another school

If you have decided to move to another school to continue your career, remember that you are in a more secure position now than you were as an NQT starting your first post. Consider what you have learnt in your first year, and the resources you have developed – all of this can be transferred to your new job.

Although your new school will have its own ways of functioning, it is the movement of teachers around the country, along with the ideas that they bring, that prevents schools from stagnating. Remember to take these items with you to your new school:

- all the resources you have produced during your first year;
- copies of other resources you have used;
- all records of your professional development;
- copies of any handbooks and policies you feel may be useful.

Don't be tempted to reinvent the wheel every time you join a new school!

ABOUT FACING NEW CHALLENGES

Although you have a whole year of teaching experience under your belt, it can be easy to feel like the 'youngster' again when you join a new school. There will be new ways of working and probably a new school day that you'll have to become familiar with, not to mention new classes to get to know. Don't expect that, just because you don't have the excuse of being an NQT, you have to know everything. You should still assigned a mentor or 'buddy' and be given a thorough induction programme. See these new challenges as learning opportunities and don't expect to absorb everything at once.

An Easter appraisal

One potentially negative aspect of working within the teaching profession is that moves between jobs tend to take place at set times through the year, and most often in time for the start of the new academic year in September. This can lead to teachers feeling trapped in a job for years at a time, if they don't take the opportunity to move at the appropriate times in the year. For this reason, it is important to do regular personal appraisals of the way you feel about the profession and your job, to ensure that you give yourself the opportunity to move on if you want to.

During your first year of teaching, the best time to do one of these appraisals is during the Easter holidays. This gives you time to move on if that is what you want to do. In subsequent years of teaching, this appraisal can be done earlier in the year, allowing you longer to make changes.

Assessing your first two terms

This appraisal is for your eyes only. Don't spend more than an hour on it and treat it not as another aspect of your Career Entry and Development Profile or a formal school appraisal but as your private opportunity to assess your position.

The following questions will help to focus your mind on your levels of satisfaction in your job:

- What have been the best events of my first two terms?
- What contributed to these events?
- What have been the worst events of my first two terms?
- What contributed to these events?
- What job satisfaction do I get?
- What would I like to change about my job?
- What factors make it difficult for me to achieve my duties?
- Does my current job allow me to move in the direction that I want my career to go?
- What other opportunities does my job offer me?
- What could I do to help me to achieve my objectives?
- What could my managers do to help me to achieve my objectives?
- Am I thriving on the demands of my job?

Is this the job for you?

It is quite usual for new teachers to go through a period of doubt about their chosen career. This can be compounded by feelings of exasperation at the length of time it takes to qualify and the amount of energy it takes to perform the functions of a teacher. Don't feel disheartened if you have these thoughts. It is virtually impossible to prepare for the emotional and physical investment that you will put into your job, which is why it is so important to ask yourself at regular intervals 'Is this the job for me?' The answer may not necessarily be 'no'.

Unfortunately, nobody can help you answer this question. Family members, partners and friends may encourage you one way or the other, but only you will be able to understand the thrill you get from a teaching day going well (when others may say to you 'How can you bear to do all that preparation every evening?') or the exhaustion you feel when, after a disappointing day, you still have 60 books to mark (when others say 'You lucky thing – a job for life and all those long holidays!').

Put yourself first, use your personal appraisal and know that you are making the decision that inspires you most.

Options to choose

> Still round the corner there may wait,
> A new road or a secret gate.
> (J R R Tolkien)

If you conclude that teaching is the career for you, your only considerations are your future professional consolidation and development. Use your personal appraisal and your Career Entry and Development Profile to discuss with mentors and colleagues how you can progress.

However, if you feel you would like to move on from teaching, there are several steps you can take.

If teaching is not for you

Under no circumstances should you consider this decision to be weak or negative in any way. There are very few people who stay within the same career all their lives, and fewer still whom this will genuinely suit.

There are three options open to you at this point:

- Decide to stay on at your school for another year. After the upheavals of joining a new institution and completing the induction year, not to mention all the materials you have had to devise from scratch, the next year may be significantly easier. It may be possible to negotiate some changes that could ease your way, or ensure that you are teaching the same year groups, to minimize the time you will have to spend on resource development. Talk to your induction tutor/mentor or confidant about the best way to go about this.
- Reduce your teaching load to part-time to allow you time to pursue other career options.
- Start to make steps to leave. Take advantage of any careers counselling

that may be on offer from your local authority and county careers service and utilize the information on careers in your local library. Be aware of your emotions while you are doing this. Don't slip into despondency or feelings of failure. As you close one door, another has to open.

Career satisfaction

For all its focus on improving your classroom performance and the achievement of your pupils, continuing and early professional development is not successful if it does not contribute significantly to your career satisfaction as well. If your need to thrive in your job is central to your plans for professional development, you can maximize the buzz you'll get from teaching and ensure that you'll reach the places you want to be.

Although external factors affect our career satisfaction – factors such as how well our managers reward/praise us for our work, and the opportunities that we may be given to link career satisfaction with professional development – we can take action, regardless of the circumstances in which we find ourselves, to ensure that we can work with vitality. These ideas may help:

- Adapt systems, within reason, to suit your way of working.
- Recognize the close connection between professional and personal development.
- Fully participate in any reviews of progress you may have.
- Link your work with your personality – are you spending most time on what suits you best?
- Recognize and celebrate (in some way) your achievements and progress.
- Spend time with like-minded colleagues, including those from other schools.
- Assist others in their professional development whenever appropriate.

Find out more . . .

- You can find out more about the Professional Standards for Teachers and about continuing professional development in general from the Training and Development Agency for Schools (www.tda.gov.uk). In particular, take a look at the national priorities for CPD. At the time of writing, these have been identified for the academic years 2007–2010 and they cover pedagogy (behaviour management, subject knowledge, supporting curriculum change); personalization (equality and diversity, special educational needs and disability); people (working with other professionals, school leadership). You can find out more on the TDA website. You may also want to explore the framework of professional standards which will help you to make sound choices in your career development. You can find this framework at: www.tda.gov.uk/teachers/professionalstandards

Appendix 1

Every Child Matters: Change for Children

Every Child Matters: Change for Children is the current Government's approach to the well-being of children between from birth to the age of 19. The aim of the initiative is to ensure that every child has the support they need to achieve the following five outcomes:

- Be healthy
- Stay safe
- Enjoy and achieve
- Make a positive contribution
- Achieve economic well-being

As you work through your induction period, it is important to keep these outcomes in mind at all times, using them as a framework for the work that you do as a teacher.

Find out all you need to know about the Every Child Matters (ECM) agenda from the ECM website (see www.everychildmatters.gov.uk).

Code of Conduct and Practice for Registered Teachers

Setting minimum standards for the regulation of the profession

This Code of Conduct and Practice was agreed at a meeting of the General Teaching Council for England on 30 June 2004 and came into effect on 1 November 2004. It is reproduced here with the permission of the General Teaching Council for England (see www.gtce.org.uk).

Introduction

The regulatory role of the Council

The standards of entry to the teaching profession are set out in the standards for qualified teacher status (QTS). In order to practise in maintained schools and non-maintained special schools, teachers are, unless exempt, additionally required to complete a statutory period of induction, and to be registered with the General Teaching Council for England (GTC).

Maintaining registration requires that teachers uphold appropriate standards of professional conduct and competence. This document sets out minimum standards expected of registered teachers and is for use within the Council's regulatory regime.

The Council's role in respect of professional standards relates both to promoting high standards and ensuring minimum standards. Since 2001, the GTC has considered cases of registered teachers whose standards of conduct or competence are alleged to have fallen below acceptable minima.

Such cases are considered at hearings before Members of the Council, comprising a majority of teacher Members with lay representation.

This Code of Conduct and Practice has drawn on the Council's experience of professionally led regulation since 2001. Whilst the provisions of the Code are based upon actions already found by hearing committees to constitute unacceptable professional conduct, serious professional incompetence or to be a relevant criminal offence, they are not exclusive. The Code will be kept under review and revised in the light of the Council's developing experience of regulation.

The Council's procedures

Most referrals to the Council arise from the requirement upon employers to refer cases where registered teachers are dismissed for reasons of misconduct or incompetence, or where they resign in circumstances where dismissal was a possibility. Supply and temporary teachers must also be referred when their employment ceases in similar circumstances. Members of the public may also make an allegation of professional misconduct, but not of incompetence, directly to the Council.

The Council does not have responsibility for considering misconduct relating to the safety and welfare of children. This remains the responsibility of the Secretary of State for Children, Schools and Families whose powers encompass teachers and other workers with children and young people. For this reason, teacher employers referring misconduct cases are required to send them first to the Department for Children, Schools and Families. The Secretary of State refers all cases of misconduct by registered teachers which fall outside this category to the Council. Incompetence cases should be referred directly to the Council where a registered teacher is dismissed for incompetence or leaves in circumstances where dismissal was a possibility. The Council expects that teachers referred on grounds of incompetence will have been the subject of significant and advanced action under formal capability procedures.

Cases are initially screened to determine whether they fall within the Council's jurisdiction. If so, they are referred to an Investigating Committee, which decides whether there is a case to answer. An Investigating Committee may take the Code into account in making this decision. Where an Investigating Committee decides that there is a case to answer, the case is heard by either a Professional Conduct Committee or a Professional Competence Committee. Such committees comprise a majority of Council members and may be supported by an additional member appointed through a public appointments process.

Hearings of the Council take place in accordance with the Human Rights Act 1998 and are normally held in public. Hearing committees comprise a majority of teacher members with lay representation. In conducting the proceedings, the Council aims for an investigative rather than an adversarial approach. Teachers may be represented in the hearing and may appeal against a disciplinary order to the High Court. If a hearing committee finds the alleged facts proved, that the facts amount to unacceptable professional conduct, serious professional incompetence or to be a relevant criminal offence, and that a disciplinary order is appropriate, it may issue one of the following sanctions:

- Reprimand, which remains on the Register for two years;
- Conditional Registration Order, which applies conditions to a teacher's continuing registration;

- Suspension Order, suspending the teacher's registration for up to two years; or
- Prohibition Order, which allows the teacher to apply for the restoration of their eligibility to register within a period of not less than two years or such other period as may be specified, including an unlimited time.

Conditions may also be added to a Suspension Order.

In determining any disciplinary order, a hearing committee will consider each case on its own facts, including the history and character of the teacher and any mitigating circumstances, and may take into account any failure by a registered teacher to comply with this Code of Conduct and Practice.

The Statement of Professional Values and Practice

In 2002, the Council published a Code of Professional Values and Practice. This code sets out the beliefs, values and attitudes which underpin the professionalism of teachers and has been incorporated into the standards for QTS. The Code of Professional Values and Practice has no direct role in relation to the Council's regulatory procedures. From 1 November 2004, the Code of Professional Values and Practice was retitled as a Statement of Professional Values and Practice.

The Council's responsibilities

The Council is concerned with the registration status of teachers, which governs their ability to teach in maintained schools, non-maintained special schools and pupil referral units. The Council is not a direct employer of teachers and is not an appeal body for decisions made under employment procedures.

The Council does not have a role in assisting individual teachers in relation to workplace or employment disputes, which is a matter for trade unions and professional associations. The Council does not inspect the standards of teaching in schools, which is a matter for Ofsted.

Registered teachers already operate within a structure of statutory duties and contractual obligations relating to employment. This Code sits alongside but does not replace these provisions, which should continue to be referred to as appropriate.

The legal background to the Code is explained further (see below).

Code of Conduct and Practice for Registered Teachers

Section 1 Unacceptable professional conduct

Under the Council's Disciplinary Rules of Procedure 'unacceptable professional conduct' is defined as 'conduct which falls short of the standard expected of a registered teacher . . . and is behaviour which involves a breach of the standards of propriety expected of the profession'. Whether a teacher is guilty of unacceptable professional conduct is a matter for a hearing committee to decide in relation to the facts of the given case, taking into account the provisions of this Code as appropriate.

Conduct relating to pupils and partners in education

Registered teachers may be found to be guilty of unacceptable professional conduct
Where they:

1   Seriously demean or undermine pupils, their parents, carers or colleagues, or act towards them in a manner which is discriminatory in relation to gender, marital status, religion, belief, colour, race, ethnicity, class, sexual orientation, disability or age
Where they fail to:
2   Take reasonable care of pupils under their supervision with the aim of ensuring their safety and welfare
3   Comply with relevant statutory provisions which support the well being and development of pupils, including where these require co-operation and collaboration with a range of agencies, as well as teacher colleagues and other adults
4   Observe confidentiality in a manner consistent with legal requirements
5   Comply with the requirements of statutory bodies relating to the examination, assessment and evaluation of pupil achievement and attainment.

Other conduct

Registered teachers may be found to be guilty of unacceptable professional conduct
Where they fail to:

6   Maintain appropriate standards of honesty and integrity in management and administrative duties, including in the use of school property and finance
Where they:
7   Misuse or misrepresent their professional position, qualifications or experience
8   Otherwise bring the reputation and standing of the profession into serious disrepute.

Section 2 Conviction of a relevant offence

The Council may also take disciplinary action where a registered teacher has been convicted of a relevant criminal offence or has accepted a caution in relation to such an offence.

Section 3 Serious professional incompetence

1   Under the Council's Disciplinary Rules of Procedure, registered teachers may be found guilty of 'serious professional incompetence' where they demonstrate 'a level of competence which falls seriously short of that expected of a registered teacher, taking into account the relevant circumstances'.

2   In assessing whether a registered teacher has demonstrated 'serious professional incompetence', hearing committees will take into account the extent to which a registered teacher has failed to maintain a level of professional competence consistent with the standards for Qualified Teacher Status, the Induction Standards and the nature of their professional responsibilities.

3   The determination of serious professional incompetence includes failings relating to management and leadership roles. Where a failure of management and leadership on the part of a head teacher is at issue, a committee may take into account the National Standards for Headship published by the National College for School Leadership (NCSL).

Further information

This section provides further information and exemplification of the provisions of the Code but does not form part of the Code.

Notes on the Introduction

The disciplinary functions of the General Teaching Council (GTC) are prescribed by legislation under the Teaching and Higher Education Act 1998 and the General Teaching Council for England (Disciplinary Functions) Regulations 2001, as amended by the Education Act 2002 and the General Teaching Council for England (Disciplinary Functions) Amendment Regulations 2003.

Section 5 (1) of the 1998 Act and the Regulations made under it make provision for the Council to issue, and from time to time revise, a code laying down standards of professional conduct and practice expected of registered teachers. Under Part II paragraph 7 of the 2001 Regulations, a committee may take into account any failure by a registered teacher to comply with the Code of Practice in any disciplinary proceedings against them.

The Council's Disciplinary Rules of Procedure and other information about the Council's work in professional regulation, including Guidance for Members of Disciplinary Committees and Guidance for Teachers subject to the Council's procedures, are available on the Council's website at www.gtce.org.uk/code The Guidance for Members of Disciplinary Committees includes Indicative Sanctions Guidance which complements the provisions of this Code by providing guidance on the determination of sanction.

Advanced notice of disciplinary hearings, held in central Birmingham, is given on the Council's website. The decisions of Professional Conduct and Professional Competence Committees are published on the Council's website for a three month period following the decision.

Further details of the Council's regulatory work, including statistical data and issues arising from casework, are contained in the Annual Report on Registration and Regulation.

Parents and members of the public wishing to make an allegation of unacceptable professional conduct against a registered teacher may find further information in the Council's publication *Complaining to the GTC – Information for Parents and the Public*, available on the Council's website. However, it should be noted that the Council is not a general complaints body and may not resolve complaints or concerns more appropriate to a school, local authority (LA) or other relevant body.

The standards for qualified teacher status and for induction are published by the Department for Children, Schools and Families. Further information on teachers who are exempt from induction is available in DCSF Guidance Document/0458/2003, 'The Induction Support Programme for Newly Qualified Teachers'. The statutory conditions of employment of school teachers in England are contained in the School Teachers' Pay and Conditions Document.

The national standards for headship are published by the National College for School Leadership (NCSL) at www.ncsl.org.uk

Notes on the Code of Conduct and Practice

In determining unacceptable professional conduct or serious professional incompetence, hearing committees will make decisions in relation to the facts of the case and by taking into account the provisions of the Code. Instances of unacceptable professional conduct and serious professional incompetence have included the following.

Unacceptable professional conduct

Paragraph 1: Demeaning or discriminatory behaviour

- Swearing at pupils and calling them by offensive names
- Making a racist remark to pupils.

Paragraph 2: Reasonable care

- Endangering pupils through instructing them to undertake inappropriate manual handling
- Failing to safeguard the health and safety of pupils by not taking reasonable steps to ensure they remained on school premises
- Intimidating a child with special educational needs.

Paragraph 3: Co-operation and collaboration

- Acting to the detriment of newly qualified and junior teachers
- Deliberately undermining the authority of the head teacher and staff colleagues.

Paragraph 4: Confidentiality

- Sending a letter to parents of children in a class, which

  - was in breach of the school's policy and guidelines with regard to communications with parents and children
  - misrepresented a confidential discussion between the teacher and the head teacher
  - invited an involvement of parents in defence of a refusal to undertake contractual obligations.

Paragraph 5: Examination and assessment arrangements

- Altering, adding to or completing scripts for Sats
- Falsifying coursework and moderating marks submitted for a GCSE examination
- Persistent failure to co-operate with arrangements for furthering the educational progress of pupils with special educational needs, including by the submission of Annual Review documentation
- Providing unauthorised photocopies of forthcoming examination papers to students at a private tutorial college.

Paragraph 6: Standards of honesty and integrity

- Failure to comply with school and LA financial and accounting procedures
- Misrepresenting the true state of school trip funds
- Theft of school property
- Submission of false mileage expenses
- Using school administrative staff and facilities for private interests
- Using school equipment to view pornography.

Paragraph 7: Professional position

- False claims to possess qualifications
- Falsifying a reference for a teaching post
- Misrepresenting the pattern of past employment on a teaching application form.

Paragraph 8: Bringing the profession into serious disrepute

Conduct in this category would include behaviour which was seriously detrimental to the standing of the profession but where no criminal offence was committed.

Conviction of a relevant offence

All criminal behaviour is a serious matter and under the provisions of Home Office Circular 45/86, teaching is a notifiable occupation. This means that the police report any conviction or caution by a teacher to the Department for Children, Schools and Families. All convictions and cautions which do not raise concerns relating to the safety and welfare of children are passed to the GTC. The role of the Council is to determine whether any given caution or criminal offence is relevant to a teacher's registration. Minor offences are considered under a preliminary procedure to determine whether there is a case for further investigation.

All criminal offending should be avoided. However, isolated Road Traffic Offences would not normally be considered as behaviour incompatible with being a registered teacher. In all cases the Council considers whether there is a trend of re-offending which may merit further action.

Criminal offences which have been determined as relevant include:

- Benefit fraud
- Indecent assault
- Inflicting grievous bodily harm
- Manslaughter
- Possession of prohibited firearms and ammunition
- Threatening or disorderly behaviour
- Unlawful wounding.

Serious professional incompetence

Serious professional incompetence has been found where there is a serious and persistent pattern of failure in terms of:

- Subject knowledge

- The ability to establish learning objectives and set appropriate activities
- The ability to operate effective assessment procedures and to mark student work
- The ability to manage pupil behaviour and thereby to ensure the safety and welfare of pupils
- The ability to follow policies and procedures and to work effectively with teacher colleagues
- The ability to adequately lead and manage a curriculum area.

Appendix 3

The Statement of Professional Values and Practice for Teachers

Reproduced here with the permission of the General Teaching Council for England (see www.gtce.org.uk).

In February 2002, the General Teaching Council for England agreed a Statement of Professional Values for Teachers *to articulate the beliefs, values and attitudes that make up teacher professionalism.*

The GTCE Statement underpins the Council's advisory and regulatory work. This version was agreed by Council in March 2006 in the light of changes to policy, legislation and the Professional Standards Framework. The Statement is kept under review to ensure it continues fully to reflect society's expectations of and aspirations for teachers, teachers' own values and aspirations, and the context in which teachers work.

The high standards of the teaching profession

First and foremost, teachers are skilled practitioners.

They have insight into the learning needs of children and young people. They use professional judgment to meet these needs and to choose the best ways of motivating pupils to achieve success. They use assessment to inform and guide their work. They are highly skilled at dealing with the rigours and realities of teaching.

Teachers inspire and lead children and young people to learn, in and beyond the classroom. They enable them to get the most out of life and develop the knowledge, skills and attributes for adulthood – so that they can achieve their potential as fulfilled individuals and make a positive contribution to society – while staying safe and healthy.

Teaching is a vital, unique and far-reaching role requiring high levels of individual knowledge, skill and judgment, commitment, energy and enthusiasm. It is one of the most demanding and rewarding of professions.

Teachers work within a framework of legislation, statutory guidance and school policies, with different lines of accountability. Within this framework they place particular importance on promoting equality of opportunity – challenging stereotypes, opposing prejudice, and respecting individuals regardless of age, gender, disability, colour, race, ethnicity, class, religion, marital status or sexual orientation.

Teachers recognise the value and place of the school in the community and the importance of their own professional status. They understand that this requires judgment about appropriate standards of personal behaviour.

The professionalism of teachers in practice

Children and young people

Teachers place the learning and well-being of young people at the centre of their professional practice.

They use their expertise to create safe, secure and stimulating learning environments that take account of individual learning needs, encourage young people to engage actively in their own learning, and build their self-esteem. They have high expectations for all young people, are committed to addressing underachievement, and work to help young people progress regardless of their background and personal circumstances.

Teachers treat young people fairly and with respect, take their knowledge, views, opinions and feelings seriously, and value diversity and individuality. They model the characteristics they are trying to inspire in young people, including enthusiasm for learning, a spirit of intellectual enquiry, honesty, tolerance, social responsibility, patience, and a genuine concern for other people.

Parents and carers

Teachers respond sensitively to the differences in the home backgrounds and circumstances of young people, recognising the key role that parents and carers play in children's education.

They seek to work in partnership with parents and carers, respecting their views and promoting understanding and co-operation to support the young person's learning and well-being in and out of school.

Professional colleagues

Teachers see themselves as part of a team, in which fellow teachers, other professional colleagues and governors are partners in securing the learning and well-being of young people.

They recognise the importance of effective multi-agency working, are clear and confident about their own role and professional standards, and understand and respect the roles and standards of other colleagues. They are keen to learn from others' effective practice and always ready to share their own knowledge and expertise. They respect young people's and colleagues' confidentiality wherever appropriate.

Learning and development

Teachers entering the teaching profession in England have met a common professional standard.

Initial education has prepared them to be effective teachers, and they take responsibility for their continuing professional development.

They reflect on their own practice, develop their skills, knowledge and expertise, and adapt their teaching appropriately to take account of evidence about effective practice and new technology; they understand that all of these are vital if young people are to receive the best and most relevant education.

Teachers make use of opportunities to take part in mentoring and coaching, to evaluate and adapt their own and institutional practice, and to learn with and from colleagues in the wider children's and school workforce.

Professional Standards for Teachers: Qualified Teacher Status

Reproduced here with the permission of the Training and Development Agency for Schools (see www.tda.gov.uk).

Those recommended for the award of QTS should meet the following standards.

Professional attributes

Those recommended for the award of QTS should:

Relationships with children and young people

Q1 Have high expectations of children and young people including a commitment to ensuring that they can achieve their full educational potential and to establishing fair, respectful, trusting, supportive and constructive relationships with them.

Q2 Demonstrate the positive values, attitudes and behaviour they expect from children and young people.

Frameworks

Q3 (a) Be aware of the professional duties of teachers and the statutory framework within which they work.

    (b) Be aware of the policies and practices of the workplace and share in collective responsibility for their implementation.

Communicating and working with others

Q4 Communicate effectively with children, young people, colleagues, parents and carers.

Q5 Recognise and respect the contribution that colleagues, parents and carers can make to the development and well-being of children and young people, and to raising their levels of attainment.

Q6   Have a commitment to collaboration and co-operative working.

Personal professional development

Q7   (a) Reflect on and improve their practice, and take responsibility for identifying and meeting their developing professional needs.
     (b) Identify priorities for their early professional development in the context of induction.
Q8   Have a creative and constructively critical approach towards innovation, being prepared to adapt their practice where benefits and improvements are identified.
Q9   Act upon advice and feedback and be open to coaching and mentoring.

Professional knowledge and understanding

Those recommended for the award of QTS should:

Teaching and learning

Q10 Have a knowledge and understanding of a range of teaching, learning and behaviour management strategies and know how to use and adapt them, including how to personalise learning and provide opportunities for all learners to achieve their potential.

Assessment and monitoring

Q11 Know the assessment requirements and arrangements for the subjects/ curriculum areas they are trained to teach, including those relating to public examinations and qualifications.
Q12 Know a range of approaches to assessment, including the importance of formative assessment.
Q13 Know how to use local and national statistical information to evaluate the effectiveness of their teaching, to monitor the progress of those they teach and to raise levels of attainment.

Subjects and curriculum

Q14 Have a secure knowledge and understanding of their subjects/curriculum areas and related pedagogy to enable them to teach effectively across the age and ability range for which they are trained.
Q15 Know and understand the relevant statutory and non-statutory curricula and frameworks, including those provided through the National Strategies, for their subjects/curriculum areas, and other relevant initiatives applicable to the age and ability range for which they are trained.

Literacy, numeracy and ICT

Q16 Have passed the professional skills tests in numeracy, literacy and information and communications technology (ICT).

Q17 Know how to use skills in literacy, numeracy and ICT to support their teaching and wider professional activities.

Achievement and diversity

Q18 Understand how children and young people develop and that the progress and well-being of learners are affected by a range of developmental, social, religious, ethnic, cultural and linguistic influences.

Q19 Know how to make effective personalised provision for those they teach, including those for whom English is an additional language or who have special educational needs or disabilities, and how to take practical account of diversity and promote equality and inclusion in their teaching.

Q20 Know and understand the roles of colleagues with specific responsibilities, including those with responsibility for learners with special educational needs and disabilities and other individual learning needs.

Health and well-being

Q21 (a) Be aware of the current legal requirements, national policies and guidance on the safeguarding and promotion of the well-being of children and young people.

(b) Know how to identify and support children and young people whose progress, development or well-being is affected by changes or difficulties in their personal circumstances, and when to refer them to colleagues for specialist support.

Professional skills

Those recommended for the award of QTS should:

Planning

Q22 Plan for progression across the age and ability range for which they are trained, designing effective learning sequences within lessons and across series of lessons and demonstrating secure subject/curriculum knowledge.

Q23 Design opportunities for learners to develop their literacy, numeracy and ICT skills.

Q24 Plan homework or other out-of-class work to sustain learners' progress and to extend and consolidate their learning.

Teaching

Q25 Teach lessons and sequences of lessons across the age and ability range for which they are trained in which they:

(a) use a range of teaching strategies and resources, including e-learning, taking practical account of diversity and promoting equality and inclusion
(b) build on prior knowledge, develop concepts and processes, enable learners to apply new knowledge, understanding and skills and meet learning objectives
(c) adapt their language to suit the learners they teach, introducing new ideas and concepts clearly, and using explanations, questions, discussions and plenaries effectively
(d) demonstrate the ability to manage the learning of individuals, groups and whole classes, modifying their teaching to suit the stage of the lesson.

Assessing, monitoring and giving feedback

Q26 (a) Make effective use of a range of assessment, monitoring and recording strategies.
(b) Assess the learning needs of those they teach in order to set challenging learning objectives.
Q27 Provide timely, accurate and constructive feedback on learners' attainment, progress and areas for development.
Q28 Support and guide learners to reflect on their learning, identify the progress they have made and identify their emerging learning needs.

Reviewing teaching and learning

Q29 Evaluate the impact of their teaching on the progress of all learners, and modify their planning and classroom practice where necessary.

Learning environment

Q30 Establish a purposeful and safe learning environment conducive to learning and identify opportunities for learners to learn in out-of-school contexts.
Q31 Establish a clear framework for classroom discipline to manage learners' behaviour constructively and promote their self-control and independence.

Team working and collaboration

Q32 Work as a team member and identify opportunities for working with colleagues, sharing the development of effective practice with them.

Q33 Ensure that colleagues working with them are appropriately involved in supporting learning and understand the roles they are expected to fulfil.

ABOUT TDA GUIDANCE FOR NQTs

As you work through your induction period, you will need to show that not only are you continuing to meet the Standards for Qualified Teacher Status but also that you are meeting the Core Standards for teachers. The Training and Development Agency for Schools has created guidance for NQTs called *Supporting the Induction Process: TDA guidance for newly qualified teachers*, which offers extensive information on the scope of each standard and examples and aspects of practice covered by the standards. You can download this guidance free of charge from the TDA website: http://www.tda.gov.uk/upload/resources/pdf/c/core_standards_guidance.pdf

You can also download the *Standards for QTS* and the *Core Standards* from the TDA website (see www.tda.gov.uk).

Professional standards for teachers: core

Reproduced here with the permission of the Training and Development Agency for Schools: (see www.tda.gov.uk).

Teachers should meet the following core standards at the end of the induction period and continue to meet them throughout their teaching career.

Professional attributes

All teachers should:

Relationships with children and young people

C1   Have high expectations of children and young people including a commitment to ensuring that they can achieve their full educational potential and to establishing fair, respectful, trusting, supportive and constructive relationships with them.

C2   Hold positive values and attitudes and adopt high standards of behaviour in their professional role.

Frameworks

C3   Maintain an up-to-date knowledge and understanding of the professional duties of teachers and the statutory framework within which they work, and contribute to the development, implementation and evaluation of the policies and practice of their workplace, including those designed to promote equality of opportunity.

Communicating and working with others

C4   (a) Communicate effectively with children, young people and colleagues.

(b) Communicate effectively with parents and carers, conveying timely and relevant information about attainment, objectives, progress and well-being.

(c) Recognise that communication is a two-way process and encourage parents and carers to participate in discussions about the progress, development and well-being of children and young people.

C5 Recognise and respect the contributions that colleagues, parents and carers can make to the development and well-being of children and young people, and to raising their levels of attainment.

C6 Have a commitment to collaboration and co-operative working where appropriate.

Personal professional development

C7 Evaluate their performance and be committed to improving their practice through appropriate professional development.

C8 Have a creative and constructively critical approach towards innovation; being prepared to adapt their practice where benefits and improvements are identified.

C9 Act upon advice and feedback and be open to coaching and mentoring.

Professional knowledge and understanding

All teachers should:

Teaching and learning

C10 Have a good, up-to-date working knowledge and understanding of a range of teaching, learning and behaviour management strategies and know how to use and adapt them, including how to personalise learning to provide opportunities for all learners to achieve their potential.

Assessment and monitoring

C11 Know the assessment requirements and arrangements for the subjects/curriculum areas they teach, including those relating to public examinations and qualifications.

C12 Know a range of approaches to assessment, including the importance of formative assessment.

C13 Know how to use local and national statistical information to evaluate the effectiveness of their teaching, to monitor the progress of those they teach and to raise levels of attainment.

C14 Know how to use reports and other sources of external information related to assessment in order to provide learners with accurate and constructive feedback on their strengths, weaknesses, attainment, progress and areas for development, including action plans for improvement.

Subjects and curriculum

C15   Have a secure knowledge and understanding of their subjects/curriculum areas and related pedagogy including: the contribution that their subjects/curriculum areas can make to cross-curricular learning; and recent relevant developments.

C16   Know and understand the relevant statutory and non-statutory curricula and frameworks, including those provided through the National Strategies, for their subjects/curriculum areas and other relevant initiatives across the age and ability range they teach.

Literacy, numeracy and ICT

C17   Know how to use skills in literacy, numeracy and ICT to support their teaching and wider professional activities.

Achievement and diversity

C18   Understand how children and young people develop and how the progress, rate of development and well-being of learners are affected by a range of developmental, social, religious, ethnic, cultural and linguistic influences.

C19   Know how to make effective personalised provision for those they teach, including those for whom English is an additional language or who have special educational needs or disabilities, and how to take practical account of diversity and promote equality and inclusion in their teaching.

C20   Understand the roles of colleagues such as those having specific responsibilities for learners with special educational needs, disabilities and other individual learning needs, and the contributions they can make to the learning, development and well-being of children and young people.

C21   Know when to draw on the expertise of colleagues, such as those with responsibility for the safeguarding of children and young people and special educational needs and disabilities, and to refer to sources of information, advice and support from external agencies.

Health and well-being

C22   Know the current legal requirements, national policies and guidance on the safeguarding and promotion of the well-being of children and young people.

C23 Know the local arrangements concerning the safeguarding of children and young people.

C24 Know how to identify potential child abuse or neglect and follow safeguarding procedures.

C25 Know how to identify and support children and young people whose progress, development or well-being is affected by changes or difficulties in their personal circumstances, and when to refer them to colleagues for specialist support.

Professional skills

All teachers should:

Planning

C26 Plan for progression across the age and ability range they teach, designing effective learning sequences within lessons and across series of lessons informed by secure subject/curriculum knowledge.

C27 Design opportunities for learners to develop their literacy, numeracy, ICT and thinking and learning skills appropriate within their phase and context.

C28 Plan, set and assess homework, other out-of-class assignments and coursework for examinations, where appropriate, to sustain learners' progress and to extend and consolidate their learning.

Teaching

C29 Teach challenging, well-organised lessons and sequences of lessons across the age and ability range they teach in which they:

(a) use an appropriate range of teaching strategies and resources, including e-learning, which meet learners' needs and take practical account of diversity and promote equality and inclusion

(b) build on the prior knowledge and attainment of those they teach in order that learners meet learning objectives and make sustained progress

(c) develop concepts and processes which enable learners to apply new knowledge, understanding and skills

(d) adapt their language to suit the learners they teach, introducing new ideas and concepts clearly, and using explanations, questions, discussions and plenaries effectively

(e) manage the learning of individuals, groups and whole classes effectively, modifying their teaching appropriately to suit the stage of the lesson and the needs of the learners.

C30   Teach engaging and motivating lessons informed by well-grounded expectations of learners and designed to raise levels of attainment.

Assessing, monitoring and giving feedback

C31   Make effective use of an appropriate range of observation, assessment, monitoring and recording strategies as a basis for setting challenging learning objectives and monitoring learners' progress and levels of attainment.

C32   Provide learners, colleagues, parents and carers with timely, accurate and constructive feedback on learners' attainment, progress and areas for development.

C33   Support and guide learners so that they can reflect on their learning, identify the progress they have made, set positive targets for improvement and become successful independent learners.

C34   Use assessment as part of their teaching to diagnose learners' needs, set realistic and challenging targets for improvement and plan future teaching.

Reviewing teaching and learning

C35   Review the effectiveness of their teaching and its impact on learners' progress, attainment and well-being, refining their approaches where necessary.

C36   Review the impact of the feedback provided to learners and guide learners on how to improve their attainment.

Learning environment

C37   (a) Establish a purposeful and safe learning environment which complies with current legal requirements, national policies and guidance on the safeguarding and well-being of children and young people so that learners feel secure and sufficiently confident to make an active contribution to learning and to the school.

    (b) Make use of the local arrangements concerning the safeguarding of children and young people.

    (c) Identify and use opportunities to personalise and extend learning through out-of-school contexts where possible making links between in-school learning and learning in out-of-school contexts.

C38   (a) Manage learners' behaviour constructively by establishing and maintaining a clear and positive framework for discipline, in line with the school's behaviour policy.

    (b) Use a range of behaviour management techniques and strategies, adapting them as necessary to promote the self-control and independence of learners.

C39 Promote learners' self-control, independence and cooperation through developing their social, emotional and behavioural skills.

Team working and collaboration

C40 Work as a team member and identify opportunities for working with colleagues, managing their work where appropriate and sharing the development of effective practice with them.

C41 Ensure that colleagues working with them are appropriately involved in supporting learning and understand the roles they are expected to fulfil.

Local authorities in England

Barking and Dagenham
www.barking-dagenham.gov.uk

Barnet
www.barnet.gov.uk

Barnsley
www.barnsley.gov.uk

Bath and North East Somerset
www.bathnes.gov.uk

Bedfordshire
www.bedfordshire.gov.uk

Bexley
www.bexley.gov.uk

Birmingham
www.birmingham.gov.uk

Blackburn with Darwen
www.blackburn.gov.uk

Blackpool
www.blackpool.gov.uk

Bolton
www.bolton.gov.uk

Bournemouth
www.bournemouth.gov.uk

Bracknell Forest
www.bracknell-forest.gov.uk

Bradford
www.bradford.gov.uk

Brent
www.brent.gov.uk

Brighton and Hove
www.brighton-hove.gov.uk

Bristol, City of
www.bristol-city.gov.uk

Bromley
www.bromley.gov.uk

Buckinghamshire
www.buckscc.gov.uk

Bury
www.bury.gov.uk

Calderdale
www.calderdale.gov.uk

Cambridgeshire
www.camcnty.gov.uk

Camden
www.camden.gov.uk

Cheshire
www.cheshire.gov.uk

City of London
www.cityoflondon.gov.uk

Cornwall
www.cornwall.gov.uk

Coventry
www.coventry.gov.uk

Croydon
www.croydon.gov.uk

Cumbria
www.cumbria.gov.uk

Darlington
www.darlington.gov.uk

Derby, City of
www.derby.gov.uk

Derbyshire
www.derbyshire.gov.uk

Devon
www.devon.gov.uk

Doncaster
www.doncaster.gov.uk

Dorset
www.dorset-cc.gov.uk

Dudley
www.dudley.gov.uk

Durham
www.durham.gov.uk

Ealing
www.ealing.gov.uk

East Riding of Yorkshire
www.eastriding.gov.uk

East Sussex
www.eastsussexcc.gov.uk

Enfield
www.enfield.gov.uk

Essex
www.essexcc.gov.uk

Gateshead
www.gateshead.gov.uk

Gloucestershire
www.gloscc.gov.uk

Greenwich
www.greenwich.gov.uk

Hackney
www.hackney.gov.uk

Halton
www.halton.gov.uk

Hammersmith and Fulham
www.lbhf.gov.uk

Hampshire
www.hants.gov.uk

Haringey
www.haringey.gov.uk

Harrow
www.harrow.gov.uk

Hartlepool
www.hartlepool.gov.uk

Havering
www.havering.gov.uk

Herefordshire
www.herefordshire.gov.uk

Hertfordshire
www.hertscc.gov.uk

Hillingdon
www.hillingdon.gov.uk

Hounslow
www.hounslow.gov.uk

Isle of Wight
www.iwight.gov.uk

Isles of Scilly
www.scilly.gov.uk

Islington
www.islington.gov.uk

Kensington and Chelsea
www.rbkc.gov.uk

Kent
www.kent.gov.uk

Kingston-upon-Hull, City of
www.hullcc.gov.uk

Kingston upon Thames
www.kingston.gov.uk

Kirklees
www.kirklees.gov.uk

Knowsley
www.knowsley.gov.uk

Lambeth
www.lambeth.gov.uk

Lancashire
www.lancashire.gov.uk

Leeds
www.leeds.gov.uk

Leicester City
www.leicester.gov.uk/city/

Leicestershire
www.leics.gov.uk

Lewisham
www.lewisham.gov.uk

Lincolnshire
www.lincolnshire.gov.uk

Liverpool
www.liverpool.gov.uk

Luton
www.luton.gov.uk

Manchester
www.manchester.gov.uk

Medway
www.medway.gov.uk

Merton
www.merton.gov.uk

Middlesbrough
www.middlesbrough.gov.uk

Milton Keynes
www.mkweb.co.uk

Newcastle upon Tyne
www.newcastle.gov.uk

Newham
www.newham.gov.uk

Norfolk
www.norfolk.gov.uk

North East Lincolnshire
www.nelincs.gov.uk

North Lincolnshire
www.northlincs.gov.uk

North Somerset
www.n-somerset.gov.uk

North Tyneside
www.northtyneside.gov.uk

North Yorkshire
www.northyorks.gov.uk

Northamptonshire
www.northamptonshire.gov.uk

Northumberland
www.northumberland.gov.uk

Nottingham, City of
www.nottinghamcity.gov.uk

Nottinghamshire
www.nottscc.gov.uk

Oldham
www.oldham.gov.uk

Oxfordshire
www.oxfordshire.gov.uk

Peterborough, City of
www.peterborough.gov.uk

Plymouth, City of
www.plymouth.gov.uk

Poole
www.poole.gov.uk

Portsmouth
www.portsmouthcc.gov.uk

Reading
www.reading.gov.uk

Redbridge
www.redbridge.gov.uk

Redcar and Cleveland
www.redcar-cleveland.gov.uk

Richmond upon Thames
www.richmond.gov.uk

Rochdale
www.rochdale.gov.uk

Rotherham
www.rotherham.gov.uk

Rutland
www.rutnet.co.uk

Salford
www.salford.gov.uk

Sandwell
www.sandwell.gov.uk

Sefton
www.sefton.gov.uk

Sheffield
www.sheffield.gov.uk

Shropshire
www.shropshire-cc.gov.uk

Slough
www.slough.gov.uk

Solihull
www.solihull.gov.uk

Somerset
www.somerset.gov.uk

South Gloucestershire
www.southglos.gov.uk

South Tyneside
www.s-tyneside-mbc.gov.uk

Southampton
www.southampton.gov.uk

Southend-on-Sea
www.southend.gov.uk

Southwark
www.southwark.gov.uk

St Helens
www.sthelens.gov.uk

Staffordshire
www.staffordshire.gov.uk

Stockport
www.stockportmbc.gov.uk

Stockton-on-Tees
www.stockton-bc.gov.uk

Stoke-on-Trent
www.stoke.gov.uk

Suffolk
www.suffolkcc.gov.uk

Sunderland
www.sunderland.gov.uk

Surrey
www.surreycc.gov.uk

Sutton
www.sutton.gov.uk

Swindon
www.swindon.gov.uk

Tameside
www.tameside.gov.uk

Telford and Wrekin
www.telford.gov.uk

Thurrock
www.thurrock.gov.uk

Torbay
www.torbay.gov.uk

Tower Hamlets
www.towerhamlets.gov.uk

Trafford
www.trafford.gov.uk

Wakefield
www.wakefield.gov.uk

Walsall
www.walsall.gov.uk

Waltham Forest
www.lbwf.gov.uk

Wandsworth
www.wandsworth.gov.uk

Warrington
www.warrington.gov.uk

Warwickshire
www.warwickshire.gov.uk

West Berkshire
www.westberks.gov.uk

West Sussex
www.westsussex.gov.uk

Westminster
www.westminster.gov.uk

Wigan
www.wiganmbc.gov.uk

Wiltshire
www.wiltshire.gov.uk

Windsor and Maidenhead, Royal Borough of
www.rbwm.gov.uk

Wirral
www.wirral.gov.uk

Wokingham
www.wokingham.gov.uk

Wolverhampton
www.wolverhampton.gov.uk

Worcestershire
www.worcestershire.gov.uk

York, City of
www.york.gov.uk

Local authorities in Wales

Blaenau Gwent County Borough Council
www.blaenau-gwent.gov.uk

Bridgend County Borough Council
www.bridgend.gov.uk

Caerphilly County Borough Council
www.caerphilly.gov.uk

Cardiff County Council
www.cardiff.gov.uk

Carmarthenshire County Council
www.carmarthenshire.gov.uk

Ceredigion County Council
www.ceredigion.gov.uk

Conwy County Borough Council
www.conwy.gov.uk

Denbighshire County Council
www.denbighshire.gov.uk

Flintshire County Council
www.flintshire.gov.uk

Gwynedd Council
www.gwynedd.gov.uk

Isle of Anglesey County Council
www.anglesey.gov.uk

Merthyr Tydfil County Borough Council
www.merthyr.gov.uk

Monmouthshire County Council
www.monmouthshire.gov.uk

Neath Port Talbot County Borough Council
www.neath-porttalbot.gov.uk

Newport County Borough Council
www.newport.gov.uk

Pembrokeshire County Council
www.pembrokeshire.gov.uk

Powys County Council
www.powys.gov.uk

Rhondda-Cynon-Taff County Borough Council
www.rhondda-cynon-taff.gov.uk

Swansea, City and County of
www.swansea.gov.uk

Torfaen County Borough Council
www.torfaen.gov.uk

Vale of Glamorgan Council
www.valeofglamorgan.gov.uk

Wrexham County Borough Council
www.wrexham.gov.uk

Education authorities in Scotland

Aberdeen City Council
www.aberdeencity.gov.uk

Aberdeenshire Council
www.aberdeenshire.gov.uk

Angus Council
www.angus.gov.uk

Argyll and Bute Council
www.argyll-bute.gov.uk

Clackmannanshire Council
www.clacks.gov.uk

Dumfries and Galloway Council
www.dumgal.gov.uk

Dundee City Council
www.dundeecity.gov.uk

East Ayrshire Council
www.east-ayrshire.gov.uk

East Dunbartonshire Council
www.eastdunbarton.gov.uk

East Lothian Council
www.eastlothian.gov.uk

East Renfrewshire Council
www.eastrenfrewshire.gov.uk

Edinburgh, City of
www.edinburgh.gov.uk

Falkirk Council
www.falkirk.gov.uk

Fife Council
www.fife.gov.uk

Glasgow City Council
www.glasgow.gov.uk

Highland Council
www.highland.gov.uk

Inverclyde Council
www.inverclyde.gov.uk

Midlothian Council
www.midlothian.gov.uk

Moray Council
www.moray.gov.uk

North Ayrshire Council
www.north-ayrshire.gov.uk

North Lanarkshire Council
www.northlan.gov.uk

Orkney Islands Council
www.orkney.gov.uk

Perth and Kinross Council
www.pkc.gov.uk

Renfrewshire Council
www.renfrewshire.gov.uk

Scottish Borders Council
www.scotborders.gov.uk

Shetland Islands Council
www.shetland.gov.uk

South Ayrshire Council
www.south-ayrshire.gov.uk

South Lanarkshire Council
www.southlanarkshire.gov.uk

Stirling Council
www.stirling.gov.uk

West Dunbartonshire Council
www.west-dunbarton.gov.uk

West Lothian Council
www.westlothian.gov.uk

Western Isles Council
www.w-isles.gov.uk

Education and library boards in Northern Ireland

Belfast Education and Library Board
www.belb.org.uk

North Eastern Education and Library Board
www.nelb.org.uk

South Eastern Education and Library Board
www.seelb.org.uk

Southern Education and Library Board
www.selb.org

Western Education and Library Board
www.welbni.org

Council for Catholic Maintained Schools
www.onlineccms.com

Acronym buster

ACE	Arts Council of England
ACW	Arts Council of Wales
ADD	Attention Deficit Disorder
ADHD	Attention Deficit Hyperactivity Disorder
AfL	Assessment for Learning
AST	Advanced Skills Teacher
BSP	Behaviour Support Plan
CAA	Computer-Assisted Assessment
CAL	Computer-Assisted Learning
CATs	Cognitive Ability Tests
CEG	Careers Education and Guidance
CEDP	Career Entry and Development Profile
CPD	Continuing Professional Development
CTC	City Technology Colleges
D&T	Design and Technology
DCELLS	Department for Children, Education, Lifelong Learning and Skills (Wales)
DCSF	Department for Children, Schools and Families (formerly known as the Department for Education and Skills)
DELNI	Department for Employment and Learning Northern Ireland
DIUS	Department for Innovation Universities and Skills
EA	External Assessor
EAL	English as an Additional Language
EAZ	Education Action Zone
ECM	Every Child Matters
EDP	Educational Development Plan
EFL	English as a Foreign Language
EHRC	Equality and Human Rights Commission
EiC	Excellence in Cities
EMTAG	Ethnic Minority and Traveller Achievement Grant
ESL	English as a Second Language
ESO	Education Supervision Order

ESOL	English as a Second or Other Language
Estyn	Her Majesty's Inspectorate for Education and Training in Wales
ESW	Education Social Worker
EY	Early Years
EYFS	Early Years Foundation Stage
FEI	Further Education Institution
FHE	Further and Higher Education
FSM	Free School Meals
FTE	Full-Time Equivalent
GEST	Grants for Education, Support and Training (from the National Assembly for Wales)
GRTP	Graduate and Registered Teacher Programmes
GTCE	General Teaching Council for England
GTCNI	General Teaching Council for Northern Ireland
GTCS	General Teaching Council for Scotland
GTCW	General Teaching Council for Wales
HEI	Higher Education Institution
HI	Hearing Impaired
HLTA	Higher Level Teaching Assistant
HMI	Her Majesty's Inspectors
HoD	Head of Department
HoS	Head of School
HoY	Head of Year
HSE	Health and Safety Executive
IAP	Individual Action Plan
ICT	Information and Communications Technology
IEP	Individual Education Plan
IiP	Investors in People
IiYP	Investors in Young People
INSET	In-Service Education and Training
ITE	Initial Teacher Education
ITT	Initial Teacher Training
JMI	Junior, Middle and Infant
KS	Key Stage
LA	Local Authority
LPSH	Leadership Programme for Serving Headteachers
LSU	Learning Support Unit
MFL	Modern Foreign Language
MFT	Management Faculty Team
MLD	Moderate Learning Difficulties
NC	National Curriculum
NFER	National Foundation for Educational Research
NGfL	National Grid for Learning

NHDP	National Headship Development Programme
NLS	National Literacy Strategy
NNP	National Numeracy Project
NNS	National Numeracy Strategy
NOF	New Opportunities Fund
NoR	Number on Roll
NPQH	National Professional Qualification for Headship
NQT	Newly Qualified Teacher
NTA	Non-Teaching Assistant
OFSTED	Office for Standards in Education, Children's Services and Skills
OTT	Overseas-Trained Teacher
PANDA	Performance and Assessment Report
PHIP	Professional Headship Induction Programme
PI	Performance Indicators
PM	Performance Management
PMLD	Profound and Multiple Learning Difficulties
PoS	Programme of Study
PRP	Performance-Related Pay
PRU	Pupil Referral Unit
PSE	Personal and Social Education
PSHCE	Personal, Social, Health and Citizenship Education
PSHE	Personal, Social and Health Education
PSLD	Physical and Severe Learning Difficulties
PSP	Pastoral Support Programme
PT	Part Time
PTR	Pupil Teacher Ratio
QCA	Qualifications and Curriculum Authority
QTS	Qualified Teacher Status
SAC	Scottish Arts Council
SACRE	Standing Advisory Council for Religious Education
SAO	School Attendance Order
SCD	Severe Communication Difficulties
SDP	School Development Plan
SEBD	Social, Emotional and Behavioural Difficulties
SEN	Special Educational Needs
SENCO	Special Educational Needs Coordinator
SLD	Severe Learning Difficulties
SLT	Senior Leadership Team
SMT	Senior Management Team
SNA	Special Needs Assistant
SOC	School Organization Committee
SRE	Sex and Relationships Education
SSE	School Self-Evaluation

STA	Specialist Teacher Assistants
STRB	School Teachers Review Body
TA	Teaching Assistant
TDA	Training and Development Agency for Schools
TUC	Trades Union Congress
UK NARIC	National Academic Recognition Information Centre for the United Kingdom
VA	Voluntary-Aided
VC	Voluntary-Controlled
VI	Visually Impaired
VLE	Virtual Learning Environment

Further reading

There are numerous books on the market that seek to support teachers in their work that you may be interested in. A browse through a good bookshop or the websites listed in this book will undoubtedly open up more possibilities, but these books are included here as good starting points to trigger your own thoughts and lines of enquiry. Don't forget, too, that your union will have several relevant publications that it would be useful to request, and the Teacher Support Network website also carries an extensive library of articles and fact sheets for teachers.

Other books published by Routledge

Holmes, E (2005) *Teacher Well-Being: Looking after yourself and your career in the classroom*

Holmes, E (2006) *FAQs for NQTs: Practical advice and working solutions for newly qualified teachers*

Holmes, E (2007) *FAQs for TAs: Practical advice and working solutions for teaching assistants*

Holmes, E (2009) *FAQs on School Inspection: Practical advice and working solutions*

Personal issues

Stress management

Grant Viagas, B (2001) *Stress: Restoring balance to our lives*, The Women's Press, London

Hare, B (1996) *Be Assertive*, Vermilion, London

Hindle, T (1998) *Manage your Time*, Dorling Kindersley, London

Lindenfield, G and Vandenburg, M (2000) *Positive Under Pressure*, Thorsons, London

Olivier, S (2002) *500 of the Most Important Stress-Busting Tips You'll Ever Need*, Cico Books, London

Peiffer, V (1997) *Principles of Stress Management*, Thorsons, London
Rechtschaffen, S (1997) *Time Shifting*, Doubleday Books, London
Wilson, P (1998) *Calm at Work*, Penguin, London

Well-being

Alexander, J (2000) *The Energy Secret*, Thorsons, London
Baker, P (2002) *Real Health for Men*, Vega, London
Chaitow, L (1998) *Natural Alternatives to Antibiotics*, Thorsons, London
Goleman, D (1996) *The Meditative Mind*, Thorsons, London
Golten, R (1999) *The Owners Guide to the Body*, Thorsons, London
Grant Viagas, B (2001) *Sleep: A natural guide*, The Women's Press, London
Mindell, E (1999) *Earl Mindell's Vitamin Bible for the 21st Century*, Warner
    Books, London

Workplace bullying

A browse of www.Amazon.co.uk will offer a wide selection of books on this
issue. Here are some of the classics:

Adams, A (1992) *Bullying at Work: How to confront and overcome it*, Virago,
    London
Field, T (1996) *Bully in Sight*, Success Unlimited, Didcot
Graves, D (2002) *Fighting Back: How to fight bullying in the workplace*,
    McGraw-Hill Professional, London

Teaching issues

Multiple intelligences

Buzan, T (2001) *The Power of Spiritual Intelligence*, Thorsons, London
Gardner, H (1993) *Frames of Mind*, Basic Books, New York
Gardner, H (2000) *Intelligence Reframed: Multiple intelligences for the 21st century*,
    Basic Books, New York
Goleman, D (1996) *Emotional Intelligence*, Bloomsbury, London
Goleman, D (1998) *Working with Emotional Intelligence*, Bloomsbury, London
Hannaford, C (1995) *Smart Moves: Why learning is not all in your head*, Great
    Ocean Publishers, Arlington, VA
Silver, H F, Strong, R W and Perini, M J (2000) *So Each May Learn: Integrating learning styles and multiple intelligence*, Association for Supervision and
    Curriculum Development, Virginia

Creativity

Buzan, T (2001) *The Power of Creative Intelligence*, Thorsons, London
Csikszentmihalyi, M (1997) *Creativity: Flow and the psychology of discovery and invention,* Harper Perennial, New York
Csikszentmihalyi, M (2002) *Flow: The classic work on how to achieve happiness*, Rider, London
Cropley, A (2001) *Creativity in Education and Learning*, Kogan Page, London
Epstein, R (2000) *The Big Book of Creativity Games*, McGraw-Hill, New York
Petty, G (1997) *How to be Better at Creativity*, Kogan Page, London

Behaviour management

Derrington, C and Goddard, H (2007) *'Whole-Brain' Behaviour Management in the Classroom: Every piece of the puzzle*, Routledge, London
Faupel, A, Herrick, E and Sharp, P (1998) *Anger Management*, David Fulton, London
Hook, P and Vass, A (2000) *Confident Classroom Leadership*, David Fulton, London

Teaching and schools

Bentley, T (1998) *Learning Beyond the Classroom*, RoutledgeFalmer, London
Craft, A *et al* (2001) *Creativity in Education*, Continuum, London
Fisher, R (1995) *Teaching Children to Think*, Stanley Thornes, Cheltenham
Fontana, D and Slack, I (2002) *Teaching Meditation to Children*, Thorsons, London
Green, C (1999) *Educational Days Out: A handbook for teachers planning a school trip*, Kogan Page, London
Smith, L and Vickers, A (1995) *Supply Teachers*, Bright Ideas series, Scholastic, Leamington Spa

The National Foundation for Education Research publishes a newsletter. To be added to the mailing list, call 01753 574123 or e-mail enquiries@nfer.ac.uk

Prim-Ed Publishing has a good selection of photocopiable resources, merit stickers and CD ROMs etc for primary-aged classes; available from Prim-Ed Publishing UK, PO Box 2840, Coventry CV6 5ZY (call 0870 876 0151; e-mail sales@prim-ed.com; or see www.prim-ed.com).

National Curriculum

The National Curriculum – Statutory Requirements for Key Stages 3 and 4 (2007) for first teaching September 2008, QCA/07/3254 (ISBN 1858389801), published 3 September 2007 and is available to order (call 08700 60 60 15).

The National Curriculum Handbook for Secondary Teachers in England –
Key Stages 3 and 4 (2005), (ISBN 1858385903) will remain available to
order and valid until August 2010.

The National Curriculum Handbook for Primary Teachers in England – Key
Stages 1 and 2 (ISBN 0113700660) remains current and valid.

National Curriculum documents are available to download from
www.curriculumonline.gov.uk

Also visit www.qca.org.uk/curriculum and www.ncaction.org.uk

Tutoring

Bullock, K and Wikeley, F (2004) *Whose Learning? The role of the personal tutor*,
Open University Press, Maidenhead

Hartley-Brewer, E (2000) *Self-Esteem for Boys: 100 tips*, Vermilion, London

Hartley-Brewer, E (2000) *Self-Esteem for Girls: 100 tips*, Vermilion, London

Marland, M and Rogers, R (1997) *The Art of the Tutor*, David Fulton, London

Marr, N and Field, T (2001) *Bullycide: Death at playtime*, Success Unlimited,
Didcot

Incentive Plus has a good selection of books for teachers on emotional
literacy, self-esteem and other issues related to tutoring. Take a look at
www.incentiveplus.co.uk for further information.

DCSF publications

Have a look at the DCSF website (www.dcsf.gov.uk/publications) for a full
list of available publications. DCSF publications are available from the
Publication Centre (call 0845 602 2260).

Education White Papers and Green Papers can also be downloaded from the
DCSF website. It is also worth browsing www.teachernet.gov.uk/
publications.

TDA publications

Publications from the TDA can be ordered on 0845 6060323, or downloaded
from www.tda.gov.uk

OFSTED publications

Have a look at the Ofsted website, www.ofsted.gov.uk, for a full list of available free and priced publications. Ofsted publications are available from the
order line (call 07002 637833 or e-mail freepublications@ofsted.gov.uk).

Index